CW01084598

NORTH KOREA IN THE 21ST CEN
AN INTERPRETATIVE GUIDE

DPRK commemorative stamp featuring the Japanese Prime Minister Koizumi Junichiro (left) and Kim Jong Il, marking their historic first meeting in Pyongyang in September 2002 – pp. 59 and 135–7

NORTH KOREA IN THE 21ST CENTURY

AN INTERPRETATIVE GUIDE

James E. Hoare and Susan Pares

GLOBAL
ORIENTAL

NORTH KOREA IN THE 21ST CENTURY
AN INTERPRETATIVE GUIDE

First published in 2005 by
GLOBAL ORIENTAL LTD
P.O. Box 219
Folkestone
Kent CT20 2WP
UK

www.globaloriental.co.uk

ISBN 1-901903-91-5 [Cloth]
1-901903-96-6 [Paperback]

British Library Cataloguing in Publication Data
A CIP catalogue entry for this book is available
from the British Library

Set in Stone Serif 9.5 on 11 pt by Mark Heslington, Scarborough, North Yorkshire
Printed and bound in England by Antony Rowe Ltd., Chippenham, Wiltshire

For all our friends who shared the experiences in Pyongyang,
but especially for Eilidh Kennedy

Democratic People's Republic of Korea, no. 4163 Rev 1, April 2003
Reproduced by permission of the UN Cartographic Section

Contents

Introduction

INTERNATIONAL COMMENTATORS have a list, rather short, of descriptions they like to draw on when writing or speaking about the Democratic People's Republic of Korea (DPRK): 'Stalinist', 'brutal', 'isolated', 'hermetically sealed'. Its leader Kim Jong Il is represented as 'reclusive' and 'secretive', his people as 'brainwashed' and 'repressed' and North Korean society as subjected to a personality cult of both Kim and his father Kim Il Sung and guided solely by the *juche* principle that the two Kims have imposed. Such words are used in the knowledge that the DPRK generally arouses irritation and puzzlement in the wider world and so, without too much offence, can be labelled in this way. They also convey the difficulty of interpreting an inward-looking and self-obsessed society that presents some highly unusual characteristics, but which takes little pains to explain itself except in a language of its own choosing.

This book, intended for the general reader, represents an attempt to explore and understand some of the motives and reasoning behind the public posture of the DPRK, a posture marked by both defiance and pride. Understanding should not be confused with condoning. There is no doubt that some of the charges against the North Korean regime have truth in them. The country pursues policies that at times bear very heavily on the population, and tactics that are seen as dangerous by both near and far neighbours. It treats very harshly those whom it perceives as lacking in loyalty. It subsumes popular needs to those of a single family. In reply to such charges, it insists that the safeguarding of independence and unity under the guidance of a single leader is the ultimate guarantee of the continued existence of the state. Dissent from within cannot be tolerated, and critics without must be confronted. One may deplore such a posture or question its wisdom, but one cannot wish it away, and there is perhaps something to be gained from trying to understand how it came about and how it might evolve.

There is nothing monolithic about the DPRK, for all the apparent uniformity of thought. At the very top, one can detect that Kim Jong Il, though he may have the final say in decision-making, must nonetheless take conflicting advice and demands into consideration. North Korean society is not a level playing field, but is consciously divided into different groups whose fortunes have always varied. The economic changes introduced in 2002 are having the effect of widening these differences. New technology is being willingly examined. Relations with the Republic of Korea to the south are now a constantly shifting area of probing and assessing. None of this, however, indicates that the DPRK is likely to fall apart soon. The economy is in poor shape, but the administrative and military structure of the country gives every appearance of solidity. Kim Jong Il has no incentive to stand down. To ask how long the regime may last is legitimate, but will get no easy answer.

As well as essaying some ideas on what makes North Korea tick, in Part II we have added some notes on travel to the DPRK and the experience of visiting, living and doing business in the country. The information presented here is not exhaustive. Two recent books, both published in 2003, provide detailed and spirited descriptions of what to see in the DPRK and Pyongyang respectively: *North Korea: The Bradt Travel Guide* by Robert Willoughby, and *Pyongyang: The Hidden History of the North Korean Capital* by Chris Springer. A number of websites, listed in the bibliography, describe the principal sights and monuments, and some offer tours. *Pyongyang Review*, published by the Foreign Languages Publishing House, is informative and clearly written. Short guides to individual sites are often sold for a small amount at a nearby booth, and maps of the DPRK and of Pyongyang are generally readily available in hotel bookshops, although you may end up with a French, Chinese or Japanese version.

We spent almost a year-and-a-half in the DPRK from 2001 to 2002 and returned for a short visit in May 2004. From an earlier stay in South Korea, from 1981 to 1985, we had come to learn a little about the peninsula and its history and society. We welcomed the opportunity for first-hand exposure to the North. Koreans both north and south are conscious of their long history as a unified state inhabited by a largely undiversified race that managed to maintain its ethnic, cultural and linguistic identity throughout periods of foreign encroachment and occupation. Such consciousness has engendered a sense of uniqueness that is at times overreaching but which has undoubtedly helped the Koreans to hold their own against powerful neighbours. Like other foreigners who have visited both halves of the peninsula, we quickly realized, not always sentimentally, that in the North we were dealing with the same people.

We have based this book on our observations in the DPRK as well as on the experiences that other foreign residents and visitors have generously shared with us. In particular we would like to thank the following for their assistance and support: Nick Bonner, Karin Bose, Gerald Bourke, Zena Bowie, Christoph Bürk, Richard Bridle, Bob Carlin, Roberto Christen, Sue Cole, Rick Corsino, James Cotton, Mike Cowin, John and Naomi Dunne, Ruediger Frank, Daniel Gordon, Bernd Hollemann, Thomas Imo, Ahmareen Karim, Eilidh Kennedy, Dave Lakin, Tomas Liew, Beth McKillop, James Mawdsley, Tony Michell, Andrew Morris, David Morton, Ueli Mueller, Jane Portal, Jodie Presnell, Bill Ross, Michael Stapleton, Hans Stehlman, Dierk Stegen, Gert Suthaus, Barbara and Günter Unterbeck. Our colleagues in the Diplomatic Corps in Pyongyang shared views and information with us for which we remain most grateful. The experience and understanding of the country among some of them far surpassed our own. We also thank our Korean colleagues in the DPRK for their patience and courtesy in dealing with such 'new creatures' as we were seen to be. We equally appreciate the support and interest our Korean friends in the South extended to us. The volume of printed and electronic sources on the DPRK is now increasing rapidly. Many of them deal primarily with strategic, security and economic issues, but some examine social and domestic problems and serve as information boards. To these scholars both recent and long-established we tender our thanks for analysis and insights. With them, as with all our sources, any faults of comprehension or interpretation are ours alone.

Our publisher Paul Norbury deserves our especial thanks for his patience and forbearance. We should also express our gratitude to those who have allowed us to use their photographs or who have eased our access to other sources of photos and illustrative material. We hope that all acknowledgements have been duly recorded.

Our stay in Pyongyang came about as a result of the decision of Her Majesty's Government in December 2000 to accord diplomatic recognition to the DPRK. Diplomatic relations were speedily established and the decision to set up resident embassies in each other's country was quickly followed up. Our final thanks should therefore go to the British Foreign and Commonwealth Office which, aware of Jim's keen support for the establishment of formal relations, asked him to go to Pyongyang to set up the first British embassy. His account of this experience forms Part III of this book. We remain grateful for the opportunity thus given and, although retired, conclude with the usual disclaimer that the views expressed in this book do not necessarily represent those of the British Government.

JAMES E. HOARE
SUSAN PARES
London, April 2005

NAMES

Korean and Japanese names normally have the family name first, followed by given names – e.g., *Kim* Il Sung, *Koizumi* Junichiro; the only exception in Syngman *Rhee* who became widely known by the Westernized form of his name. Korean proper and place names have been given in the romanized forms that correspond to the simple versions of the McCune-Reischauer romanization as it has been employed by both North and South Korea. Practice has diverged slightly between North and South. The preference in the North is for the separation of the three elements in a proper name; thus, Kim Il Sung. In the South, the second two elements are generally, though not invariably, hyphenated; thus, Kim Dae-jung. Where other Korean terms are employed, they appear in the form current in the society in which they are used, giving, for instance, *juche*. Chinese names and words follow the pinyin romanization. Japanese names appear in the Hepburn romanized form.

VISAS

There is no United States consulate/embassy in Pyongyang and no North Korean one in the US. There is a NK mission to the UN in New York but it does not issue visas. There are no travel agents in the US dealing with North Korea. Indeed, tourist visas are not issued for US or Japanese citizens, and business visas are normally issued in Beijing. Even Britons living outside the UK are likely to be directed to the NK Beijing embassy for visas. For further details see pages 144–150.

▶ Part I

Understanding the DPRK

1

Politics with North Korean Characteristics

POLITICAL FORMATION OF THE NORTH

THE UNITY THAT had marked Korean history for over a thousand years was rudely shattered in 1945. On purely arbitrary grounds, and despite the hopes of Koreans of all political shades and none, the peninsula was now divided along the 38th parallel. The initial division for the practical purpose of effecting the Japanese surrender soon developed into a political separation as the United States and the Soviet Union failed to agree on the country's future, and by the autumn of 1948, the line had become fixed as two separate states emerged on the peninsula. That in the southern half was seen as part of the 'free world' of capitalist-orientated free market economies, with democratic governments elected by fair elections that would make possible a change of government. The North, by contrast, was viewed as a one-party state, following Marxist-Leninist political and economic goals. The reality was that in 1948, neither state really matched up to these shorthand descriptions.

The Soviet occupation forces do not seem to have had any particular plans for Korea. Their entry into the war had been late, and Japan was their main preoccupation. The experience of state creation in Central Asia may have helped in their approach to Korea, as did the existence of Koreans in the Soviet Union – though before the war, Stalin had been so concerned about this group's possible links to Japan that he had all Soviet Koreans moved from the border region to inland republics. The first instinct of the Soviet forces, as it was of the Americans who would follow some weeks later, was to treat the Koreans as enemy aliens and Korea as a conquered country. The Japanese were disarmed, and the Soviet troops set about stripping Japanese factories of their contents to take back to the Soviet Union. The Soviet occupiers did not make the mistake of using Japanese to maintain law and order, as the United States did in the South, but they continued to use Japanese-trained Koreans and kept on many Japanese managers and technicians until 1948 to do work for which Koreans had not been trained.

In fact, since Korea was still essentially one country in the autumn of 1945, the Soviet forces faced the same type of political turmoil and struggle for power among political groups, some right, some left, that the Americans would meet in the South. The strongest group at first in the North were the Nationalists, led by the conservative leader, Cho Man-sik. They placed themselves at first under the short-lived Korean People's Republic, formed in Seoul, but when that failed to get recognition, they organized their own 'North Korean Five Provinces Administrative Bureau', with Cho as chair. The bureau failed to make headway against the growing number of 'People's Committees', and it was with the latter – increasingly left-wing – groups, that the Soviet occupiers began to work.

To help with the administration, the Russians used a number of Koreans from the Soviet Korean community, since these were seen as both more reliable and probably better trained than native Koreans. In what would become a highly significant development, they brought in Korean guerrilla leaders who had fought against the Japanese and who had been forced into the Soviet Union by Japanese pressure in 1940–41. Among them was Kim Il Sung, who arrived in Pyongyang in either September or October 1945, in the uniform of an officer of the Red Army. The Soviet authorities did not designate Kim as the leader of North Korea. Rather, he would gradually ease himself into that position over the next three years.

The division of the peninsula left Communists in the North cut off from the party leadership in Seoul. Although the Communists, like most Koreans, opposed both the continued division of the country and the Allies' proposed trusteeship, they eventually shifted their position on the latter point to fit in with Soviet ideas. By December 1945, Kim, riding this wave, had become head of the northern branch of the Korean Communist Party and was engaged in pushing the Nationalists to one side. Cho Man-sik was placed under house arrest in January 1946. The domestic Communists also found themselves sidelined as Kim, still officially in a subordinate role, gradually came to dominate. He was number two in the North Korean Workers' Party (NKWP), formed in July 1946 in succession to the northern branch of the Korean Communists. Moreover, he had already been chairman of the North Korean Provisional People's Committee since February of that year. Under the Russians, the Committee was now the government of the northern half of the peninsula.

The formal political structure of the Democratic People's Republic of Korea (DPRK), as originally set out in 1948, and still officially in place, provides for what had by then become the classic Marxist-Leninist state. This structure incorporates a cabinet and an executive headed by a prime minister, in theory answerable to the national parliament, or Supreme People's Assembly (SPA). The latter, however, meets for only a couple of days each year, to hear an account of the previous year's budget and to endorse the new one. Otherwise, its power devolves to a standing committee, which meets more frequently, but is in reality no more powerful. The actuality for much of the DPRK's history has been that all power lies with the Korean Workers' Party (KWP) and those who lead it. Two other parties formally exist, supposedly speaking for groups that have long since disappeared, such as the bourgeoisie (represented by the Korean Social Democratic Party) and the peasants (represented by the Chondoist Party – there is also a religious group, Chondogyo, associated with this party). When challenged on why they should exist, since the groups that they stand for have long disappeared, the reply is that they now represent the descendants of those who once fell into these categories. This also reflects other aspects of DPRK society, where what matters is not what you are now, but what your family once was. There is, in other words, no escaping one's past.

These minor parties have neither power nor influence, and describe their main role as supporting the KWP. Their leaders appear on some ceremonial occasions, such as the opening of the SPA, and it is possible to visit the party offices. These contain no pictures of the supposed party leaders, only the usual pictures of Kim Il Sung and Kim Jong Il found in all buildings. Accounts of their official programmes give no hint of different policies from those of the KWP; indeed, for both groups, support for the policies of the KWP is the main party plank. Incomprehension meets enquiries about why one party should have a picture of another's secretary-general on the wall. The unspoken question is: who else would you put there?

This one-party dominance was not always the case. Even the NKWP was not a united group in 1948. (It merged with the South Korean Workers' Party in 1949 to form the KWP.) Several strands had come together to make up this political entity. They included Koreans returned from the Soviet Union, Koreans from China, those from South Korea, indigenous groups, and Kim Il Sung's guerrilla fighters. Even though some of the latter had for a time functioned with the first two groups, they remained apart and after 1948, formed a distinct entity. In contemporary North Korea, they and their descendants are the only group that matters, but this did not happen at once. The others were neutralized or eliminated over many years, as real or imagined threats to the growing dominance of Kim Il Sung. Neither the Russians nor the Chinese supported the groups that they had originally sponsored, when Kim moved against them. The Korean War and the failure of southern groups to rise up to support the invading People's Army were used to denounce the South Korean

Communists. Even then, Kim and his supporters were not totally secure. Only in 1972 was he able to change the constitution to reflect his and his northern supporters' authority. Then it was that Marxist-Leninism became associated with the indigenous *juche** philosophy, attributed to Kim Il Sung. Then also was Pyongyang, Kim's home town, proclaimed the capital of the DPRK, replacing Seoul.

That process took twenty-six years and it would be another eighteen before Kim Il Sung felt strong enough to have his eldest son formally and publicly recognized as his successor. Although Kim Il Sung has always been seen as leading DPRK politics, his absolute dominance had taken time and much effort to achieve. In the process, Kim hijacked the KWP. From being a Marxist-Leninist party, it was turned into a support system for Kim Il Sung and increasingly for his family. The outward features of a Marxist-Leninist party are there, particularly in the emphasis on democratic centralism, a system whereby there is consultation at every level, but ultimately, it is the top echelon of the party that decides, and since the top echelon of the party is now Kim Jong Il, he makes the final decisions.

Kim's position as ultimate leader, as was his father's before him, is boosted in several ways. Among the most important elements is the indoctrination system.

THE INDOCTRINATION PROCESS

All through life, North Koreans are bombarded with the same message: the DPRK is strong and will prevail against the hostile forces of imperialism because it is armed with the juche creed, which puts man in charge, and because the Korean people have had the wisdom to choose as their leader first Kim Il Sung and then Kim Jong Il. Unification will come under the Kims' leadership. Times may be hard, and life may be a struggle, but since the North Korean people are independent, they are in reality better off than those who superficially appear more prosperous. Collective effort will produce results. The message is present on every street corner, on television and the radio, and is steadily reinforced through compulsory study and reading.

From the cradle to the grave, the party guides all aspects of life. From a very early stage, in some cases at three months or so, children attend institutions for long periods at a time, returning to their families late at night or sometimes only at weekends. In the case of

---

**Juche*: rarely translated, the term expresses the concepts of self-reliance and independence of thought in solving problems. Presented as a guiding principle, *juche* calls on the people to be masters of their destiny, while accepting central leadership, and to avoid spiritual deference to outside influences. We discuss aspects of *juche* throughout the book.

multiple births, children are usually taken wholly into care from the outset. This is presented as evidence of party and state care for children, but there are other interpretations. Some see these policies as designed primarily to free the parents for work, others as making it easier to indoctrinate children from their earliest days about the benevolence of the party and the leadership. Whatever the purpose, the indoctrination certainly happens. Visitors to baby homes, orphanages, boarding schools and ordinary schools soon become aware of the all-pervading cult of personality that surrounds the children. They sing of the benevolence of 'Grandfather' Kim Il Sung and 'Father' Kim Jong Il, whose photographs appear in all rooms and whose care and interest in children are often shown in wall paintings in classrooms or corridors. The martial ethos of the DPRK is there as well. Children's songs are of being soldiers or living bombs for the revolution. Pictures of bright-eyed little generals, sailors or, as role models for girls, army nurses, are as widespread in and outside schools and children's homes as are the equivalent adult images on the streets.

The curriculum, as far as one can tell, reinforces this approach. History naturally reflects the official state line. The claimed role of the Kim family dominates recent historical periods, while earlier history reflects the official view of the role of the northern part of the peninsula. The Japanese and the Americans come under fierce attack as imperialists; few other countries feature. Kim Il Sung liberated the peninsula in 1945; the Soviet forces that actually did the deed are now rarely mentioned, and North Korean children will be generally unaware that it was Chinese intervention that saved the DPRK in 1950. Even apparently neutral subjects such as mathematics can be brought into play on the regime's behalf. Maths problems are sometimes presented along the lines: 'If one hand grenade can kill ten wolf-like Yankee imperialists, how many will be killed if ten hand grenades are used?' This example comes from material in use in Pyongyang's Foreign School; material used in the ordinary Korean schools seems unlikely to be less extreme.

The indoctrination process continues into tertiary education. It follows both formal lines, by means of regular classes in the study of the works of Kim Il Sung and Kim Jong Il, and informal methods, such as involvement in mass displays and demonstrations. These can be very demanding. During our time in Pyongyang, which coincided with the rehearsals for the 2000 Arirang festival, the foreign teachers in the universities noted that their students were often absent from classes for long periods. In one case, a second-year language class appeared at the beginning of the academic year and then did not show up again until the final term. Yet, these students were specializing in foreign languages, which, the authorities repeatedly claimed, occupied the highest priority, having been endorsed by Kim Jong Il himself. Even when no mass games are scheduled, students take part in planting, harvesting and other agricultural activities, militia training and a whole host of *ad hoc* meetings and rallies.

Indoctrination does not cease with the end of schooling or university. Most young people, male and female, have to spend time in the armed forces. Up to mid-2002, the majority of university students outside the military's own colleges would spend only a short period on military training. For example, Kim Jong Il himself did a few weeks with the military when he graduated from Kim Il Sung University in 1963.* Since summer 2002, however, university graduates, male and female, along with other young people between school-leaving age and the age of twenty-six for men and twenty-three for women, can expect to do several years with the armed forces. These new rules may reflect the regime's concern about the reliability of younger people, who lack their parents' and grandparents' direct contact with war and revolution. Whatever the system, it is likely that the children of the élite will be able to evade the regulations. Once young people have passed through these stages, they become workers in whatever field the party decides to employ them. There is no sign that young people rebel against this practice, which after all reflects the traditional way in which the young found work. As far as one can tell, none, whatever their background, are left to fend for themselves – indeed, until the recent emergence of private or quasi-private shops and restaurants, it is hard to see what any who fell outside the system could do to keep themselves alive.

Within the work unit, the relentless indoctrination to be loyal to the leadership and to support society continues. There are compulsory study classes in the works of Kim Il Sung and Kim Jong Il that appear to take up a sizeable portion of the day. Saturday afternoon is a prime time for such study. In addition, there may be rallies and meetings, to reinforce the lessons learnt on study days. For most people, including government officials, the collectivist ethos is further reinforced by what is called 'social work'. On Saturdays and Sundays, women and children can be seen working in groups cleaning grass and weeds from the tramway lines in Pyongyang. We even noticed a young mother with her baby strapped to her back stooped in such a task, and elderly women are also present in large numbers. Each Friday, ministry officials will leave their desks and engage in productive labour. In the bitter winter of 2000–01, even the sick Minister of Foreign Affairs, reportedly on a dialysis machine

*The shortness of his service does not prevent it from being marked at a number of 'revolutionary sites' at which he camped or otherwise served. The most famous is in an attractive valley near Pyongyang airport. There a red star identifies the spot in the neat dining-room where he sat, and his utensils are preserved.

twice daily, went to help build the unification monument that sits astride the main road south to Kaesong. So strong is this emphasis on the collective – which echoes many of the practices of traditional society – that North Koreans who end up in the South find it an unfriendly place, where everybody is out for their own interests.

Mass organizations mop up any spare time that might be left. Children from eight upwards join the Young Pioneers. All those who have served in the military are enrolled in the reserve forces and remain formally part of the reserves until retirement between fifty-five and sixty. How often they are expected to take part in exercises is not clear, but in and around the cities and in the countryside, they can be seen parading with dummy rifles and practising manoeuvres. In addition, those between fourteen and thirty, including those in the military, must join the Kim Il Sung Socialist League, as the old Socialist Youth League became following Kim's death in 1994. Since the late 1950s, workers in all institutions have been organized into work teams. These are not only concerned with production but are important vehicles for social control and indoctrination. Women have the Women's Democratic League, in theory to defend their rights, in practice to reinforce their loyalty to the leadership.

The constant indoctrination aims not only to ensure loyalty, but also to keep people's minds focused on how they should conduct their lives. As beneficiaries of an enlightened socialist culture, they should in particular be careful about their appearance and let it display a good moral and mental state. To that end, a media campaign has been running over the autumn and winter of 2004–05, centred on Pyongyang television, to remind men of acceptable standards in hairdressing and to warn against copying foreign styles in hair and dress. Desirable haircuts are of varying degrees of shortness, suitable for the 'Army First' era. Smart shoes are also demanded. Those detected in public sporting long hair have been named and shamed on television. Such emphasis on personal conformity to collective standards is not new: hairdressing establishments have long required customers, both male and female, to choose from a sample of approved styles, which are displayed in wall posters. Nor is the North Korean authorities' preoccupation with appearance unique to them. In the 1970s, young South Korean men with long hair might have it forcibly cut short, and ten years later, mini-skirted females faced abuse on the streets of Seoul.

THE TWO KIMS

The extraordinary devotion to Kim Il Sung during his lifetime and now to his memory, and the continuing respect paid to Kim Jong Il, are not just the products of caution and regimentation. Kim Il Sung in particular, eulogized as the benevolent 'father' of his people, was clearly able to tap into a deep emotional vein in North Korean society. His personality, marked by ruthlessness – whence the epithet 'Stalinist' – but also by great vision and a highly personal approach, stamped itself on the society he sought to create. His experiences as an outlaw and guerrilla fighter against the Japanese in Manchuria encouraged a vein of resourcefulness, even daring, in him which showed itself in an ability to outmanoeuvre opposition and envisage new solutions. In pursuing his goals, he demanded much of his people and pushed them to extremes. His pre-eminent position, allied perhaps with a fear among those around him of thwarting him, gave him rein to set the tone of society and to impose his personal tastes. In this way, a number of idiosyncrasies still prevalent in North Korean society made their appearance. It seems no detail was too small. Thus, he is credited with banishing bicycles from Pyongyang during his lifetime, because they were not fitting for a modern capital (and in any case were a Chinese habit). Disabled people and even pregnant women were said to have been similarly banned from the capital, presumably because they were unsightly. Both categories of citizens have now re-appeared on the Pyongyang streets. Bicycles were allowed after Kim Il Sung's death, but women were still debarred from riding them in Pyongyang in 2002 with the argument that their anatomy does not suit them for bicycle-riding (!) or that they are not sufficiently agile. In rural areas, however, they are free to ride bicycles and it seems they may now be able to do so in the capital.

The sense of apartness that surrounded Kim Il Sung and still surrounds Kim Jong Il is noticeable in the treatment of any site or building associated with one or both of them. When visiting such a site, it is soon clear, even without prior confirmation, that one or other has visited in the past. Where the Kims have passed by, there will be a plentiful use of materials to mark and decorate the site; examples include the Ryongmun caves near Mt Myohyang and the vast display halls for the gifts received from international guests at Mt Myohyang. In a country suffering from major shortages of electricity, these are kept lit and air-conditioned at all times. Each Kim has given his name to a different species of flower: Kim Il Sung to the Kimilsungia orchid, Kim Jong Il to the Kimjongilia begonia. Such is the aura surrounding these two men that these plants are carefully grown in heated glasshouses for presentation as prized gifts, and no Korean will collude in throwing one out. In 2002, a vast exhibition hall solely for the display of these plants appeared on the banks of the Taedong river, in addition to the separate houses devoted to each at the Botanic Gardens.

THE ROLE OF THE ARMED FORCES

The military have always been important in the DPRK. Indeed, in the official historiography, there was an army before there was a party. The experience of the Korean War and the belief in a continued threat to the DPRK's survival from the United States and the Republic of Korea have led the country to put a high premium on the armed forces. They play an important role in training the young and in fostering patriotism and loyalty to the leadership. One foreign scholar sees the armed forces and the guerrilla groups from which they originally developed as providing the key to the continued existence of a 'guerrilla dynasty'. Assessments of the role of the military and of the impact of the armed forces on the country at large are difficult for the outsider. The military keep very much to themselves, avoiding contact with foreigners. Even the defence attachés of supposedly friendly countries such as Egypt, Libya and China say that they are not invited to witness exercises or to visit military units – standard practices in most other countries – and complain of lack of access to anything beyond military guesthouses. Non-military inquirers often find it hard to get even that far.

That said, the military are prominent. According to estimates such as those made by the International Institute of Strategic Studies in London, the DPRK has more than a million soldiers under arms, and many more serve in Red Guard or militia units. DPRK officials deny that the numbers are this high. In discussion, the Korean Workers' Party, for instance, maintained that there were no more than 500,000 service personnel, which would make the armed forces comparable to those of the ROK (numbered at 687,000 in 2004). Outside observers stick to the higher figures. Men and women in uniform are everywhere, though not always performing military tasks. The largest groups of soldiers we saw in Pyongyang and elsewhere were engaged in construction or agricultural work. Apart from military parades, the only armed soldiers or militia normally visible were on ceremonial or sentry duty outside government buildings. During our time in the DPRK (2001-02), military parades consisted only of people; no equipment beyond cars, trucks and motor cycles ever appeared. The pictures of rockets, tanks and armoured personnel carriers so often shown on Western television to accompany stories about the DPRK date from before 2000. The consensus among diplomats was that the lack of fuel and the generally aged nature of the weaponry for display persuaded the North Koreans not to parade it.

In the early days of the DPRK and during the Korean War, Kim Il Sung frequently appeared in military uniform, but thereafter he was normally seen in civilian clothes even when visiting military establishments. His son, Kim Jong Il, occupies the position of chairman of the National Defence Commission (NDC), officially described as the top post in the republic, but does not appear in military uniform; such photographs of him in military garb to be seen are in a few selected places associated with the armed forces.

Since the announcement of Kim Jong Il's election to the post of head of the NDC in September 1998, there has been a strong propaganda emphasis on 'Army First' – *songun* in Korean – policies, a doctrine that had begun to emerge soon after Kim Il Sung's death in 1994. How much this new line has changed the existing emphasis on the importance of the armed forces is hard to say. The main outward evidence of the policy is Kim Jong Il's apparent preference for the military above the party, as shown by his frequent visits to military establishments and his apparent avoidance of formal meetings with the KWP. The official line is that ever since he visited a tank unit in 1960 with his father, he has seen the importance of the military. South Korean sources have argued that this involvement goes back to his childhood in and around military establishments, his experiences during the Korean War, and his realization that the group most likely to rally round him are his father's former comrades-in-arms, who now occupy the top echelons of the military system. What the 'Army First' policy, now introduced untranslated into discussions and publications as *songun*, does not seem to mean, as some imply, is that the army gets the first choice of what is available. Rather, it is an exhortation to follow the army's lead and to learn from the army's example of sacrificing all for the country. The emphasis given to the policy, however, does indicate the very important role that the armed forces play in support of the political structure.

At the same time, while the military are highly regarded, they are not cut off from the rest of society. The army has always been well represented in the KWP and continues to be. Delegates to the Supreme People's Assembly include many military figures. At the day-to-day level, many military personnel live among their fellow citizens rather than in cantonments. In the countryside, the military not only run their own farms, but also work some farms jointly with civilians and frequently help at busy times such as rice transplanting and harvests. All the signs are too that the military and their families have not escaped the food shortages that have hit the DPRK since the early 1990s. South Korean sources have reported that DPRK soldiers who are occasionally washed up dead in the South are much smaller than their southern counterparts, and even in Pyongyang, few of the military look any better fed or appear to be notably better housed than their civilian counterparts. It is hard to imagine, therefore, that troops in remote areas where there are constant shortages are much better off. The military may support the regime but the regime does not always appear to support the military.

THE LEGAL SYSTEM

A formal legal system does exist in the DPRK. There are individuals who claim to be lawyers. There are police forces, including traffic police. Basic laws, including the civil and criminal codes and a family law, are available in published form, including in English translations, and laws are promulgated from time to time. A major revision and expansion of the criminal code was undertaken in April 2004. Law in the DPRK derives from European law, through the Japanese and former Soviet systems. However, despite its formal framework, the DPRK legal system appears subject to the same characteristics as other aspects of North Korean society. Legal matters are secret and even the existence of crime is sometimes denied to outsiders. Yet, in Pyongyang and other places, many apartments have bars that cover their windows often up to the third floor. Many foreigners have experienced robberies. While we were in the DPRK, several foreigners lost bicycles, and parts disappeared from cars. One ambassador lost his golf clubs when his official car was broken into. Requests to visit courts and prisons are turned down, sometimes with the assertion that neither exist in the DPRK. In 2002, in the wake of international concern about the plight of DPRK refugees returned from the PRC, the DPRK authorities said they might allow resident diplomats to visit holding camps and similar facilities on the border with China; but in the event, nothing came of the proposal.

Built into the fabric of North Korean society is a system of classification dependent on the notion of reliability. Social ranking is based on the state's perception of an individual's loyalty to the leadership and of his or her family's trustworthiness in an earlier generation. Following a reassessment in 1958–9 of the population's allegiance to the regime, society was divided into three broad categories: those, somewhat over a quarter of the people, whose loyalty was judged secure; a wide middle group, assessed at around 45 per cent, deemed wavering in their support; and a remaining group, again over a quarter, perceived as potentially hostile. These distinctions still prevail, as far as is known, and are said to be broken down further into fifty-one sub-categories. These classifications control residence and access to promotion, education, welfare and even rations. Such minute ordering of society has long origins in Korea. Formal distinctions of rank were introduced in the sixth century, under the Silla dynasty (*c.* AD 300–668), were perpetuated by succeeding dynasties and were reinforced by Confucian precepts. In the DPRK, the concept of ranking continues to be accepted, although with a special twist that carries with it the implication that certain groups of people deserve to be penalized.

The decade 1995–2005 has brought with it change, sometimes disruption, in North Korean society and the loosening of former constraints on enterprises and individuals. This measure of relaxation has allowed some enlargement in institutional and personal autonomy, but has also encouraged illegal or lax behaviour. South Korean legal experts who have been able to study the revised criminal code report that many of the new clauses deal with what is regarded as deviant economic and social activity. In an attempt to rein in undesirable practices, the DPRK appears to be setting legally sanctioned activities against those it judges harmful. The revised code is said furthermore to propose confining itself only to those activities that are prescribed as crimes.

It remains to be seen how the administration of justice and punishment will actually work out, how it will deal with what might be viewed as 'political' offences and how those judged politically unreliable will continue to be treated. Defectors have testified that the DPRK is a country where decisions that would be taken on legal grounds elsewhere are made on arbitrary bases, and where punishment is harsh and unrelenting. Some offences and punishments have no counterpart elsewhere. ROK sources have frequently reported that senior officials are sent away from Pyongyang for offending the leadership, and that this is in itself a punishment, given the benefits of living in the capital. To this banishment may be added the equivalent of hard labour through agricultural or factory work. Hitherto, criminal offences have incurred the basic penalties of death or 'reform through labour', generally accompanied by deprivation of civil rights. Reform has meant hard labour; but the 2004 revision of the criminal code has introduced an additional, alternative sentence of light labour without suspension of civil rights, which may be aimed particularly at those guilty of economic offences. The new provision may also mean that decisions such as those described above, taken formerly on arbitrary grounds, will now be made within the framework of the criminal code.

A world of labour camps exists, where, by all accounts, conditions and standards of treatment are among the worst in the world. The DPRK has denied the harshest excesses but has admitted the existence of 'reform through labour' camps. Reports say that such camps are found in the more remote areas and their inhabitants are likely to have suffered badly from food and other shortages during the lean years of the 1990s, quite apart from the standard poor regime in the camps.

North Koreans deny that there are human rights' violations, and profess themselves amazed, for example, at child abuse in other countries. DPRK officials see criticism of their human rights' record and of their legal apparatus as just another part of the international attack on the country's socialist system, and reacted angrily to the United Nations' resolution of April 2003 condemning the DPRK's human rights' abuses and to the North Korea Human Rights Act passed by the US Congress in October 2004. While the DPRK lasts, direct confrontation is unlikely to effect much change, although it might lead to greater efforts to hide what is there. From 2000 onwards, the European Union and individual EU countries began discussing such issues with the DPRK, with some effect. The DPRK eventually entered into a dialogue and allowed some of their officials to go for training on human rights' issues. The nuclear crisis has affected both approaches. It has reduced the DPRK's willingness to continue the dialogues and has led it to decline offers of training, even where these were still available.

HOW AND WHY THE SYSTEM WORKS

In the months that followed the death of Kim Il Sung in 1994, there was concern among some academic commentators that the DPRK did not appear to be following its own rules on the succession and other related matters. Such trust in the country's observance of constitutional niceties would be hard to substantiate from its previous history, and since 1994, at no point have anything like the official state or party procedures been followed. Kim Jong Il became secretary general of the KWP by acclamation and thus by what appear to be unconstitutional means, and the manner in which his state appointment as head of the National Defence Commission came about was hardly in accordance with constitutional propriety. This sense of singularity is also true of the continued position of Kim Il Sung as formal head of state as set out in the 1998 constitution. International protests from countries that declined to address ambassadorial credentials to or to receive them from a dead president have led to some modifications. No longer are such documents prepared in the name of Kim Il Sung. In other ways, however, he is still head of state. The small Pyongyang diplomatic corps can expect to visit the Kumsusan Memorial Palace, his working palace in life and now his final resting place, on occasions such as New Year's Day and Liberation Day. It makes a somewhat sombre start to festive holidays. No DPRK function is complete without a toast to the 'Eternity of Kim Il Sung', and attempts to use alternative formulae whereby the late president is included but not deified do not go down well with protocol officials.

These developments nonetheless provide clues to how the system works. Although there have been state and party constitutions since the earliest days of the DPRK, they are not regarded in the same way as such documents are in other countries. States have such documents and so therefore does the DPRK. As with business contracts, however (see chapter 7), such documents are not the last word on anything. If what is wanted can be done within the terms of a particular constitutional document, well and good; formal procedures will be put in place. If not, then no matter, the constitutional provision will go by the board. The details are different, but in essence, this is not far removed from the attitudes South Korean leaders such as Syngman Rhee and Park Chung-hee took towards the constitutions that sought to bind them.

As far as one can tell, government (which here includes party, state and other actors, including the military) in the DPRK operates less on formal, legal principles than on *ad hoc* solutions to problems. Adrian Buzo, a former Pyongyang-based Australian diplomat and now scholar, sees in this approach echoes of the guerrilla campaigns of the 1930s, but that is only one strand. In modern DPRK practice, one can discern Soviet concepts of state structure, the practical approach of the guerrilla fighters, the arbitrary power of the Japanese colonial government (or the Japanese authorities in Manchuria in the 1930s), and even the methods and approach of the Choson-dynasty monarchs. What is lacking is any appreciation of democracy and democratic methods, except in the debased form of 'democratic centralism'. How could it be otherwise? The DPRK has never known democracy in any real form. Its leaders learnt their craft of government from entirely authoritarian traditions, and such traditions have made their mark deep on North Korean society.

Kim Il Sung's long period of leadership allowed him to move away from the *ad hoc* approach of the earlier years, and while he was president, formal constitutional practices were often followed. However, even Kim Il Sung worked outside the system to make sure that Kim Jong Il would succeed him. Perhaps because of his father's attitudes, Kim Jong Il seems to have no particular reverence for the formal rules and appears content to work as much outside them as within them. His liking for the army rather than the party has been noted, and rumour has it that he prefers to deal with a few chosen relatives and acquaintances rather than to work through formal state or party structures. Unsurprisingly, such characteristics are found elsewhere in the system as well. Officials do not necessarily keep to their own rules, or they can invent new rules as it suits them – this can make working with the North Koreans very frustrating indeed! In terms of operating, it means one should never take no for an answer – there is, if you have time and patience, a way around most apparently impenetrable blocks. Those who have lived and worked in other East Asian countries will not be surprised at these North Korean characteristics.

Since the establishment of the DPRK in 1948, there have been those who have predicted its imminent demise. They have seen, not a state that had its roots deep in Korean culture, but something imposed from outside, and therefore easily toppled. The reality is different. While the Soviet forces in 1945–8 provided the space in which the DPRK could establish itself and indicated a form and style for its new administration, they were by no means the sole creators of the North Korean state. The impetus for that came from the Koreans. Soviet structures may have been introduced, and at first, Kim Il Sung and his colleagues may have looked closely to the Soviet Union as a model for the organization of society and the economy, for the role of the army and above all for the leading position of ideology. At the same time, the new state drew on Korean traditions as well: a deep-seated attachment to Confucian principles, above all, the mutual relationship between ruler and ruled with its exchange of benevolence against loyalty; and an acceptance of the values of order and hierarchy in the interests of stability. It is for such reasons that, despite all the problems of recent years, the DPRK survives. The majority of people have never known anything else. They inherited a tradition of harsh and autocratic rule from the colonial period. Today's powerful framework of indoctrination, backed by a major security apparatus whose origins go back far beyond the revolutionary fervour of the 1940s, makes it difficult for individuals to oppose the system. What would they offer instead? Most have known and can know nothing else. Loyalty to leaders and acceptance that leaders know best has been inculcated from their great-great-grandparents and further back, and is not something easily overcome. For those with any sort of position in the DPRK, the continuation of the present system offers them their best chance of a future. From Kim Jong Il downwards, looking south offers few prospects worth contemplating. The ROK has been rough on former presidents; how much rougher might it be on former enemies? Even today, apparently settled into democracy, one of the ROK government's priorities appears to be to search out those whose parents or grandparents can be charged with collaborating with the Japanese. A few years back, the then ROK foreign minister lost his job because he had been forced to serve briefly with the North Korean army during the occupation of Seoul in 1950. Even junior DPRK officials are aware that ordinary state employees in the former German Democratic Republic lost heavily following German reunification. Such a prospect is not appealing, however difficult life is at home. A few have defected, though this is no easy task, but most have remained and seem likely to do so as life becomes marginally better after the bad years of the 1990s. The DPRK will be with us for some time to come.

2

The Role of History

BRIEF OVERVIEW OF THE HISTORY OF THE PENINSULA

ARCHAEOLOGICAL EVIDENCE indicates that the Korean peninsula was inhabited as early as Palaeolithic times (before 10,000 BC). Little is known of the way of life of the first peoples on the peninsula. They were hunters and often cave-dwellers, who used very rough stone tools and knew the use of fire for heating and cooking. It is thought, however, that the ancestors of today's Koreans were a later group of settlers, whose activities can be dated to the Neolithic period (*c*. 5000–1000 BC). It seems generally accepted that these peoples had their origins in Central Asia rather than in what is now China. They not only inhabited the Korean peninsula but were also spread widely over what is now northeastern China; while between the second century BC and the fourth century AD there were also Chinese colonies on the peninsula.

Neolithic remains are few. Pottery and polished stone tools, common to northeastern China and the Korean peninsula, are about all that has been discovered so far. These early people were hunters and gatherers, who also fished, often some way out to sea, if the fish bones that remain are an accurate guide. Later, these same people began to practise agriculture. Caves continued in use, but pit dwellings were also constructed, and the *ondol* underfloor system of heating, distinctive to Korea, had already evolved. Some dwellings were grouped together, and therefore may indicate a more sophisticated form of community life. Scholars debate whether these people had a form of clan society, with elected rulers, but the evidence is tantalizingly slight.

Despite claims of '5000 years of history' made both North and South, the reality is that it was only at the end of Korea's Iron Age, around the third century AD, that the first recognizable states begin to emerge on the peninsula. This is the era known as the Three Kingdoms period: Koguryo in the north, and the first to emerge, Paekche in the centre, and Silla in the southeast. Some historians add a fourth kingdom, Kaya, located in the region of the Naktong river in the far southeast of the country. Silla eventually absorbed Kaya in the sixth century. These kingdoms were heavily marked by Chinese culture, language and political structures. Chinese influence penetrated the peninsula by land and sea, and many travellers went from the peninsula in search of knowledge and trade.

United Korea

Silla further subdued the other two states and in AD 668 succeeded in uniting most of the peninsula with the help of the Chinese Tang dynasty. Despite this support, Silla eventually drove out the Tang forces, a move that helped to create a sense of separate identity among the peoples on the peninsula. Nonetheless, Silla's links with Tang China remained strong, and Chinese influence was widespread among the Silla aristocracy. The Silla capital at Kyongju was laid out on Chinese lines, and from China came Confucian and Buddhist teaching. Chinese architecture and other arts and sciences also made a deep impact on the peninsula, although the Koreans modified and developed in their own way the skills that they acquired from China. In turn, the Koreans carried these modified arts and sciences to Japan.

Silla's decline began with power slipping away from the centre to local magnates, with a resulting loss of revenue. The growth of Buddhist monasteries also undermined the centre's revenue-raising powers. For a brief period around the beginning of the tenth century, three separate kingdoms re-emerged. The division did not last, and under Wang Kon, the Koryo kingdom (AD 918–1392) succeeded Silla. The name Koryo reflected that of the ancient Koguryo kingdom. From the term Koryo, through the Chinese, the West derived the name 'Korea'.

Wang Kon moved his capital to his home area in the centre of the peninsula, to the city known since 995 as Kaesong. Koryo's rulers widened the aristocratic base and allowed for a degree of mobility between lesser and upper nobles. Confucian doctrine, with a strong emphasis on obedience, reinforced aristocratic rule, but Buddhism was the court religion, while native shaman rites were also held in high esteem, particularly at times of danger. During the Koryo period, the border of the Korean state settled along the Tuman and Amnok (Yalu) rivers. Koryo was a time of remarkable artistic advancement in ceramics, painting, poetry, sculpture and printing. While developing their own techniques, Korean artists and craftsmen continued to draw on and refine those from China, and Korea remained a channel for passing skills to Japan.

Korea's new border brought it into direct contact with the Mongol people, whose state of Liao was to the north of the Tuman river. As

China fell apart under Mongol pressure, Koryo deemed it sensible to pay tribute to Liao and other Mongol states, rather than to the remnants of the Song dynasty. Koryo's international position became more complicated when the Mongols established the Yuan dynasty in China in 1271. Mongol pressure to incorporate the Koreans into their empire increased. The Koreans resisted, but Korean troops were compelled to join the Mongol forces in two attempts to invade Japan, in 1274 and 1281. All this put a huge strain on Koryo society. The peasantry suffered because of demands for increased production to meet the costs of fighting. The close links between the Koryo kings and the Mongol emperors were emphasized by the practice whereby the Korean crown prince took a Mongol bride and lived in the Mongol capital of Dadu or Khanbaliq (modern Beijing), before ascending the throne. Even the collapse of the Yuan dynasty brought little relief, for the resulting fighting in China spilled over periodically into the Korean peninsula. Added to raids from China were more systematic attacks by 'Japanese' pirates (in reality probably a mixture of Japanese, Chinese and Koreans), in the late fourteenth century. Diplomatic attempts to stop these failed, and instead the raids increased the importance of the Koryo military. Meanwhile, the ruling classes were split over whether Koryo should continue to support the failing Yuan in China, or switch its allegiance to the rising, native Chinese Ming dynasty. One Koryo general, Yi Song-gye, who thought opposition to the Ming was mistaken, staged a *coup d'état* and proclaimed himself king of a new Choson or Yi dynasty in 1392.

The Yi (Choson) dynasty

This dynasty (known by both names of Yi and Choson) ruled Korea until 1910. The capital was moved from Kaesong to Hanyang (modern Seoul), which became the economic, social and political centre of the country – a position it held in a unified Korea until 1945, and which it still holds in modern South Korea. Buddhism, favoured by Koryo, now took second place to the doctrines of Confucianism. This philosophy placed a strong emphasis on social order and education. It came to dominate most aspects of Korean life, and its influence remains strong in both Koreas today. Buddhism did not disappear; it continued to be supported at a personal level, but it faded from the central position it had once occupied, and its monks moved from the cities to more remote areas.

Periodic unrest in Korea's neighbours brought problems. During the late fifteenth and early sixteenth centuries, Japanese pirates once again raided Korea's coasts. Political turmoil in Japan meant that no central authority existed to control these raiders. Although Japan regained stability at the end of the sixteenth century, Korea continued to suffer. The Japanese ruler Toyotomi Hideyoshi's attempt to conquer China inevitably involved the Korean peninsula. Hideyoshi's invasion, known to the Koreans as the Imjin Wars, lasted from 1592 to 1597. The conflict devastated the peninsula and only ended with Hideyoshi's death.

The pressures in China as the Ming dynasty declined at the end of the sixteenth century also affected Korea. The Manchu rulers, anxious to secure their flank as they attacked Beijing, invaded Korea twice, in 1627 and 1636. During the first Manchu attack, much of the northern half of the peninsula was laid waste, and the court fled from Seoul to the nearby island of Kanghwa. The Manchu only withdrew when the Koreans acknowledged the suzerainty of the later Jin empire that the Manchu had created. When the Manchu proclaimed the Qing empire, replacing the Ming as rulers of the whole of China, in 1635, the Koreans refused to accept the change. The Manchu invaded once more. The Korean king and the court again fled. Eventually, the Koreans accepted the Qing, joining with their new overlords in the final overthrow of the Ming empire. Despite such upheavals, Korean links to China under the Yi dynasty were at their strongest, surviving even the transition from the Ming to the Qing dynasty in 1644, and lasting until China's defeat by Japan in 1895. Korea's rulers saw their country, in Confucian terms, as the younger brother of China.

Circumstances were such, however, that Korea, from the seventeenth century onwards, increasingly turned in upon itself. The country was never entirely isolated from the outside world, but it tended to treat it with considerable wariness. Regular diplomatic missions were sent to Beijing, relations were maintained with the Tokugawa rulers who had succeeded Hideyoshi in Japan, and the Japanese established a permanent trading establishment in the far south of the country. Trade continued, so that by the late nineteenth century, many Koreans were using Western goods bought from Chinese and Japanese peddlers. At the end of the eighteenth century, Roman Catholicism, introduced through China by Koreans visiting the Chinese capital and developed at first by Koreans without outside assistance, took root and from the 1830s eventually led to a clandestine French missionary presence in the country. The Korean authorities were aware of the international links of the Catholic church and tried to destroy its presence on Korean soil through the persecution of native and foreign Catholics; yet the faith survived.

Opening to the outside world

The Korean refusal to contemplate change meant that the country was poorly placed to resist Western and Japanese overtures in the latter years of the nineteenth century. As first China and then Japan were drawn from their relative isolation, it was inevitable that there would be pressure on Korea. From the end of the eighteenth century, when Captain Broughton of the British Royal Navy visited Pusan, a steady stream of foreign ships entered Korean waters. They met strong defiance. The Koreans rebuffed Western attempts at trade, sometimes with force. An American merchant ship, the *General Sherman*, attempted to sail up the Taedong river towards Pyongyang in 1866. The river was low and the ship became trapped. When the Koreans tried to persuade it to leave, the crew fired on them. The Koreans retaliated by burning the ship and killing all aboard. At Kanghwa island in 1871, the Koreans defeated an American naval expedition sent to punish those responsible.

The persecution of Catholic missionaries and their flock, seen as dangerous forerunners for Western expansionism, also intensified in 1866. The French sent an expedition to Kanghwa, with the intention of capturing Seoul, but in the end, it fared little better than the Americans. These hollow victories created a false sense of security at the Korean court, which proved no match for a more determined approach. This came in 1876, when the Japanese forced Korea to sign its first modern treaty, in an echo of similar treaties forced on China and Japan since 1842. The Koreans looked to China for support, but the Chinese, battered by years of Western pressure, had little constructive advice to offer. Western countries quickly followed the Japanese example, and the 'opening' of Korea began, to traders, diplomats and missionaries as well as to new ways of thought.

During the next thirty years, a nominally independent Korea found itself at the mercy of the great powers around it. British and American merchants, strongly represented in China and Japan, wanted new outlets for trade. The treaties signed after 1876 led to the opening of several ports for trade with Korea, but these ports never achieved the same importance as their counterparts in China and Japan. Russia, steadily expanding eastwards, reached Korea's borders in 1860. This development worried the British, who saw any advance by Russia as a threat to their imperial interests. Competition between China and Japan for control of the Korean peninsula only ended with the Japanese defeat of China in 1895, in a war mostly fought on the Korean peninsula, although Korea was officially neutral.

Despite some attempts at reform in Korea, by the turn of the century, the outside world saw the country as ripe for take-over. The Anglo-Japanese Alliance of 1902, together with the indifference of the United States, left the Japanese a clear hand in Korea. The only challenge was from Russia, which came to a head in the 1904–05 Russo-Japanese War. The Russian defeat paved the way for the Japanese to establish control over the peninsula. Korea became a Japanese protectorate in 1905, and the Japanese hold on the kingdom grew steadily stronger in the following years. Any opposition was ruthlessly suppressed. In 1909, a Korean patriot assassinated the first Japanese Resident-General, Prince Ito Hirobumi, at Harbin. The following year, the Japanese completed the process of take-over, formally annexing the peninsula as a colony.

Colonial rule

Thirty-five years of harsh colonial rule followed. Korean resentment at Japanese control led to a number of uprisings and protests, the largest of which was the *samil* (Three One, or 1 March) uprising of 1919. As before, all such resistance was met with great savagery. At the same time, Korean opposition to the Japanese developed outside the country. In north-east China, generally known in the West at that time as Manchuria, where the Japanese puppet state of 'Manzhouguo' was established in 1932, guerrilla bands, often made up of mixed Chinese and Korean forces, harassed the Japanese, often carrying out raids on Korean territory itself. In Shanghai, members of a Korean government in exile plotted against the day of their return to Korea. Both activities were of marginal importance in the colonial period and never threatened Japanese domination of the peninsula, but were to have a considerable impact later.

In recent years, it has been conceded that Japanese rule brought incidental benefits to Korea, such as the development of a modern administrative system, the promotion of education, new roads and railways, and the beginning of industrialization. Such changes, however, were primarily designed to benefit Japan. Road and rail links, for example, were constructed to facilitate Japanese trade. Education was limited as far as Koreans were concerned; the high rate of illiteracy in both Koreas in 1945 amply demonstrated that. After the outbreak of full-scale hostilities between China and Japan in 1937, the demands on Korea became ever greater as Japan moved steadily towards a total war footing. Now Koreans were supposed to speak only Japanese; even Korean names could not be used. Huge economic demands came from Tokyo, with more and more Koreans pressed into service for the war effort. They included many women, known euphemistically as 'comfort women', who were forced to become prostitutes for

Japanese forces in China and later in Southeast Asia. As with earlier economic developments, some Koreans benefited from Japan's wartime needs. A number of those engaged in agriculture or manufacturing gained as the war progressed; while many who joined the Japanese military were selected for officer training. For most Koreans, however, the war meant harder work and fewer rewards.

Division and civil war

As noted, the end of the Second World War brought freedom from Japanese rule, but not the independence that the Koreans expected. The sudden collapse of Japan in August 1945 caught the Allies by surprise. There had been little post-war planning at that stage either for a defeated Japan or for a liberated Korea. To effect the Japanese surrender, the Soviet Union and the United States agreed to the division of the peninsula at the 38th parallel into Soviet and American zones. Nobody saw this as a permanent division. Nonetheless, a temporary arrangement quickly set into permanence when the two superpowers failed to agree on a unified government for Korea. At the same time, political attitudes were hardening in both North and South. Two separate states emerged in 1948: the Republic of Korea (ROK), proclaimed on 15 August, with the American-educated veteran independence campaigner Syngman Rhee as its president; and the Democratic People's Republic of Korea on 9 September, led by a relatively unknown former guerrilla leader, Kim Il Sung, who was head of the NKWP and premier. Each state still celebrates its national day on these dates. In broad terms, North Korea's leadership came from the guerrilla bands that had operated from Communist-controlled areas in China and the Soviet Union in colonial days, and from Koreans settled in the Soviet Union. In South Korea, the top leadership came from exile groups in China and the United States.

Between 1948 and 1950, both Korean states claimed the allegiance of all Koreans, called for early reunification and indulged in much military jockeying for position along the 38th parallel. Communist guerrilla fighters kept up campaigns in mountainous areas of the South. The potential for a wider armed conflict was always present, though South Korea was weaker in military terms than the North. Although the United States' occupation forces had begun creating a South Korean army, this process was not completed by the time US troops withdrew from Korea in 1949. South Korean forces had little armour or artillery, and there was no air force. The North Koreans had large stocks of equipment left behind at the departure of Soviet forces in December 1948, including tanks and military aircraft. They had been able to incorporate into their new army large numbers of experienced Korean fighters who had fought with the Chinese Red Army in the civil war in China. The Chinese Communist victory over the Nationalists and the establishment of the People's Republic of China (PRC) in October 1949 meant that many of these experienced soldiers were free to return to Korea. Soviet advisers had remained behind to help train these forces.

It was against this background that the DPRK, with the tacit agreement of both the Soviet Union and the newly established PRC, and with promises of more equipment and supplies from the former, attempted to achieve reunification by force in June 1950. The bid was nearly successful, with North Korean forces taking Seoul within three days and then pushing the ROK government down to a tiny enclave around the port city of Pusan. Intervention by the United States and United Nations (UN) stopped this headlong progress and instead pursued the North Koreans north. The advance had, in any case, began to run out of steam as North Korean lines of communication became over-extended and the expected uprising in support of the 'liberators' failed to materialize. By October 1950, South Korean forces were at the Amnok (Yalu) river, with UN forces close behind, North Korea's survival was only possible because the PRC entered the war in October-November 1950 to save it from defeat at the hands of the UN forces. After three years of fighting, the war ended on 27 July 1953 with an armistice agreement signed on the one side by the DPRK and the 'Chinese Peoples Volunteers', and on the other by the United Nations' Commander. Under its terms, a Military Armistice Commission, made up of representatives of the two sides, would supervise the armistice arrangements. The South Korean president, Syngman Rhee, regarded the armistice as a betrayal and refused to sign it, but eventually agreed to abide by it. Korea remained divided, but now with the added legacy of the bitterness of war to complicate the issue of reunification.

The armistice agreement is the only agreed arrangement for the peninsula, and it remains in force to this day. The North Koreans have regularly called for its replacement by a peace treaty between themselves and the United States, whom they have always regarded as their real opponent in the war, rather than the United Nations. In their view, since the ROK was not a party to the armistice, it should not be a party to a peace treaty, a position opposed by South Korea and the United States. After 1991, when the UN Command (UNC) appointed a South Korean general as its head, the North Koreans largely withdrew cooperation with the UN side of the Military Armistice Commission, although they agreed in June 1998 to resume talks, provided an American headed the UNC team.

The Korean War left both Korean states devastated. Millions were dead, homes destroyed, and families split. For most of the next twenty years, both North and South Korea put most effort into rebuilding and reconstruction. The wish for reunification did not disappear, but it was subordinate to the process of state-building and economic development.

North Korea since 1953

Until the early 1970s and possibly later, the DPRK probably had the economic edge over the ROK, as it rapidly industrialized with Soviet and East European assistance. Indeed, Japan and North Korea were recognized at that time as the two leading industrialized countries in East Asia. Its success came at a huge political and social cost. Effectively, ordinary civil society disappeared, as the state absorbed all social organs. In political terms, Kim Il Sung gradually eliminated his main rivals in a style reminiscent of Stalin, so that by the early 1970s, he was the unchallenged leader of North Korea. The result was one of the most tightly ruled political units in the world, with power centred on Kim and a small group of supporters drawn from his own family or from those who had fought with him in the guerrilla war against Japan. Together they formed the core of the Korean Workers' Party. Unable to decide on an appropriate successor, he eventually selected his son Kim Jong Il for this role in about 1973. The son remained in the background for another ten years, receiving training for the succession in a series of party and government posts, and referred to only as 'the Party Centre'. From the early 1980s, he began to appear in public, often by his father's side. While his father's title was always translated into English as the 'Great Leader', the younger Kim's title was 'Dear Leader'; he remained a more shadowy figure than his father, known for his interest in the arts, for his links with the military, and, according to the more lurid stories, for heavy drinking and outbreaks of temper. When Kim Il Sung died in 1994, Kim Jong Il succeeded him in practice, but not in title. It was not until 1997, when he became secretary-general of the KWP, that he formally assumed any of his father's titles. In September 1998, he also became effective head of state, but not president. The constitution was changed so that the presidential title is reserved for the deceased Kim Il Sung, while Kim Jong Il ruled as head of the military. For ceremonial purposes such as receiving ambassadorial credentials, the head of the Presidium of the Supreme People's Assembly stands in for the 'eternal president'.

The DPRK's economic strength began to falter in the 1970s (see Chapter 3). The insistence on developing heavy industry as the lead sector strained an economy that needed large inputs of capital.

Military budgets imposed a further burden. The need to prove constantly the superiority of the North Korean economic model, while subjugating the economy to ideological and political ends, confined it in a straitjacket and stunted its growth. Productivity was dropping, and the workforce's willingness to accept largely moral incentives was diminishing. Equipment supplied or bought in the 1950s and early 1960s was wearing out, and the fall in commodity prices, which occurred after the 1973 world oil crisis, hit the DPRK badly. Some new equipment was bought, but, finding that it could not pay for it, North Korea defaulted on its debts. The country suffered as China moved towards a market economy after 1978, and the Chinese began to demand the end of 'friendship prices'. When the Communist system collapsed in the Soviet Union and Eastern Europe, the DPRK's loss of material assistance and favourable trading terms was particularly damaging.

To make matters worse, a series of natural disasters then struck between 1994 and 1998 (see chapter 4,) causing immense damage to an agricultural structure that was already in difficulties through years of over-exploitation. Unable to feed its people, and with little idea of what to do next, the DPRK government appealed for international humanitarian aid. Despite the growing international concern about the DPRK's nuclear programme, help was forthcoming from international bodies and even from countries such as the United States. Over ten years on, the DPRK is still receiving such assistance. Although some trade with the ROK has replaced that lost with the fall of the Soviet Union, and China has continued to trade at subsidized prices and to give aid, it is clear that the North Korean economy is in a very weak state. The one industrial area where there are still signs of activity is in the production of military equipment, including missiles. Some of this is for the North's own use, but it also exports both weapons and missiles. While it is not in breach of any international law in doing this, nevertheless, its indiscriminate sales to unstable regions have become a matter of international concern.

To help what even they could see was an economy in trouble, the North Koreans announced a series of economic reforms in summer 2002. These included a massive devaluation of the North Korean won; wholesale and consumer price increases; decentralization of management responsibilities; and an unsuccessful attempt to create another special economic zone near Sinuiju on the border with China. A switch from the dollar to the euro for international and domestic transactions involving foreign currencies came later – there had been an earlier and unsuccessful attempt to switch from the dollar to the deutschmark. More promising is the development of an economic zone at Kaesong, just north of the line of division with the South, where joint North Korean-South Korean enterprises are envisaged. The economic reforms have brought problems for sections of the population, and their underlying rationale and direction are not yet clear.

THE HISTORICAL UNDERPINNING TO THE REGIME

All Koreans draw on the same historical background. In both North and South Korea, as in modern China, history is not some abstract or optional subject. It is a constant part of each Korean state's efforts to claim legitimacy and in particular, an important element in each state's claim to represent all the Korean people. The story that both states tell is obviously broadly similar, but there are important differences in the way that the historical record is interpreted and presented, long before one gets to 1945 and the division of the peninsula. In the DPRK, that record is used to back up the claims of the DPRK to leadership in matters such as reunification, and the particular claims of Kim Il Sung and Kim Jong Il to lead the Korean people. The account is detailed and tortuous, but offers a stunning, if extreme, example of how history, no matter how ancient, can be pressed into the service of modern political aims.

Even before approaching an analysis of the material itself, problems of sourcing and doctrine arise. One concerns the provenance of records. The earliest surviving Korean manuscript records date only from the thirteenth century, and are not very reliable. Produced by scholars anxious to prove that Korea enjoyed the same historical longevity as China, they are heavily influenced by the Chinese chronicles. Other written accounts have survived on stone steles and in various other inscriptions, but in general, the historical record is highly dependent on Chinese and, to a lesser extent, Japanese materials. These outside accounts are important but, of course, their compilers often had their own points to make about the relationship between Korea and its neighbours.

The Japanese colonial period adds a further complication to Korean history, as does Korean suspicion of much Japanese scholarship relating to the peninsula, since it is seen as *parti pris*. Yet it was in the colonial period that the study of Korea's archaeology really began, and whatever the motives of those undertaking the task, there was also much sound scholarship, which helped to form the basis of historical study in both Koreas after 1945.

Another factor is that, even among professional historians, the narrative of early Korean history is constantly shifting. New archaeological finds since 1945 have pushed back the earliest dates for human occupation of the peninsula and have led to many modifications of earlier accounts. Thus, it was only in the 1960s, for example, that the first clear evidence emerged of a Palaeolithic culture in the Korean peninsula. Since then, several sites have been discovered, confirming that the interpretation of the first finds was not mistaken. Paradoxically, at the same time, while much must be presumed lost because of the ravages of both war and development, these two activities have also uncovered many sites.

The North Koreans face a further problem. Marxism-Leninism may not be noticeable in the political structure of North Korea today, but it has certainly influenced the way that history is looked at in the DPRK. Marx laid down that societies follow the pattern of a slave-holding society that gives way to a feudal structure, which in turn is replaced by a bourgeois state. North Korean historians have insisted that this is the pattern found in Korean history also and have felt obliged to present that history within a framework into which it may not altogether fit. Although historians outside North Korea generally accept that slave-holding in Korea persisted right up until the nineteenth century, and that nothing resembling European feudalism ever existed in Korea, North Korean historians maintain that the early slave-holding states on the peninsula gave way eventually in the first century BC to the Three Kingdoms, which were feudal in character. Feudalism, in this chronology, lasted until the late nineteenth century, when the bourgeois revolution began in the face of domestic repression and external aggression. The bourgeoisie failed to liberate the country, and it was only with the advent of Kim Il Sung in the 1920s that the next, and final, stage of a socialist revolution could be achieved.

Against the background of such general considerations, a number of specific issues have arisen for North Korean historians and archaeologists. The interpretations they have chosen, or have been obliged, to put on these issues add a very particular colour to the DPRK's presentation of history.

Tangun

Among the myths that ancient Koreans used to explain their origins, one particular legend emerges, that the first state on the Korean peninsula was the kingdom of Choson, founded by Tangun in 2333 BC. Tangun, also known as Wanggom, established his capital at Asadal, which has been identified with Wanggongsong, in the region of modern Pyongyang. The acceptance of this as historical fact is complicated by the belief that Tangun was of divine origin, the offspring of a son of the Lord of Heaven and a bear that had become a woman. Having founded his kingdom, Tangun ruled for 1,500 years, and eventually died aged 1,908.

To most Koreans, Tangun has remained a legend. In the early years of Japanese colonial rule, a new Korean religion emerged under Na Chol, which treated Tangun as a real person and claimed to revive the religion that Tangun had practised. Na Chol committed suicide in 1916, and the religion moved its headquarters to Manchuria in northeast China, where it remained until 1945. Taejong-gyo, the religion of the great founder, still survives, with a minute following in South Korea.

In North Korea until the 1990s, Tangun appeared in historical accounts as an important but undoubtedly legendary figure. Then Tangun was enrolled in support of the Kim Il Sung dynasty. A tomb outside Pyongyang had, from the sixteenth century onwards, been identified as Tangun's tomb but this was seen as part of the legend rather than an indication that the site really was his burial place. In 1993, however, North Korean archaeologists announced that the traditional tomb site not only had been excavated but that datable remains had been found in such a condition and quantity that the age and sex of the skeletal remains could be identified. The date of the tomb was fixed at 5011 BC, by a technique known as electron-spin resonance. Within the year, North Korean archaeologists publicly identified the remains as those of Tangun and his queen, and went on the record as saying that 'Tangun now stands as a historical figure as our founding ancestor'. Later, both Kim Il Sung and Kim Jong Il endorsed the claims; no North Korean scholar can now challenge this verdict. A majestic, and totally unhistorical, tomb marks the site, which has become a place of pilgrimage. (The tomb, and other sites mentioned below, receive fuller descriptions in chapter 8.) South Korean archaeologists and historians have challenged both the methods used and the conclusions drawn. The claimed use of electron-spin resonance techniques has been questioned on the grounds that it does not work for this type of dating. Others have pointed out that the contents of the tombs, even as described by North Korean scholars, bear much more resemblance to artefacts of the later Bronze Age (middle of the first millennium BC) than to those of the period at which Tangun is supposed to have lived. The North Koreans have ignored such critical comments.

The reality is that this is more an example of the continued struggle between North and South for political legitimacy than a real contribution to historical scholarship. It is, in fact, an exemplary exercise in the reconstruction of history. By positively identifying this tomb with Tangun, North Koreans are asserting the claim of Pyongyang as a historical capital of the nation. Those, therefore, who currently occupy Pyongyang share in the city's historical legacy.

The Chinese connection

Considerations of national autonomy affect the North Korean view of the next stage in Korea's history, the states led by Kija Choson, *c.*1122 BC, followed by Wiman Choson in 194 BC. Whether Kija and Wiman were real figures or not, they are rejected by the North Koreans since they seem to be of Chinese origin and indicate that for some period the peninsula was under close Chinese control. Thus the once-famous temple to Kija that stood in pre-war Pyongyang is no longer acknowledged. North Korean scholars also dispute the existence of the much better documented Chinese 'commanderies', or military colonies, that once existed in the Korean peninsula and in what is now northeast China. Established about 108 BC during the Chinese Han dynasty (206 BC–AD 220) as a means of controlling the Korean peninsula, the commanderies lasted until the most important of them, Rangrang (Lelang in Chinese) was finally suppressed in AD 313. Although a district of modern Pyongyang takes its name from Rangrang, and tombs excavated during the Japanese period are clearly visible beside the Unification Arch on the southern edge of the city, North Korean scholars deny that the area was under Chinese influence, arguing that if such commanderies existed at all, they were much further north in what is now China. Evidence of Chinese-style artefacts and tomb layout are cited as evidence of trade and influence, not occupation. Some scholars, indeed, will deny the very existence of remains from this period.

Koguryo

The period of the commanderies overlaps with the emergence of the three proto-Korean kingdoms of Koguryo, Paekche and Silla. Traditional dates for the kingdoms place their foundation in the first century before the Christian era, but in reality, it is well after that period that discernible political entities emerge on the peninsula. North Korean accounts place particular emphasis on the most northerly of the three kingdoms, Koguryo, attribute a founding date of 277 BC to the kingdom (well before the traditional date of 37 BC) and credit it with a history stretching over nine centuries. Of central importance is the fact that in the middle of the fifth century AD, the Koguryo capital, originally sited on what is now the Sino-Korean border, moved to the area in which Pyongyang now stands. In another piece of imaginative reconstruction, the tomb of the legendary founder of Koguryo, King Tongmyong, has been 'discovered' to the east of Pyongyang, and another elaborate tomb and a rather simple temple have been reconstructed to mark the site. The area does have long historical associations, but there is no particular reason to assume that King Tongmyong, if he existed, is buried there. Certainly, the expressive scenes of his life, including his chariot pulled by dragons, and the pictures of the happy lives that people led under him, owe more to the artists' imagination and knowledge of a much later period in Korean history than they do to what is actually known of the origins of Koguryo.

A complicating factor is the Chinese assertion that Koguryo was as much a Chinese kingdom as a Korean one. This claim has been emphasized more to South Korean scholars (and politicians) seeking to project Korean identity and claims into what is now China's northeastern provinces than it has to the North Koreans. Nonetheless, the issue was sufficiently delicate to complicate for a while the North Korean application to have a number of Koguryo tombs inscribed as World Heritage Sites. In the end, tombs in both the DPRK and on the border in what is now Chinese territory were inscribed simultaneously at a World Heritage Committee meeting held in China in July 2004.

Of all the three kingdoms, the martial Koguryo most appeals to the North Koreans, but even they have to admit that it was the more southerly Silla kingdom that finally unified most of the Korean peninsula into one. Silla achieved this by bringing in outside forces in the form of the Chinese Tang dynasty, whose troops eventually defeated and occupied Koguryo. Although Silla later turned against the Tang and succeeded in driving them out, they had, in North Korean eyes, begun a tradition of *sadae*, or 'looking up to the great', that would bedevil the peninsula for over a thousand years. (Its modern equivalent is 'flunkeyism', used by the North to castigate the South for its subordination to foreign interests in allowing the continued stationing of US troops on its territory.) In addition, the fact that it was Silla and not Koguryo that achieved unification is a setback in the eyes of the DPRK, since the martial Koguryo state is regarded as more 'progressive' than Silla. At the same time, the DPRK praises the cultural achievements of the Silla kingdom, both before and after its unification of the peninsula. Such achievements are, however, attributed to the talents of the Korean working people rather than the effete aristocracy.

Koryo

Unified Silla, established in AD 668, lasted until the beginning of the tenth century. Growing disorder marked the later years of the dynasty, and for a time the earlier three kingdoms re-emerged.

Between 918 and 938, one of the leaders of these later three kingdoms, Wang Kon, founded a new unified dynasty, which he called Koryo. Since Wang Kon's power-base centred on the old Koguryo kingdom, the title of the new dynasty consciously echoed that of Koguryo. Koryo's capital was at what is now Kaesong, the southernmost city in the DPRK. Perhaps because Koryo developed out of the northern half of the peninsula, it has proved more acceptable to North Korea than its predecessor. During the 1990s, the tomb of Wang Kon, or Wang Taejo ('Wang the progenitor', as he is generally known), one of the few royal tombs in North Korea, was refurbished, apparently on the direct orders of Kim Il Sung, who considered that the original tomb was not grand enough for the founder of the Koryo dynasty.

Koryo's success in establishing Korea's frontiers along the Amnok (Yalu) and Tuman rivers and its resistance against incursions from what is now northeast China are both highly evaluated in North Korea, but its inability to resist the Mongols from 1270 to 1392 tells against the dynasty in North Korean accounts. As with Silla, the dynasty's artistic and cultural achievements win high praise, but its close links with China even before the subservience to the Mongols are a further example of sadae tendencies among the ruling class.

Yi (Choson)

Even greater censoriousness extends against the Choson or Yi dynasty that succeeded Koryo in 1392, and for similar reasons. Its founder, Yi Song-gye, is doubly condemned. Not only did he abandon a military campaign that would have, North Korean historians claim, ensured Korean control over lands beyond the Amnok that had once been Koguryo territory, but he did so to appease the Ming dynasty that had replaced the Mongol Yuan dynasty in China in 1368. Then, once established, the new rulers of Korea proceeded to seek endorsement from the Ming and continued to do so all through the dynasty, ensuring that the dynasty became thoroughly sinicized.

This record of failure, as far as North Korean historians are concerned, was made more dismal by the dynasty's inability to cope with the external pressures that beset the peninsula from the late eighteenth century. The arrival of Catholicism marked the advance guard of imperialist aggression, a development confirmed by the clandestine arrival of French missionaries. Their capture and execution by the dynasty led to a French naval expedition against Korea in 1866. The French attack on Kanghwa and an abortive expedition against the capital are adduced in North Korean circles as proof both of the hostile intentions of the French and the failure of the dynasty to act.

Another momentous event in 1866 was what many Koreans see as the first aggressive act by the United States against the country. In North Korean accounts, there is no doubt on the matter. An American warship, the *General Sherman*, sailed up the Taedong river and tried to force the barriers at Pyongyang. Outraged at this violation of Korean sovereignty, the people of Pyongyang rose up against the aggressors and, led by one Kim Ung U, attacked the ship, which was set on fire and all its passengers and crew killed. Not only did the ordinary people of Pyongyang act when the court proved powerless, but Kim Ung U was the great-grandfather of Kim Il Sung. Much of this is myth. The ship was a merchant vessel and was not even owned by Americans but by British, who had leased it to a group of Americans. Like many ships sailing the China coast, she carried guns against pirates. Kim Ung U is a comparative latecomer to the scene, for earlier North Korean accounts make no mention of any such person. However, he is now enshrined in the role of leader, and it would be a brave person in North Korea who questioned this.* From the *General Sherman* incident onwards, Korea, in North Korean accounts, was entering the bourgeois revolutionary phase, which proved a total failure.

Kim Il Sung

With the Japanese take-over of Korea in 1910, a new star soon appears on the horizon. From his birth in 1912, Korean history as taught in the North becomes synonymous with Kim Il Sung (1912–94) and his family. His father, Kim Hyong Jik (1894–1928), a teacher, is credited with playing a major role in opposing the Japanese; as with his great-grandfather, there appears to be little historical evidence for these claims. Kim Il Sung himself, at the age of seven, supposedly went to Pyongyang in March 1919 to take part in the nationwide anti-Japanese protests that broke out that month. Six years later, aged thirteen, he set off on the long struggle to overthrow the Japanese and liberate the country. At Kujang, on the way to Mt Myohyang, travellers can admire a thatched inn where Kim is said to have stayed in 1925 on his way north to China. He did not return home until 1945 when his task had been accomplished.

Now the myths flow thick and fast. Kim Il Sung, as the years

* That said, when challenged, some North Koreans accept that the story of the *General Sherman* as presented is not wholly accurate, though we never went so far as to question the existence of great-grandfather Kim.

have gone by, has become the only effective guerrilla leader in the anti-Japanese struggle, while the efforts of those who fought for Korea's freedom elsewhere are dismissed as further examples of the failure of the bourgeoisie to handle the Japanese. Kim founded the Communist Party, or Korean Workers' Party, as it would later become, and the Korean People's Army. Under his leadership, the latter held down the Japanese for years in both Korea and in north-east China, winning major battles against better equipped forces. To support this assertion, not only are minor guerrilla skirmishes built up into major engagements, but there are regular discoveries of 'evidence' proving the passage of the guerrilla forces. Thus, in various parts of the country, trees bearing carvings by passing guerrillas that praise the wise leadership of Kim Il Sung are regularly 'discovered' and preserved. Even at Kim's birthplace at Mangyongdae, just outside Pyongyang, a place completely under Japanese control, there are trees so carved.

To intensify the credentials of the dynasty, the birth of Kim Jong Il, Kim Il Sung's eldest son and later successor, is supposed to have taken place in a log cabin on the sacred mountain, Mt Paektu, in 1942. The two Kims and Kim Il Sung's first wife, Kim Song Jok, the mother of Kim Jong Il, are consequently now known as 'the three generals of Mt Paektu'. Like other buildings associated with the Kim family, the log cabin has survived the vicissitudes of both the Pacific and the Korean Wars, in pristine condition, and now forms one of the major set pieces for any visitors to the region. Yet diplomats and others who went to Mt Paektu in the 1960s and early 1970s have no recollection of visiting the log cabin, or even of being told of its existence.

The reality seems to be that after a period as a guerrilla fighter both on his own and with the Chinese Communist forces in north-east China, Kim Il Sung moved to the Soviet Union and was commissioned in the Red Army. It was probably in Russia that Kim Jong Il was born, in 1941, not 1942, and it was there that the Kim family seems to have spent the war years. Far from Kim having liberated Korea in 1945, as the myths claim, he was not even in the first batch of Soviet forces to cross into the peninsula, but arrived later, and in Soviet uniform.

Just as the Soviet (and United States) role in defeating Japan receives short shrift in modern North Korean accounts, so do the period of the Soviet occupation and the Soviet role in the establishment of the DPRK in 1948. The monuments to the Soviet liberators are there in Pyongyang, as is the Soviet graveyard, but not much is made of them now. Since the 1950s, the historical spotlight has been increasingly focused on Kim Il Sung alone, to the exclusion of those who fought with him and who also played a role in the formation of the republic.

3

Rise and Fall of the North Korean Economy

1945–1990: DEVELOPING THE ECONOMIC BASE

The situation in 1945

THE STATE THAT EMERGED in the north after liberation in mid-August 1945 found itself with somewhat over half – around 55 per cent – of the territory of the peninsula. The figure for the total land area of the DPRK varies, according to the sources, between approximately 120,000 sq. km. (about 46,300 sq. miles) and approximately 122,000 sq. km. (around 47,000 sq. miles). The better and more extensive cultivable land was in the south of the peninsula, which, partly because of that, had the larger population, about twice that of the north. This imbalance was sustained by a flight of population from north to south in the face of land reform from 1946 and then war, and by the repatriation of Koreans back from Japan from 1945. The ratio of around 2:1 persists to today.

In other respects, North Korea gained in the division. The geological formation of the peninsula had laid down deposits of exploitable minerals throughout all parts, but more plentifully in its territory. Many of the most productive gold mines, worked since the mid-1890s, were in the north. In addition to gold, other non-ferrous metals still under exploitation are copper, lead and zinc. Iron ore deposits are particularly rich at Musan, in the north of North Hamgyong province, and in the region south of Pyongyang. Metals needed in the production of alloys are also abundant: tungsten, molybdenum, nickel and chrome. The country's reserves of magnesite and graphite are considerable. To these resources can be added deposits of anthracite, especially around Pyongyang, and bituminous and lignite coal, scattered throughout other areas.

The Japanese colonial administration first exploited this natural wealth in a systematic way to develop an industrial base in the peninsula. The presence of iron ore and coal around Pyongyang led to the siting in 1919 of an iron processing plant at Songnim, south of the capital (there is still an iron works at Songnim, which is just holding on). In the northeast, coal was again first used to power industry, as iron ore came by rail from Musan to the coast. But with the damming and diversion of the headwaters of the Changjin and Pujon rivers in South Hamgyong province, the Japanese were able to apply hydroelectric power from the early 1930s to the development of heavy industries – steel, chemicals and fertilizers – along the northeast coast. A railway line extended up the coast by 1928. The workforce expanded through migration from provinces to the south, and a number of new towns were established. In the northwest, the construction of the Supung dam on the lower reaches of the Amnok river in the early 1940s added to the hydroelectric network.

The Japanese were also the first to impose a system of railways on the peninsula. By 1904–05, a trunk line from Pusan in the southeast corner ran via Seoul and Pyongyang to Sinuiju on the Amnok (Yalu) in the northwest. The line was eventually double-tracked. (Alas, the section from Pyongyang to Sinuiju has now been reduced to a single track in many places.) It was linked to the rail system in China by a bridge over the Amnok. Work on the first bridge across the river started in 1909 and was completed in 1911. This bridge, and the second one alongside it, were bombed during the Korean War by US aircraft. A truncated section of the old bridge extends as a pier from the Chinese side to halfway across the river and is now a tourist attraction. The Japanese laid other lines into the interior of the north to facilitate the exploitation of natural resources.

After the annexation of the Korean peninsula in 1910, the Japanese colonial government undertook a reafforestation programme to reintroduce some forest cover after the earlier constant exploitation of wooded areas for fuel and for various forms of economic activity. The mismanagement of forest areas had led to the denuding of much of the countryside, especially on the west. The British traveller Isabella Bird Bishop, in her account of her visits to Korea between 1894 and 1897, remarked on the 'long treeless valleys' from which even brushwood had disappeared on the route from Kaesong to Pyongyang. (Sadly, the impression is much the same somewhat over a century later.) The Japanese efforts were largely negated by their own need to strip Korean forestry reserves to meet the demands of the Japanese war drive, and the DPRK started out with depleted forestry stocks.

The value of the Japanese legacy should not be exaggerated. Japan developed both industry and communications in the Korean peninsula primarily in furtherance of its own plans for territorial and political gain in East Asia. Particularly as the Pacific War (1941–5) progressed, Korean resources, human, agricultural and industrial, were pressed into support of the Japanese war effort. With the Soviet army threatening defeat, the Japanese destroyed industrial installations, rolling stock, infrastructure, and communication lines. (Soviet occupation forces inflicted further losses on the north when they removed industrial plant in 1945.)

A planned economy

From the outset, the intention in North Korea was to develop a planned socialist economy that would act as a base for communism. Whatever the example and encouragement conveyed through the Soviet occupying forces in the north of the peninsula from 1945 to 1948, Kim Il Sung and his new organs of power went straight to the point, with laws in 1946 to reform land tenure and labour relations and to nationalize industry, banks, communications and transport. Forests and natural resources were nationalized the following year. Land reform was achieved very rapidly through the confiscation of land owned by Japanese and Korean landowners and other disfavoured elements and its free re-distribution to farm workers and landless peasants. A more thorough refashioning of the agricultural sector, however, was intended, aimed at the collective ownership of land, and between 1954 and 1958, farmers were progressively organized into a system of state and collective farms. As it moved during the 1950s to consolidate its hold over the means of production, the state emphasized the need to squeeze out all private trading in favour of a state system of marketing and distribution.

In 1948, the principle of economic planning was enshrined in the first constitution of the new state and remained an essential component in the two subsequent constitutions of 1972 and 1992. One-year plans of rehabilitation were implemented for each of 1947 and 1948 and a two-year plan for 1949–50. The Korean War broke the sequence, and the economy was placed on a war footing. To cope with post-war reconstruction, a three-year plan was imposed for 1954 to 1956. Thereafter, a series of more extensive plans, of varying duration, emphasis and success, succeeded each other until 1993. Gaps for 'readjustment' broke the continuity on several occasions. The five-year plan (1957–61) was completed a year early. The first seven-year plan, scheduled for 1961–67, was extended to cover the entire decade, to 1970, before it was declared completed. The third seven-year plan (1987–93) is accepted as having failed, and the three years following, 1994–96, were designated again as a period of readjustment. Since 1994, no plans have been announced. Nonetheless, the planning apparatus remains in existence and officials claim to be working to (undisclosed) plans. Some observers have suggested that the annual budget may have become the vehicle through which the government of the DPRK implements economic policy.

Kim Il Sung co-opted the economy into the task of proving the superior nature of socialism. The labour force was composed of workers who were also to show the worth of socialist norms. To this end, he exhorted them by political means as much as, if not more than, by material incentives (though systems of bonuses did, and still do, exist). The guiding principle of *juche* – self-reliance, which Kim first expounded in December 1955 as an ideological tool – was being applied to the economy a year later. Soon after, during the five-year plan (1957–61), three further movements were launched, all reminiscent of similar campaigns in China and all aimed at improving work-style and productivity. These were: the *chollima* (literally, 'thousand-*li* [mile] horse') campaign, introduced in 1959 to encourage work teams to greater efforts through emulation; the Chongsan-ri village management movement, imposed by Kim Il Sung in 1960 after a period of time he spent in the village of Chongsan (between Pyongyang and Nampo); and the Taean work-style, introduced in 1961 in emulation of a heavy engineering works in Taean, a small town likewise on the way to Nampo. The essential feature of both the Chongsan-ri and the Taean work-styles was the combining of party guidance with economic management and technical expertise. The latter area was sacrosanct, and the party representative could not interfere in technical matters. These campaigns may have boosted productivity at the time: but by late 2003, Chongsan-ri, though still described as a model farm, appeared to be experimenting with small-scale private enterprise; and trees are growing out of the abandoned factories in Taean. What seems to have survived is the Taean style of tripartite leadership, which is still being instilled into the country's managers.

The DPRK's devotion of nearly half a century to the principle of the planned economy has not in the end brought it much benefit once the immediate needs of national rehabilitation had been satisfied and the economy entered a more complex phase. Errors in planning and management have played their part. In particular, the intertwining of political demands with economic necessities has proved damaging, leading, as it has, to at times unrealistic expectations of what the economy could actually deliver.

Industry

In the early decades of the DPRK, heavy industry was regarded as the key element in the progress of the state plan, and the measure of its success. Kim Il Sung was doubtless encouraged in his decision to launch the construction of the DPRK's economy on the back of heavy industry by the existence of an industrial base, including hydroelectric schemes, in the north of the peninsula, together with a workforce already accustomed to the discipline of factory work, and an abundance of mineral resources. Agricultural development was of course essential to ensuring national self-sufficiency, but both the agricultural sector and light industry received inferior levels of investment to heavy industry. Among the explanations offered in the DPRK's handbook for 1958 for the priority accorded to the latter sector after the Korean War was its help in ending the 'backwardness of light industry' and in 'improving systematically' the people's living conditions. Kim Il Sung's insistence on the primacy of heavy industry does not appear to have been accepted by all of his colleagues. Among the charges against two of them purged in 1956 was their alleged criticism of such policies.

There were further ideological and demographic twists. Among the categories into which the population was re-classified after 1945 – workers, peasants, intellectuals and small traders – workers, following the general Marxist-Leninist line, constituted a 'leading class' of which the agricultural population was 'the powerful ally'. The politically more reliable industrial workers were to take a 'guiding role' towards the rural areas and help them towards collectivization. As heavy industries expanded their bases in the big urban centres, many of them on the northeast coast, the numbers of such workers grew, drawn into the cities, and the balance between the agricultural and urban populations began to shift towards the latter. The ratio is now estimated at 60:40, urban to rural.

The years from 1945 to 1950 were devoted to establishing a new style of economy through nationalization and land reform, to securing the people's living conditions and to rehabilitating and expanding war-damaged installations. Starting from a low base, output was bound to rise. These efforts were negated by the ravages of the Korean War, but the three-year post-war reconstruction plan (1954–6) was again productive, as it restored the industrial base with much input of raw materials, machinery and equipment from the Soviet Union, China and Eastern Europe. Industries under development during the three plans that ran from 1954 to 1970 included the extractive and power sector, the machine-building industry, chemical and fertilizer industries, ferrous and non-ferrous metallurgical plants and the cement industry. Such a programme demanded huge amounts of capital, and large sums were indeed invested in industrial construction, more than in any other sector. The necessary funds, aside from what foreign aid might provide, were to come from domestic reserves, raised through increased productivity, economies and extended operation of equipment. As a formula, it was inadequate. The small domestic market within which the economy functioned could not provide the necessary base for high growth rates; the labour force itself seems to have been insufficiently large for the tasks imposed on it; the defence sector made heavy demands; and foreign funds declined.

Problems started to emerge from the mid-1960s, the decade of the first seven-year plan. Slow-downs were identified in the extractive and energy sectors, which threatened to put a brake on production in other industries. (Shortfalls in these two sectors continue to plague the economy to this day.) From the first half of the 1960s, too, economic data became increasingly rare, an indication perhaps that targets were not being met. The country, recognizing the need for technical modernization, looked during the six-year plan (1971–6) to Japan and Western partners for necessary imports, but found itself unable to pay for what it had ordered and retreated back into policies of self-reliance, while still emphasizing the requirement to modernize. Production seems to have stagnated during the 1980s, though the period was marked by small measures to loosen up formerly rigid systems in the management of the economy and by renewed overtures to the outside in the form of a Joint Venture Law in 1984. Deficiencies in the production of electric power, steel and chemical fibres were of particular disappointment in the implementation of the third seven-year plan (1987–93). In a swing away from the earlier prioritization of heavy industry, agriculture, light industry and foreign trade were identified as areas to be promoted during the subsequent three-year period of adjustment (1994–6).

A buoyant start in the late 1950s and early 1960s allowed a doubling in the DPRK's manufacturing capacity and permitted North Korea to hold its own with the ROK in many areas of economic activity into the early 1970s, after which the South started to pull ahead. Although the economy reported positive growth right through to the end of the 1980s, the underlying pattern, from the late 1960s onwards, was of a gradual decline in productivity, and the rate of growth slowed during the 1980s until it appears to have slid into the negative register for much of the 1990s. Manufacturing and mining still contributed to the North Korean economy through the 1980s, but industry seems now to have largely lost its role as a powerhouse, and other ways have to be found of keeping the economy going.

Agriculture

The agricultural sector in the DPRK has had heavy loads thrust upon it. On a narrow base of arable land of somewhat over two million hectares (7722 sq. miles) for all types of crop – no more than twenty per cent of the country's total land area – it has been required to feed a population that has more than doubled since 1945. At the same time, it lost a large number of workers early on, drafted into the manufacturing sector to push forward the DPRK's industrial development. A further constant difficulty is the harsh climate. The number of frost-free days is estimated at 190 at the most and can be as low as 130, depending on location. Good cultivable soil, dependent on alluvial deposits and loam, is distributed unevenly, with most of it on the west side of the country and in a small strip along the east coast. Some 10 per cent of arable land has been reclaimed from the sea. Erosion, particularly through heavy summer rainfall and floods, is a recurring problem. In order to produce the good yields necessary to meet demand, farmers must extract a high rate of utility from the land. Close planting, *juche nongbop*, the practice of juche in farming, is a characteristic of Korean rice cultivation.

In conjunction with the industrialization of the country from the 1950s through to the 1970s, programmes were put in hand to mechanize and modernize agriculture, to bring electric power to the countryside and thus improve irrigation through pumping stations, and to boost the production of chemical fertilizer. Agricultural output rose as a result, and the export value of some items in the sector was recognized. Self-sufficiency in food production was taken as a marker of the country's independence, and claims were made at various times that it had been achieved. Some flexibility, however, seems always to have been permissible in the practice of juche, and rice, for instance, might be exported to earn foreign exchange, while cheaper grains were imported for domestic consumption. Now the support that agriculture received in earlier decades from the industrial sector has fallen away, machinery is wearing out, electricity is failing, the necessary 'high-value' inputs often have to be provided from outside the country, and the soil is losing its fertility.

As noted, the framework within which agriculture was to operate was very early laid down: a collective system through which the foodstuffs essential to the functioning of society would be drawn off, after those producing them had taken their requirements, and then distributed in an orderly fashion to the rest of society. In return, agriculture would receive the support of other sections of society in meeting those needs it could not satisfy from its own resources. The organization of agriculture along collective lines was completed by 1958, by which time the average cooperative farm had

275–300 farming households and around 400–500 hectares (988–1235 acres) of land. The *ri* or village was taken as the basic unit of the farm. The workforce was divided into work teams and again into sub-work teams. Extra voluntary labour has always been drafted in as required from the military or civilian population. The present number of cooperative farms is upwards of 3000, each with an average area of 300 hectares (740 acres). Their task is to produce the staple cereal crops. Some 500 state farms (possibly fewer, possibly more) undertake more specialized work, such as livestock-rearing and breeding, fruit-farming, fish-rearing and seed-supply. Military farms, established in remote and difficult areas, attempt to open them up to cultivation. The third element in land holding is the private family plot. Estimates of the size of these plots vary greatly, from 10 to 100 sq. m. (107 to 1076 sq. ft.).

The collective organization of agriculture is sometimes criticized as contributing to its present failings. Yet the system, as well as representing the working out of Kim Il Sung's policies, has its roots both in the history of the peninsula under the Japanese colonial apportioning of the land among large landowners and many small tenant farmers, and in a wider East Asian tradition of cooperation in the cultivation of rice. After liberation from Japan, some measure of land reform was necessary. Two campaigns to redistribute land were mounted in the South between 1948 and 1952. What distinguishes the North Korean experience was the subsequent progression from land reform to collectivization, and the adoption of the cooperative principle as the organizational basis of agriculture and the means of providing the rural population with health, educational and cultural facilities.

Foreign aid and trade

As a planned economy, the DPRK operated within the wider orbit of the Communist system, and especially at first the Soviet system, of command economies. North Korea was never a formal member of the Council for Mutual Economic Assistance (CMEA), the former Communist economic community generally known as COMECON, that functioned until 1991, but participated in some of its activities, doubtless preferring not to put itself too closely under Soviet economic domination. Nonetheless, the country willingly accepted transfers of economic aid, technology and training, raw materials and equipment from the Soviet Union, China and the countries of the former East European Communist bloc. Such assistance included whole industrial plants, hospitals, renovation of the railway network, and East German help with the reconstruction of a whole city, Hamhung. To begin with, the DPRK built the value of such aid into its budgetary calculations. (The Communist bloc's financial contribution during the three-year plan (1954–6) has been estimated at forty per cent of budgetary revenue. North Korean figures are considerably lower.) The DPRK obviously found no difficulty in squaring its policy of juche with at times a large measure of reliance on foreign assistance. Juche does not in fact entail isolation, rather, self-sufficiency, and the DPRK clearly felt able to justify such assistance as one of several ways of attaining that goal. Right up to the mid-to-late 1980s, North Korea was entering into agreements with the Soviet Union over trade and for the supply of large-scale projects, including a nuclear power plant, and was making similar agreements with China. Only the collapse of the Soviet Union in 1991, the accompanying disintegration of the East European Communist bloc and Russia's and China's need to trade in hard currency have brought an end to such arrangements.

As with economic assistance, foreign trade was accommodated as a means to achieving self-sufficiency. Its role was to raise foreign currency and acquire goods and equipment that could not be produced domestically. It has generally played a subsidiary part in the North Korean economy, constituting less than ten per cent of GNP. Nonetheless, the volume of total trade rose enormously between 1946 and 1990, from US$22.8 million to US$4.77 billion according to the South Korean economist, Hwang Eui-gak. Throughout that period, the DPRK ran an almost consistent trade deficit. North Korean exports have always consisted largely of minerals, ferrous and non-ferrous metallurgical products, chemical products, semi-finished goods, and agricultural and marine products. (Rockets and arms are a more recently acknowledged category, though the trade may have started in the 1980s.) For decades, the DPRK's trading partners were primarily its Communist allies with whom trade was conducted within the framework of agreements, mainly in the form of barter trade, with transfers in non-convertible currencies. During the 1960s and the early 1970s, however, the DPRK, aware of the need to modernize through the acquisition of new technology, began to trade with non-Communist partners in Asia, Africa, the Middle East and Europe. It increased imports of technology to encourage production and boost export earnings and for a while succeeded. Exports of minerals were to pay for imports. But the first half of the 1970s, an era of high oil prices, was an inauspicious moment for trade in primary commodities, and the DPRK suffered badly. The country had to renege on its foreign debts and has never recovered a foreign credit rating. The country's trade debts, some US$2.0 billion in 1974, reached US$6.78 billion in 1989. In 1987, after various attempts at negotiating a rescheduling agreement had failed, the DPRK's Western commercial bank creditors declared it in formal default on US$750 million in debt; and it owes even larger sums to its former Communist partners.

The DPRK began to experiment again with foreign cooperation in the 1980s, when it introduced a Joint Venture Law in 1984 and related legislation in 1985. The hope was to encourage foreign investors, including those from non-Communist countries, to help modernize areas of the Korean economy through the input of funds, technology and equipment and technical skills, and from there to build up businesses with the potential to earn foreign currency. The overwhelming share of investment funds came from members of the pro-DPRK section of the Korean community in Japan, though the Soviet Union and China also participated in a few enterprises. From 1985, a number of joint ventures were launched, several in the form of industrial enterprises, others engaged in food processing. Many of the new enterprises were in and around Pyongyang, where they widened the capital's service sector with the construction of restaurants, shops, the Ragwon Department Store, the Pyongyang golf course and the Yanggakdo Hotel. This last, which took nearly ten years to complete, began with a French partner. Still unfinished is the Ryugyong Hotel, known to Koreans as the '105–storey building'. This enterprise, too, is said to have initially had a foreign partner, but the deal fell apart, and the vast pyramid, crowned with a crane that has never been retrieved, now adds a surreal touch to the Pyongyang skyline and is incorporated into paintings of the city's horizon.

From the late 1980s, a new trade partner began to emerge: the Republic of Korea. As part of wider policies aimed at the reduction of tension on the peninsula and at engagement with the North, the then president of the ROK, Roh Tae-woo, announced in 1988 that South Korean private companies would be permitted to engage in exchange of commodities with the DPRK and that commercial vessels from the North might visit ports in the South. Excluded from such exchanges were certain goods with military and technical applications. This opening was immediately seized upon by Chung Ju-yung (1915–2001), founder and honorary chairman of the Hyundai Group, who was born in Tongchon county in Kangwon province just north of the DMZ. In January 1989, he visited the DPRK, met Kim Jong Il and initiated discussions on the Mt Kumgang tourist project.

1990–2005: TRIALS AND CHANGE

During the years since 1990, the people and the government of the DPRK have had to contend with difficult changes that have affected the lives of many, often for the worst. In the end, self-sufficiency eluded the country again, and despite its professed determination to make itself independent of external forces, it suffered some of the consequences of the political and economic upheavals among its Communist allies that culminated in German reunification in 1990 and the break-up of the Soviet Union in 1991. Declining productivity in industry and continuous reliance on favourable aid and trade terms from these partners and from China, meant that the DPRK was ill-equipped to cope with the new economic relationship, based on payment in hard currency, that these countries demanded. With food production failing from the outset of the 1990s, the DPRK was even less able to absorb the effects of a series of natural disasters that hit the country each year from 1994 to 1998. Arable land – possibly fifteen per cent of the total arable area – and emergency food reserves were so devastated by floods in 1995 that the government appealed that year to the United Nations for food aid assistance (see Chapter 4).

The country's economic difficulties were reflected in nine consecutive years of negative growth from 1990. A visiting fact-finding mission from the International Monetary Fund was told in 1997 that between 1992 and 1996, GDP had shrunk from $20.9 billion to $10.6 billion and industrial output had contracted by sixty-six per cent and agricultural output by forty per cent. (Other estimates suggest less severe contraction.) Only from the end of the 1990s has the economy registered a small upward turn, thanks to better harvests, continuing hard work from the labour force and a steady flow of international assistance.

Agriculture

Agriculture, once cast in a secondary role to industry, now shows more vitality than the industrial sector and, with fisheries, originates a large share of exports. Since 2001, the government has been able to channel funds, equipment, fuel and energy into the sector and to improve irrigation, and it has benefited from international donations of fertilizer, largely from South Korea (the bags seen lying by the side of fields openly marked 'ROK' are witness). Agricultural rehabilitation is also a target for aid agencies and Non-Governmental Organizations (NGOs). While the material supplies the latter bring are welcomed, it is less certain how readily their technical advice is taken, although some has been followed up.

The problems facing the agricultural sector nonetheless remain enormous if it is to meet the country's need for upwards of five million metric tons of cereals each year (to provide which actual production should be over six million metric tons, to take account of post-harvest losses, seed requirements, animal feed and other uses). The UN's World Food Programme (WFP) and the Food and Agriculture Organization (FAO) have estimated shortfalls of around one million tons every year since 1995–6, even in years of good harvests. The DPRK imports around 100,000 metric tons of grains a year through commercial channels; and it still maintains a stockpile of unknown proportions. The resulting gap in supplies is nonetheless considerable and has lead to many appeals to international organizations.

One of the most pressing needs is to extract as much output as possible from the soil. Every scrap of usable land is cultivated in the countryside, and spare plots such as river embankments and office yards are sown to maize in the cities. Of the DPRK's total cultivable area of somewhat over two million hectares, around one million hectares (3861 square miles) are suitable for the cultivation of annual staple food crops – rice above all, but also maize, potatoes, wheat and barley. Other cereals can be grown on marginal land: soybeans, essential to the Korean diet, are planted along the banks of rice fields and pathways; fruit and nut orchards occupy hilly slopes. A valuable crop is ginseng, of which the North Korean variety is highly prized. The choicest land for the cultivation of staple crops is the 'cereal bowl' in the central, southwest and southeast parts of the country, where up to 180 frost-free days from May to October can be counted on and double cropping is possible. Vegetables can run to two or three growing seasons a year. Potato cultivation, traditionally confined to the high northern parts, has been extended under official encouragement to southern areas where a double season is usual. Double cropping used to be practised in North Korea, in the 1950s, but was at some point abandoned. The practice was reintroduced as a joint initiative of the FAO, the UN Development Programme (UNDP) and the DPRK government in 1996–7 and has now been extended to all areas except the north. Winter or spring wheat, barley, greens and potato are grown from October to May-June, then the same land is planted to rice and maize or to wheat and potato again. Wheat and barley may also be inter-cropped with other crops. Double cropping, however, puts a severe strain on the soil.

Such intensive use of the soil needs constant application of water, fertilizer and pesticides, good-quality seeds and seedlings, plastic sheeting to construct shelters for winter seed nurseries, fuel, energy, and the use of mechanization and manpower. Of these constituents, only the last can be assured. Use of chemical fertilizers, once liberal, has dropped to about one-third of pre-1989 rates, and the country's fertilizer plants are obsolescent. To replenish the soil in the rice fields, fresh earth is brought from elsewhere and organic manure applied. There is no domestic production of pesticides, fungicides or herbicides. The farm machinery and mechanized equipment still in use is not being adequately renewed or maintained, and spare parts and fuel, though now rather more plentiful, are still lacking. Somewhat over half of the country's 64,000 tractors – two per 100 hectares (247 acres) – are operational, failing Kim Il Sung's injunction in 1978 that there should be five to ten tractors per 100 hectares. Of those still working, some are miracles of patching up and improvization. Such shortages mean that ploughing, rice transplanting and harvesting once done by mechanized means are now often the task of manual and animal labour, with consequent delays in the agricultural timetable and losses to the harvest. In scenes reminiscent of earlier times, farmers cut the rice with sickles and bind it in sheaves to be carried from the fields. The Korean ox with its reddish-brown hide is frequently seen ploughing or pulling a cart.

Even the irrigation system can fail, sometimes through drought, but often because of ageing equipment and lack of electricity to power the pumps. With the aim of extending a gravity-fed system that would link in with the existing irrigation network, a 148-km. (92-m.) waterway has been completed with funding from the Organization of Petroleum-Exporting Countries, leading from Kaechon in South Pyongan province across rice-growing areas to the Nampo region. Two further such waterways are planned. Doubtless, much of the construction will be manual.

In an attempt to expand the area available for rice farming, the government is pushing ahead with levelling and realigning land in the arable plains north and south of Pyongyang and in Kangwon province. The intention is to produce uniform irrigated plots of a uniform depth, capable of sustaining larger tractors. Other means of extending cultivable surfaces are less promising. Land reclamation is costly; while terracing of hill slopes and cultivation of the thin hillside soil, often involving disturbance of the natural cover, can lead to erosion and soil degradation. The underlying granite fissures react under the impact of heavy summer rains and can produce enormous amounts of rubble, soil and silt to be washed down. Deforestation is illegal, but the felling of timber and clearing of undergrowth, primarily for firewood and to sell, are widespread. At one time, the government encouraged cereal cultivation on steep slopes, but now discourages it. Nonetheless, hillside and forest plots are still being cultivated privately, some by farmers and forestry workers, others reportedly by urban workers who walk long distances into the mountains to raise a few crops, which they can keep for their own use. In some areas individual farmers are being permitted to work land previously held by the collective. Although farmers are required to sell their staple crops to the state, to support the Public Distribution System (PDS), they may sell their surplus produce in the markets.

The North Korean countryside is an active place, populated by humans but also by flocks of chickens, geese and guinea fowl in the fields and of ducks in the rice paddy. Individual farmers raise pigs, rabbits and sometimes dogs in their garden plots. Often these animals and poultry are sold to buy cereals. White goats browse everywhere, always with a goatherd in sight. The government encourages them as a source of milk and animal protein, even yoghurt, but also because they do not compete with humans for grain and thrive on marginal hilly land. Some cooperative farms already have quite large herds of goats, and they are also raised by individual households. Oxen do consume grain, but the increasing need to use them for ploughing and hauling means that they must be supported.

Industry, energy and infrastructure

It is clear that the balance between economic sectors in national production has changed considerably. In 1987, for instance, the combined share of manufacturing and mining in total production could be estimated at 60 per cent, that of agriculture, forestry and fisheries at 20 per cent. By 2000, the latter sector was judged to contribute 30.4 per cent, against 25.4 per cent for mining and manufacturing (17.7 per cent for manufacturing). During the same period, the service sector expanded to account for 32.5 per cent of production in 2000.

Visual evidence confirms the impression of a loss of industrial capacity, even in Pyongyang, where the view from any high point yields few signs or sounds of manufacturing activity. Derelict buildings and machinery occupy one whole quarter in the capital; and the situation is far worse in the former industrial bases in the north-east of the country. The difficulty is in turning such impressions into precise information. The figure above for the extractive and manufacturing sector – around 25 per cent of GDP – indicates continuing industrial activity, and there is even a possibility that such activity may be slightly increasing, at least in certain areas, judging by the greater number of productive smokestacks in spring 2004. A look at DPRK export items helps to define some areas of industry. Gold and zinc are still being mined, though in smaller quantities than in the past. Steel and metal products, machinery and transportation equipment also appear, as do chemical and mineral products. Another important export category comprises textiles and garments. Electronic and electric goods, computer software and assembled television sets make up a further group. The share of goods for export produced in the light industry sector is expanding, by contrast with the diminishing share from heavy and the extractive industries. Within the country, coal, cement and timber are still important commodities. Garment and footwear production and food processing for the domestic market are clearly important, while the newly developing IT sector requires electronic and software products. Although very little is known about the production of military hardware and rockets, the existence of such a sector implies a continuing input of steel and metallurgical products and of electrical and electronic systems. General industrial production is thought to run at thirty to forty per cent of capacity. All sectors are liable to be affected by a recurring shortage of electricity; though it is likely that the defence sector and export industries may have the first share in energy and resources.

Shortfalls in fuel and electricity have long been a constant aspect of daily life in the DPRK, though there are some signs that supply may be slowly improving. Power resources are centred on Pyongyang, and the capital is still able to put on a good show of illuminations for festivals and national celebrations and to floodlight its monuments. In May 2004, the blacked-out districts that two years before had been a feature of the capital by night, were sufficiently lit; and trams and trolleybuses seemed to be running well, where formerly they had piled up in long queues, halted by an electricity outage or a broken overhead connection. Some factories, at least in Pyongyang, said they relied on 'private lines' of supply – possibly generators. The situation in other towns in 2001–02 was known to be worse, with electricity cut off one day a week in winter, as in Hamhung, or long daily periods without power, as in Kaesong. We could not discover what the present situation is in these cities.

The problem of power generation has been particularly severe since the floods of 1995–6, which damaged hydroelectric schemes in the northwest of the country and flooded coal mines. Up until then, much of the country's power came through its large hydroelectric installations, which fed into a national grid. Since 1996, coal-fired power plants have provided the bulk of electricity (as the black smoke enveloping the capital's principal power station at peak times attests; the plant is now forty years old). Coal supplies themselves declined throughout the decade 1990–2000, as coal has become increasingly difficult to extract from the ground, and many new mines are quite small. The grid has suffered heavy transmission losses and no longer operates nationally, leaving a system of smaller, isolated grids. Small- and medium-scale power installations serving local needs supplement the large plants, some of them thermal, others hydroelectric. Oil, which has to be imported, is principally used in transport, and only two power plants were oil-fired. Where China and the former Soviet Union once supplied the DPRK with oil at 'friendship' prices, the commodity now has generally to be purchased with hard currency, and imports have dropped since 1991. Under the terms of the US-DPRK Agreed Framework of October 1994, which provided for an international consortium, KEDO, to construct two light-water nuclear reactors, partly to meet some of the North's need for energy, the US had been providing 500,000 metric tons of heavy fuel oil a year, which was to continue until the reactors were completed. With the collapse of the Agreed Framework, these supplies have ceased. The inclusion of equipment for the energy-producing sector among recent imports from the European Union is a good sign; three large power stations are said to be under construction; and old power plants are being reconstructed and modernized. North Korean attendance at an international conference on renewable energy in Germany in 2004 would suggest some interest in new approaches.

The other big impediment to economic productivity is the poor state of the country's infrastructure. The railways largely carry freight, including coal. Much of the network – nearly 80 per cent – was electrified at an early date, but is now affected by power stoppages, and engines are frequently diesel-fuelled. Maintenance of rolling stock and tracks is inadequate. Journey times can now be extraordinarily long: 15–19 hours from the northeast coast to Pyongyang, 30–40 hours from the capital to visit Mt Paektu. The road network is hardly better. Only some 8 per cent of the 23,500 km. (14,3000 miles) of surfaces are paved, maybe because the roads were not primarily intended for heavy goods, and passenger traffic has been little developed. Car journeys over dirt and stone roads are consequently protracted and uncomfortable. Road repairs are rudimentary: hot tar poured on the surface, or soil laid on the road. Expressways link Pyongyang with Nampo, Kaesong, Wonsan and the Kumgang mountains, Mt Myohyang and Sinuiju. The first four carry generally light traffic; indeed, lorries are banned from the Nampo and Mt Myohyang expressways for fear of damaging the surface. The highway to Wonsan, completed in 1978, is kept in reasonable condition. By contrast, the road to Sinuiju, completed in 1995, has since deteriorated into a dirt road for considerable stretches. Yet this road, to the Chinese border and the Amnok (Yalu) river bridge, over which large quantities of goods are imported, is a lifeline along which container lorries and bulk liquid carriers must jolt. Pyongyang and some other cities have public transport systems, but there appear to be no buses linking these towns, and people in the countryside must walk, bicycle or catch a lift from a passing truck. Many of those on foot are heavily laden.

Information technology (IT)

This lively and growing area of activity in the DPRK is one that fascinates many young people. Kim Jong Il and his family are said to take a close interest. The sector received a boost in an editorial of 9 January 2001 in the party newspaper *Rodong Sinmun*, which emphasized the value of new technology. Within the country, the Pyongyang University of Computer Technology was established as early as 1985, Kim Il Sung University has a faculty of computer technology, and Kim Chaek University of Technology is another centre. South Korean IT specialists have lectured at other institutions, the Ministry of Education has run computer training centres since 2000 and some schools and children's palaces also offer courses. Other institutes, such as the Pyongyang Informatics Centre, promote the commercial and scientific applications of IT, some of them collaborating with ROK companies in joint ventures in the DPRK and China. Computer technology is used in weather forecasting and is reportedly being gradually applied to the railway system. An excellent electronic map of the Korean peninsula and a scientific and technological electronic dictionary, *Kwangmyong 2001*, are available, as are other works of reference. Development of software programmes has been underway since the mid-1980s. Software, game design and animation are all produced for export and computers are also assembled for export. Inside the country, there is a market for second-hand computers. IT experts know how to design websites. An international 'technology and infrastructure' exhibition, the first in the DPRK, was held in September 2002 with foreign participation.

The DPRK is cautiously establishing relations with the international IT community. It uses servers in China, Japan and Singapore to run websites. In November 2003, it announced the launching of an international email service, an advance on an earlier email relay system that had been routed through the Silibank server in Shenyang in China or through a server sited at Pyongyang airport. Use of that system had been confined to registered customers in business and government and among the foreign community, and the new service will demand identification and a password. Cost will again be a factor, as it was for the earlier system, in determining use. Access to the Internet is said to be through the Ministry of Posts and Telecommunications and will be restricted to approved users. In September 2003, hopes were aired for developing a broadband system and for linking the domestic intranet, which has functioned since 2001, to the Internet, in the interests of creating a better environment for business. Kim Chaek University of Technology hopes to develop an electronic library that will be linked to the Internet and form a pivotal point in North Korean exchanges with it. The Korean telecommunications authorities appear to have entered into negotiations in 2003 with a German entrepreneur to develop Internet and email links. An Internet café operated for a while in Pyongyang in 2002, but at $10 an hour was too expensive for many Koreans and offered a restricted range of options.

The government promotes research and production, but also acts as regulator and censor. It permits some use of IT by commerce and bureaucracy, but information and communication are another matter, particularly between the two Koreas. The ROK government permits viewing of North Korean sites, but no further use, and does not sanction unauthorized contact by its citizens with the North. Some kind of cyberwar between the two sides is without doubt being waged. Inside the DPRK, the government remains obsessed with security and control. For a year, it refused to allow the installation of a secure satellite communications system in the British embassy in Pyongyang, but relented and now permits the use of satellite communications, including satellite telephones, within the country. The introduction of mobile telephones has been a saga still without an end. In the autumn of 2003, the authorities permitted the sale of foreign-made mobile hand phones in Pyongyang, and launched a mobile telephone system in the capital that was reported to have attracted around 3000 subscribers. By early 2004, officials were regularly using mobile phones, though presumably only for internal calls, and the signs were that the network would extend to other cities. Foreigners, hitherto denied access to the system, were to be permitted to use it for overseas calls, on payment of a large fee. Then suddenly, in May 2004, the right to use a mobile telephone was withdrawn from all users, Korean and foreign. Foreigners must continue, as before, to deposit their mobiles at the airport on arrival, to collect them again on departure. The source of this confusion lies doubtlessly in the anxieties and obduracy of the security services. Communication in the DPRK cannot be taken for granted.

The DPRK is a member of SWIFT and INTELSAT and has had a DHL office since November 1997.

Foreign trade and investment and special zones

Foreign trade was identified in 1993, together with agriculture and light industry, as an area to be promoted in the search for economic improvement. Even before then, the DPRK's trade partners and patterns of trade had been changing, from a situation in 1990 where trade with the Soviet Union constituted around half of North Korea's foreign trade, to the present listing of China and the Republic of

Korea as the country's first and second trading partners, with Japan in third place. Trade with the PRC in 2003 is reported to have reached US$1,020 million, that with the ROK US$720 million. These figures indicate not only a rise in trade with these specific partners, but also an upswing in the total volume of the DPRK's foreign trade, which was said to have dropped in 1999 to US$0.5 billion. Such figures, however, cannot be taken as a firm indication of the state of play. Although many imports must be paid for in foreign exchange, trade between the two Koreas, for example, often takes the form of an exchange of commodities or may be regarded as internal domestic trade, and there are reports of continued barter trade with cross-border provinces in China. At the lowest level, individuals 'import' consumer goods and even machinery by conveying it as checked or 'carry-on' luggage on aircraft and ferries. The traveller approaches the Air Koryo counter at Beijing airport through vast amounts of cartoned goods and luggage for each twice-weekly passenger flight.

China itself has supplied the DPRK with large quantities of oil, grain and coal, and is the source of many consumer goods, but the terms on which it provides these commodities are not known. Trade with China is said to run at a deficit; that with Japan and South Korea is in surplus. Japan takes agricultural products, particularly the delicious Korean mushrooms, and in return exports vehicles and specialized machinery, as does the EU, which has recently exported equipment for energy generation, construction, the agricultural sector and food-processing to the DPRK. The Japanese-Korean Chongryon association in Japan, established in 1955, created and dominated much of Japan's trade with North Korea, but its numbers are falling and its financial clout is waning as a result of irregularities in its credit network and losses in its business activities. Its ability to continue supporting investment in the DPRK on the scale of the late 1980s is now in doubt.

By contrast, the two Koreas are becoming increasingly enmeshed in their trade relationship. Backed by agreements on economic cooperation between the two states, by a non-tariff agreement and by legislation on both sides facilitating economic contacts, inter-Korean trade grew to US$441 million in 2002 and, as seen above, reached US$720 million in 2003. Major North Korean exports to the South are agricultural and marine products (around 47 per cent in 2000), gold ingots, chemical products, machinery, light consumer goods, and textiles and garments, electronic and electric goods processed or semi-processed on commission and frequently transhipped through China. The ROK exports steel, metal and chemical products, machinery, textiles and food products. Aid items, such as fertilizer, and 'non-trade' items for cooperative ventures augment this commercial trade. The latter items include fuel oil, equipment and materials for trans-border road and rail projects and the Mt Kumgang tourist programme, and, until recently, the continued delivery of material for the construction of the two light-water reactors at Kumho in South Hamgyong province. Prompted by the availability of a disciplined, well-educated, yet low-wage, workforce and also, sometimes, by sentiment, South Korean businesses are slowly moving towards investment and joint venture cooperation in North Korean enterprises, especially in textiles, IT and food-processing. To encourage their participation, the North Korean government gives tax breaks and has reportedly offered to cut workers' wages. The Pyonghwa motor company, which has strong links with the Unification Church, has set up a car-assembly plant in the Nampo export-processing zone to produce Fiat-type cars, and, in a first for North Korea, advertizes its products on Pyongyang billboards. (The Samsung logo has also appeared in a Pyongyang stadium.) The biggest player is Hyundai, whose Asan group runs the Mt Kumgang project and is much involved in the Kaesong industrial park, which exported its first products, kitchenware, to South Korea in December 2004. Chinese entrepreneurs are also being courted. The No.1 Department Store in central Pyongyang is reported to be passing under Chinese management on a ten-year lease. The store, hitherto more often closed than open, may now operate on a reliable basis. Investment from foreign, i.e. non-Korean, sources is being solicited under the management of the External Office of Trade, under direct control of the cabinet.

The concept of special zones has been much favoured by the North Korean authorities, who see in them a way for intensified promotion of foreign exchange-earning businesses and activities that will nonetheless impinge little on the surrounding society. The Mt Kumgang tourist project, closed off from the rest of Kangwon province, is a case in point. From 1991, the DPRK has joined in international discussions to develop the Tuman river area, a project backed by the UNDP, and that same year announced plans for its own Free Economic and Trade Zone at Rajin-Sonbong, just below the mouth of the Tuman. Progress on the Tuman river project has faltered, inhibited perhaps by China's and Russia's interest, as well as North Korea's, in creating their own special economic zones in the area. Development of the Rajin-Sonbong zone was facilitated through an extensive series of laws from 1992 on foreign investment in the DPRK. A number of foreign businesses have visited the zone, but to date, investment has been sluggish and only the tourist projects appear to have got off the ground. Poor communications and the weight of regulations may be deterring factors. The 500,000 metric tons of fuel oil supplied by the US under the terms of the Agreed

Framework were being sent to the oil-fired power plant at Sonbong and the termination of this supply can only have an adverse effect on the zone's operation. A proposal in 2002 to establish a special zone at Sinuiju, facing the Chinese city of Dandong across the Amnok, that would specialize in IT development but also offer tourist attractions, has irritated the Chinese, who were not consulted and who are anxious to develop their own free-trade zone in Dandong. The Sinuiju zone was to function as a 'special autonomous region' with its own governor and legal structure and a visa-free regime. Chinese patience snapped when Yang Bin, a Chinese with Dutch nationality and an associate of Kim Jong Il, was nominated governor. Yang owed taxes in China and while there was tried and imprisoned. The Nampo and Kaesong projects, carefully planned and enjoying South Korean participation may have a better chance of success. A road link has been opened between the ROK and Kaesong and electricity is being supplied to the Kaesong project from the South.

The management of foreign trade, as is customary in a command economy, has always been in the hands of official organs operating through trading firms. There are said to be around one hundred such firms. In 1998, the newly-formed Ministry of Foreign Trade subsumed many of the government trade organizations. The trade units run by the Korean Workers Party and the Korean People's Army are as important as the Foreign Trade Ministry. The party, for instance, manages Daesong Trading, rumoured to be connected with Kim Jong Il. It certainly produces and markets a very palatable red wine, the product of a joint venture with China! It is further supported by its own bank, Daesong Bank, and other banking institutions. The army has its own trade organs and bank, Kumsong Bank, and its own factories. Beyond these, other ministries and individual cities, provinces and counties run their own trading activities, often in competition with each other, in the search for foreign currency.

It is one thing to prioritize foreign trade, another to realize the hopes pinned on it. In both quality and output, North Korean products need to make considerable strides. Where quotas are open to, for example, textiles, the DPRK is not taking up its allocation. The involvement of multiple state, party and army organizations in foreign trade obscures the role the sector can play in boosting national finances. The continued preference for soft trading terms suggests the country cannot shake off the attractions of dependency.

Where does the money come from?

Finally, the question has to be asked: how, in the face of evidence of economic difficulties, does the DPRK manage to acquire the foreign exchange vital to its functioning? Hard currency now flows freely within the country since the abolition of the 'convertible' won used formerly in dealings with foreigners. All foreigners are required to pay for goods and services in euros (which replaced dollars as the officially preferred hard currency in December 2002, but which, it is rumoured, may yield again to dollars), thus stimulating the circulation of foreign exchange, and Koreans are also entitled to use this means of payment if they have the right currency. External trade and foreign investment produce a certain amount of foreign earnings. Other ways of engendering foreign exchange have been exploited over the years; but the search for hard currency has been sharpened by the requirement on work organizations to strive for financial independence in support of national prosperity.

The outstanding example is the Korean People's Army, which can be claimed to run a 'second economy'. Part of this economy is devoted to its own welfare, but overseas sales of arms, weapons and even missiles, produced within the DPRK, which have been going on since the 1980s, are presumed to pass through its hands and its own banking institutions. Its clients are said chiefly to be a number of Middle Eastern and African states. It is impossible to tell if any of the funds generated by such sales find their way back into state revenues or if the army retains them for its own needs.

The export of labour and services is another source of foreign exchange. In an economy where private recruitment and employment of personnel are virtually unknown, these transactions must clearly be handled by official organs. North Korean bodyguards, presumably from the military, have been supplied to a number of heads of state in Africa. In the Russian Far East, North Korean workers have been employed since the late 1960s in logging camps in the Khabarovsk region. Agreement to continue the Soviet arrangement was renewed with the new Russian government in 1995. Between 15,000 and 20,000 loggers are reported to be working, often in very harsh conditions and under the surveillance of North Korean security guards. The DPRK receives around thirty-nine per cent of output. Other workers, similarly recruited through official channels for labour in mines and on construction sites, have now apparently joined the loggers in the Russian Far East. About 2,500 North Koreans are said to work in the Maritime Territory (which includes Vladivostok). The big fear on the Russian side is of attempts at defection by this labour force.

Within its own borders, the DPRK has been earning annual fees since 1998 in overflying rights for civilian aircraft. It also receives payment from an unexpected source, the US, in return for its formal assistance since 1996 in locating and disinterring the remains of US soldiers killed in the Korean War. One potential source of funds has so far eluded the DPRK: the reparations for the colonial period that it demands from Japan. The joint North Korean-Japanese agreement signed in September 2002 during Prime Minister Koizumi's visit to Pyongyang committed Japan to economic cooperation with the DPRK. Further exchanges, however, have stalled on the issues of Japanese citizens abducted by the North during the 1970s and 1980s and the North's admission of its nuclear programme.

The DPRK has used its connections with fellow Koreans to extract funds. As seen above, the Chongryon organization in Japan has been a source of investment in North Korean enterprises, but has also channelled remittances to the country as sums brought in by Chongryon visitors to the North or through banks. The flow of funds fell sharply during the 1990s as Chongryon grappled with its own financial problems, and it is not clear how substantial they are now. Cooperation between the ROK and the DPRK has cost and continues to cost South Korea large sums of money. Hyundai's involvement in the Mt Kumgang tourist project has necessitated enormous outlay in construction and maintenance charges and materials and in regular fees to the DPRK, regardless of the profitability of the project. The ROK government now underwrites the burden. It has further emerged that Hyundai, presumably with government knowledge, paid over some US$500 million to the North to ease the path to the summit meeting in June 2000 between President Kim Dae-jung and Kim Jong Il.

Such means of raising hard currency must all be accepted as lying within the DPRK's rights, however regrettable or distasteful others may find them. But other methods attributed to North Korea of winning foreign exchange can only be regarded as unlawful. As early as the mid- to late-1970s, stories were surfacing of arms- and drug-trafficking and of smuggling of duty-free and counterfeit goods, ivory and endangered species, by North Korean diplomats and other officials. Such reports have continued and have increased during the 1990s and beyond. There are suspicions that the DPRK has been cultivating opium for processing into heroin and is dealing in amphetamines. Drugs are thought to be distributed through North Korean trading houses and cargo boats, with the help of criminal gangs and even through diplomatic channels. Counterfeit US dollar notes, particularly $100 bills, used to circulate in Pyongyang and were the subject of frequent jokes among the foreign community. The story goes that when one embassy complained to the bank about the number of false $100 notes it had received and returned them, they were quietly replaced with genuine ones. The introduction of the euro will have presented new challenges.

Given the structure of the North Korean economy and the close involvement of official organs in foreign trade, such dubious activities must be conducted with the knowledge of the state. Rumours that the gains from such trade are channelled towards the leadership simply cannot be proved; and all these activities are deniable, despite the testimony of non-Korean authorities that have seized shipments of drugs in recent years. It is equally impossible to know the full value of this suspected illegal trade.

Changes to the economy

The news in July 2002 that the North Korean government was introducing price and wage increases and abolishing subsidies produced eager speculation among foreign commentators that at last economic reform was on its way. Talk of a market economy, even capitalism, in the DPRK seems at present premature and does not tally with the leadership's professed intentions. The regime long reacted with hostility to the economic reforms initiated over the past two decades and more in China and then in Russia and Eastern Europe, and has set its face against structural reform of its own economic system. The government's hope seems to be that setbacks will be overcome and that socialist policies can be restored. At the same time, it has been urging fundamental changes in both thinking and work-style to find practical answers to economic problems. The emphasis, as presented in the Party newspaper in January 2001, was to be on IT development, science and technology. A dual strategy of technological advance and experimentation with untried measures emerged as the official plan to cope with current problems.

The large rises in wages for selected categories of workers and in the prices of commodities and the costs of basic services that the government implemented from 1 July 2002, along with the withdrawal of state subsidies, had apparently been announced in the preceding May. The price of rice and maize shot up (to fixed levels), public transport fares increased and a rental system was introduced in place of formerly free housing. As an inducement to increase output, prices paid to farmers for their produce also rose proportionately. The rate of the won against the dollar, then standing at 2.16 won, rose a hundredfold to around 230 won. The Public Distribution System has been whittled down to those without other means of support, and the need to pay for commodities is leading to the monetarization of the economy. The changes took some getting used to, and wage earners who rejoiced in their first enlarged pay packet were less happy to see how much of it they had to part with in the shops. Prices increased, in fact, by a factor of twenty-six, outstripping eighteen-fold rises in salaries (as revealed in the summer of 2004 by a government economist). The price of rice rose by 550 times. The first impact of the new system seems to have been inflationary. In an attempt to reduce the amount of money in circulation (and, it has been suggested, to finance wages in the interval before price reforms started to work), the government introduced interest-free ten-year life bonds in March 2003. During the summer of 2003, the won reportedly floated against the dollar at a rate of 900 won to the dollar, close to the prevailing black market rate. By spring 2004, official rates of exchange had come down to around 140 won=one US dollar and around 173 won=one euro. In the markets, they might be far more advantageous.

In raising prices, the government may have wished to allow the state-owned shops to match the farmers' markets and thus compete with them. The popularity of these markets among those with the means to patronize them has increased to the point where, in the late 1990s, around half the population was estimated to be using them daily. In addition to the vegetables that farmers are authorized to send to market from their private plots, the markets sell meat and fish, consumer goods, and furniture. They are a phenomenon that had been tolerated, if grudgingly, since the early years of the regime, despite attempts to end private trading. Kim Jong Il is said in particular to resent them. In June 2003, however, they were officially recognized as forming part of the economy and operate with legal approval under the simple name of 'markets'. An arrangement that was offering a persistent challenge to the government has now been co-opted into the system. Besides the markets, informal 'frog markets' – so called because the sellers would leap up and run away if disturbed – might spring up in a neighbourhood, as when, in the winter of 2001–02, we found ourselves walking through a large selection of goods that included meat, grain, wedding rings, shoes and oil lamps, laid out on pieces of paper or cloth on the bare ground in a Pyongyang district. A 'private economy' of personal services such as dressmaking and hair-cutting, repairing bicycles, renovating apartments, photographing people in public places, private trading, in, for instance, gold, paintings and antiques, and second-hand cars and consumer goods, and selling on the street or by the roadside, has also emerged since the early 1990s. Various institutions have opened up their premises for informal shopping in local and hard currency. In early 2004, around 500 private businesses were said to be renting space in state-owned buildings in Pyongyang, paying a fee based on their incomes and fixing their own prices for goods and services.

The other aim of recent economic reforms has been to improve management and accountability in enterprises. In October 2001, Kim Jong Il reportedly directed that the numbers of party officials assigned to factories and public enterprises should be cut and their managerial rights transferred to specialised managers, a repudiation of the earlier work styles devised by his father. Performance in a job was to become a factor in determining pay, rising from a minimum wage level. Under supervision and within a framework of capped prices, enterprises were to take responsibility for drawing up production plans, setting standards and prices for their goods, appointing their own officials and for selling their output. After fixed reimbursements to the state, they were to be free to invest profits back into their business or to award bonuses to employees. On the downside, enterprises could no longer count on the state for machinery and subsidies. Planning and management of production for most goods was to pass to local authorities, with the centre determining total output for each province. Decentralized accounting systems have been in place for some time; and provinces have been free for several years to conduct their own trade. In the agricultural sector, a certain freedom in decision-making is also passing down the management line. Farmers, for instance, may decide what crops to grow and market from their private plots. The drive towards decentralization and enterprise-level responsibility looks set to continue in 2005 with the expansion of reforms in the factory and corporate sector that will, it is reported, replace state-fixed prices with market prices and end state planning in production and sales. Regular payment of taxes would be required, as would settlement of bills through banks (the intention here doubtless being to discourage barter trade).

These changes had their smaller-scale precedents in earlier decades as the government experimented with slight changes in the working of the system, in general away from centralized decision-making towards a modest extension of autonomy at provincial, county and enterprise level. The reforms put into effect in neighbouring countries may have appeared to the DPRK leadership as lapses from socialist principles, but may nonetheless have pushed it into considering the needs of its own economy. In conversation with foreigners, officials talk openly of the need to operate at a profit and eliminate debt. Gradually, the country is starting to educate some of its brightest talent in market practices through training abroad or by inviting foreign consultants including Westerners to lecture in the DPRK.

How are changes working out?

Two years on, the scene had changed somewhat in Pyongyang and possibly elsewhere. Energy supplies seemed to have improved and with them industrial activity; although it is difficult to know if there is a direct link between the reforms instituted in 2002 and the enhanced levels of electricity and production. A greater level of commercial activity was apparent in the introduction of pavement and roadside stalls, some of them tented, others more solid, in both Pyongyang and the countryside, selling bottled water, soft drinks, biscuits, candy and dried foodstuffs. Some of those in Pyongyang clearly stayed open until late at night. The newly constructed Tongil indoor market that opened in October 2003 in a southern suburb of Pyongyang caters primarily for Korean shoppers, but will let foreigners in to look and, if they can produce won, to make purchases. The one thing they must not try to do is to take photographs. The market offers a rich array of fresh produce, light consumer goods, clothes, furniture and consumer durables such as freezers and TV sets. A licence to sell at Tongil market was reported to cost US$30, with a fixed sum payable thereafter each time the stall was used. Various retail associations supply goods. The stallholders are almost all women, dressed in smart uniforms. Stewards, again mostly women carefully police the markets. They also adjudicate in disputes and keep an eye on foreigners. More markets of the same kind are planned. Other local markets remain closed to foreigners. A few foreign women have managed to make it once into other local markets before they were escorted out. They report that the range of goods they saw available was as extensive as that at Tongil and the prices slightly lower.

Prices are nonetheless undoubtedly high. Those at Tongil market would make a dent in many monthly budgets, and indeed, it is clear that even for middle-ranking cadres, most of their salary goes on food, once rent and utilities have been paid. The average cost of rice at Tongil market in May 2004 was 250 won per kilo. WFP reports of later that year detailed greatly increased prices of 600–700 won per kilo. Prices of oil and maize have also risen sharply. The average worker's wage appears to be 2000 won a month. Skilled workers can earn at least twice that. Government cadres may not do so well. Retirement is set at sixty for men and fifty-five for women, but pensions are not large. To live reasonably well, a family needs more than one monthly salary. Although details of the distributive network are no longer clear, the impression is that the PDS may operate a separate network where prices of basic commodities are much lower for its particular clients: at 44 won per kilo for rice and 24 won per kilo for maize. For other citizens, the necessities of life are still available and still guaranteed at distribution points (possibly the same as those used by the PDS) in the neighbourhood where they have their family registration. These commodities have always had to be paid for, but now cost more.

The comparatively thriving commercial scene and the readiness of Koreans to talk about the impact of economic changes on their lives serve to emphasize the continuing rigidity of other aspects of the economy. Despite Kim Jong Il's reported insistence that managerial specialists should take charge of business management, it seems that the style of management still taught to cadres is the Taean system of collective leadership apportioned between party workers, factory managers and technicians. Holding companies, which in turn are under the control of local party committees or government ministries, appear to continue to operate and finance factories; they are not truly independent. There appear to be no rights of dismissal or redundancy at factory level; this would be against the 'spirit of society', we were told. The way out of a situation such as a contraction in the workforce brought about by the extensive automation of a plant would be to reassign the redundant workers to another section. The continuing inability of government institutions handling economic-related affairs to produce any statistics or to offer a coherent account of the recent reforms and how they are working out is disquieting. The reversal of decisions on mobile telephones and possibly on the use of the euro, and the unease of some at the presence of foreigners at Tongil market, suggest conflicting voices in a debate that is conducted out of the hearing certainly of outsiders and possibly also of most Koreans. Change in the economy may indeed be progressing step by step and in accordance with the DPRK's own ways and style, as officials have said, and the government may feel it has achieved some of its goals, but a sense of hesitancy still marks the whole reform process.

4

Society

ELEMENTS OF SOCIETY

Population and cities

A CENSUS CONDUCTED in 1993 indicated a total population of 21.2 million for the DPRK. The current figure (2002) has generally been put at a little over 23 million, but this has been topped by an estimate, attributed among others to Kim Jong Il himself, of a population of 26–27 million. This compares with a figure for 2001 for the ROK of 47.34 million. The balance between the sexes in the 1993 census was 48.7 per cent men to 51.3 per cent women; this ratio is likely to have remained much the same. The generational structure in the DPRK favours the young and those in early middle age, and one sees relatively few elderly people. Rapid and deliberate moves towards urbanization in the late 1950s accompanied the drive to industrialization and resulted in an urban population of around 62 per cent of the total population. The country is divided into nine provinces – North and South Hamgyong, Ryanggang, Jagang, North and South Pyongan, North and South Hwanghae, and Kangwon – and three cities administered directly by the state – Pyongyang, Nampo and Kaesong.

The largest city in the DPRK is the capital, Pyongyang. Its population is generally said to be around 2.7 million, but again, a higher figure of 3.8 million, this time from pro-North Korean sources in Japan, emerged at the end of 2003. No other city approaches this size. Nampo, which serves as the port for Pyongyang, is the second largest, with 731,448 inhabitants. On the eastern seaboard, the Hamhung-Hungnam industrial conurbation in South Hamgyong province has a population of 709,730, and Chongjin, another industrial centre further north in North Hamgyong province, records 582,480 inhabitants. (The figures for these three cities date to the 1993 census and have probably increased.) The ice-free port of Wonsan on the east coast and Sinuiju at the western end of the Sino-Korean border are other important towns. The fertile western provinces of North and South Pyongan and the industrialized eastern provinces of North and South Hamgyong are the most heavily populated.

Family life

The charge used to be laid against Communist regimes that they sought to destroy family life. The DPRK has had its share of such criticism, but the situation in which the family finds itself in North Korea is somewhat complex. Rather than dismembering the family, the state has co-opted it into furthering its grand project of building a socialist society. The Family Law of the DPRK, promulgated in 1990, defines the family as the 'basic unit in society' and marriage as the foundation of a family (cohabitation is not acceptable). In so doing, it acknowledges one of the most important of Korean beliefs, that all adults should marry and continue the family line. What have been dismantled in the North are the extended family and the clan, rooted in family property. Land redistribution, followed by the organization of farmers into collective farming, broke up the old patterns of land-holding. The drive towards industrialization took many peasants off the land and into cities. As a result, the North Korean family is primarily a nuclear family, a social unit with no independent economic status. Rather, adult members of the family, male and female, are all expected to contribute to the general economic welfare of the country.

The pressures on family life are centrifugal. Both parents are expected to work outside of the home and to attach themselves to a work unit that controls much of their daily activity, organizes outings and supervizes political study sessions. The DPRK does not appear to have a policy on family size; but most families have two children. From the age of three months, a baby may be placed in a daily or even weekly or monthly nursery before being enrolled in kindergarten and then school. At eight years, he or she may join the Young Pioneers (distinguished by their red neck scarves). Older children, students and women have their own organizations. The emphasis is on activity within a group – in itself, not an alien concept to most Koreans – and on conformity with the vision of society laid out by Kim Il Sung. As a result, the population can be very speedily mobilized and expects constantly to be called out for various forms of 'voluntary' work such as digging trenches for pipes or rehearsing for a parade. This appropriation of individual and family time in the name of mass activities can on occasion seem very harsh, as when a neighbourhood was roused at 4 a.m. for rehearsals.

Nonetheless, a family's right to live as a unit and to care for its members does not appear to be challenged. It is accepted that a courting couple may wish to spend time together. If they hold hands, that is no longer frowned upon. The practice of generations living together, formalized in the traditional requirement that the eldest son look after his parents and unmarried siblings, is not uncommon in the DPRK. The ideal arrangement is probably the one that has the son's (widowed) mother living with her son's family and taking care of all household tasks. Her daughter-in-law can work with an easy mind, the children can be looked after if they are sick and the grandmother has accommodation and access to food. (A grandfather may be less useful, since his role in life is said to be 'smoking and drinking'!) Personal property is permitted by law and may be passed on to inheritors. Though an apartment cannot be inherited in this way because it has been rented from the state, it has been possible, if one has a sufficient amount of hard currency, to 'buy' the interest in it on a private basis in order to secure a change of occupancy. Revisions to the criminal code in April 2004, perhaps reflecting such practices, now make it possible to inherit a home. Parents who are in a position to do so try to ensure that their children get a good education and are as concerned as parents elsewhere to know who is telephoning their son and who his friends are. On the downside, a serious offence such as defection may bring down punishment by association on other members of the defector's family, including spouse, parents and siblings, in the form of a spell in a labour camp and permanent relocation from Pyongyang.

This framework for family life is closely tied in with the continuing ability of the state to meet material needs. Now that the PDS is being scaled down amidst price rises and the spreading use of cash in obtaining food (see Chapter 3), many families are coming under stress. Those with more than one wage earner in good jobs or with access to food supplies or to hard currency are managing to get by, yet even they are starting to admit to difficulties. Those with adult members out of work or in low-paying jobs or who cannot find or afford supplementary food supplies are facing hardship. The gaps in society are widening.

Children and the elderly

Kim Il Sung hailed children in the DPRK as the 'kings of society'. He appears in several paintings surrounded by children. Certainly, much has been done to promote their welfare and elevate their status. Since its establishment in 1948, the state has instituted free, compulsory school education, has passed laws recognizing the needs of children (1976) and prohibiting labour under sixteen

(1978), has defined the civil rights of children in the country's Civil Law (1990) and legislated for their protection in the Family Law (also 1990). That same year, the DPRK acceded to the international Convention on the Rights of the Child. It has been working since 1985 with the UN Children's Fund – UNICEF and in 1995 invited UNICEF to establish a resident office in Pyongyang.

If they are seen as kings, this is in part a reflection of the high value that Koreans have always placed on children as guarantors of the continuity of the family. In the DPRK, children have a particular role as inheritors and upholders of the socialist state. To that end, as already seen, they are exposed from an early age to an intensive process of socialization. Children's 'palaces' in Pyongyang and the provinces provide extra training in the sciences and arts for gifted children. Here are nurtured the music and dance troupes so beloved of Koreans and a source of amazement to foreigners, who marvel at the proficiency, even if they have doubts about the taste and spontaneity of it all – twenty little heads all bowing in exactly the same gesture over their instruments. All children are encouraged to sing and learn musical instruments, wherever their school or nursery.

Some children, however, are faring less well than others are as care structures fail. Pyongyang, with its population of highly favoured citizens, is generally able to maintain its children in good health and spirits, although even there you may see grubby children playing in the dust or shod only in gym shoes with no socks in icy weather. In other parts of the country, children and their clothes have an unwashed look, because soap is in short supply, and children's health has often deteriorated, especially in the north and northeast. They are particularly vulnerable to the continuing food shortages, the effects of which are clear in reduced resistance to illness and in small, underweight children. Koreans say that the present generation of children will be no taller than their grandparents. A range of institutions at provincial level care for children from birth to sixteen years whose parents have died or are unable to care for them. Some have been abandoned altogether and have been obliged to fend for themselves, even in Pyongyang.

At the other end of life, the old present a similar spread of good or bad fortune, from the grandparents walking with their grandchildren beside the Taedong or the old men sunning themselves by the banks of the Potong river, to the elderly women who tramp through the streets laden with huge sacks. Perhaps in recognition of their need, old women are permitted to sell minuscule amounts of goods by the roadside or glean ears of rice in a harvested field; and they are given a lot of leeway to drink, sing and dance in the parks on Sunday afternoons and holidays. Life expectancy, which by 1984 had risen to seventy-four, was estimated at between sixty-nine and seventy-five in 1997. Sad stories are reported of elderly people giving up their rations to other family members or of dying alone in winter in unheated apartments or on the stairs of high-rise blocks. If children and the elderly constitute, as it were, a barometer of the well-being of the Korean people, the reading is only fair.

Women

By the time of Korea's liberation from Japanese colonial rule, women had to some extent shaken off earlier restrictions on their activities. Some of them had already studied at school or university, one or two engaged in political activity, and others were already working in factories. Many women, however, were illiterate. They still had to subordinate their interests to the needs of their husbands' families and in particular to produce sons to continue the male line.

Kim Il Sung's new regime struck quickly at the lineage principle when in 1946 it redistributed land to peasant farmers, including women, and introduced a law on sex equality. The following year it replaced family registration based on male lineage with a new registration system. Without land and a clan kinship structure, the patrilineal family could no longer thrive. Women benefited from the rapid drive to literacy that followed liberation and from legal protection of maternity leave and appropriate conditions of work for pregnant and nursing mothers. From the outset, Kim Il Sung appears to have taken a close interest in women's emancipation, intervening to oppose male resistance to female participation in voting in the 1946 elections, encouraging women to engage in public and political affairs and underlining the need to reduce their burden of housework and childcare through the provision of nurseries. His aim, however, was specific: to bring women into the labour force, both as a means for them to achieve independence and in support of the national economy. He was successful, in that women have remained in the work force, albeit bunched in agriculture, light industry and the service sector and health and primary education and now in market trading. As in most societies, whatever their political colouring, women have only occasionally penetrated the highest reaches of the North Korean power structure, although at middle levels, they emerge as formidable chairwomen of cooperative farms or municipal management committees. The organization representing their interests, the Korean Women's Democratic League, is wholly under party control. In 2001, the DPRK acceded to the international Convention on the Elimination of All Forms of Discrimination Against Women (CEDAW).

The Marxist basis of the DPRK's policies on women, that they are emancipated through collective labour, allows no place for feminist theory or practice. Indeed, feminism is rejected as bourgeois and individualist, and there are no centres for women's studies at the universities. The female role model is Kim Jong Suk, mother of Kim Jong Il and Kim Il Sung's first wife. (She died in childbirth at the age of thirty-two.) Her loyalty to Kim and her care for her family are the qualities for which she is praised.

The political and family security and economic standing of women in North Korean society are assured by law. They no longer face pressure to produce sons, but must still think of marriage by twenty-six, to escape becoming an 'old slipper'. They are expected to dress conservatively. For a long time, trousers on women were only permitted in the winter months and then for outdoor wear; now, it seems, in a further small relaxation, women may wear them when they want to. Male authority is circumscribed, but still expresses itself through attitudes of superiority and talk of 'women's work', usually of a menial kind that no man would do, although he might supervise it, to 'ensure it is being done correctly'. Women are the physical load-carriers, whatever their age and however heavy the burden. In the home, moreover, they may find themselves expected to undertake every household task, in addition to their professional work. One woman we met spoke bitterly of being 'one skirt' who had to look after 'four trousers', none of whom appeared to lift a finger to help her. (In this respect, North and South are not so far apart; attitudes may be changing in the South, but such views on the differentiation of male and female spheres would be readily recognized in the South.) Men smoke heavily, smoking being seen as a sign of manhood, and drink a lot, with consequent domestic violence. Extra-marital affairs are known, and reports circulate of prostitution. In conversation, Korean men dismiss the possibility of homosexuality in society.

What is emerging, however, in assessments of the impact of malnutrition in recent years, is evidence that pregnant women and nursing mothers are suffering fairly high rates of anaemia and malnutrition – possibly 30 per cent – expressed in low intakes of food with calorific value and of iron and folic acid. The combination of work and communal activities outside the home with primary responsibility for the care of the family within it, often on an insufficient diet, is taking its toll.

THE WELFARE OF SOCIETY

Health

In 1953, a universal health system was introduced in the DPRK, free at the point of delivery. In keeping with the pattern of comprehensive party and administrative structures throughout the nation, the state early on instituted an extensive framework for the delivery of health care. This stretches from the section doctor and Red Cross first-aid post at village level up through the clinic staffed by a doctor, nurse and midwife at every *ri* or *dong* (the lowest administrative unit in rural and urban areas respectively), to county or district medical hospital and services. On top of these, come the provincial or city specialized hospitals, and eventually the big hospitals in Pyongyang – the Red Cross, university and maternity hospitals – and in some other cities – the National Orthopaedic Hospital is in Hamhung. The Ministry of Public Health is in charge of much of this provision. In the late 1950s, Red Cross teams from the Soviet Union and East European Communist states provided medical services in support of the North Korean effort and constructed several hospitals.

The framework is still in place, so that the greater part of the population has access to medical attention. Doctor-patient ratios would appear to be good, with, for instance, one section doctor responsible for between one hundred and four hundred families. Health checks and immunization are easily implemented through the ri and dong clinics. The larger factories and collective farms have their own clinic and children's homes and large nurseries may have their own doctor. Public health provision at county and provincial levels includes anti-epidemic stations, water-treatment plants and medical warehouses. The comprehensive care available through the 1950s, 1960s and 1970s improved children's health, raised life expectancy and wiped out communicable diseases. A system of social insurance benefits for industrial and office workers offered them free medical treatment, assistance in disability and pensions in old age.

The tragedy is that through economic decline and isolation for the past few decades from knowledge of medical advances in the rest of the world, the content of much medical care has fallen away, despite the willingness and competence of doctors. Libraries stopped taking foreign medical journals in the 1970s, and few doctors seem to have studied abroad since that period. Malaria and tuberculosis have made a return, though both these diseases are being held in check. Western drugs, in constant short supply, are provided largely though the international aid effort, and traditional medication is often administered. The country has no system of pharmacies operating outside of the state structure. General anaesthetics are unavailable, and equipment has not been replaced for decades, so that x-ray machines, where they exist at all, are operated without film, to the grave harm of staff. Hospitals may lack running water because of broken pipes and pumps and are often unheated in winter and short of food. Village health services now receive very little support from the national budget; yet the World Health Organization judges that it is at the village and county level that the system should best be built up. Care for the disabled is often inadequate. Bright spots are the renewed success of the child immunization programmes, especially against polio and measles; and the fact that AIDS does not seem to have taken hold in the country. During the SARS epidemic of 2003, the DPRK put itself in quarantine for several months by forbidding travel to and from China, and no cases were reported; but bird flu erupted in early 2005.

'The arduous march'

Such is the phrase Koreans use to describe the hardships of the years 1995–7, when natural disasters compounded the deficiencies of a failing economy to produce widespread shortages of food and other resources and in some areas famine. The intended analogy is with Kim Il Sung's long struggle against the Japanese. By spring 1998, the worst hardships were judged to be over, and from that year the Korean population was directed into a 'socialist forced march' as the country slowly emerged from the privations of the earlier years. The sequence and dynamics of this famine period are still hard to grasp, with many gaps in understanding and information scattered between various reports and studies, but the outlines of what happened can be pieced together to some extent.

NATURAL DISASTERS AND THEIR IMPACT

In 1994, hailstorms affected the DPRK. In August 1995, heavy floods struck the country. Among the regions badly hit were the northwestern provinces of North and South Pyongan and, further south, North Hwanghae province, all vital to agricultural production. The following year, fresh floods compounded the damage. The floods of 1995–6 were estimated to have affected up to half of the area given over to agriculture. In 1997, drought affected many parts of the country and tidal waves then hit North and South Pyongan provinces again, as well as South Hwanghae, flooding farmland and claiming lives. In 1998, heavy rain, hail, strong winds and again tidal waves struck the country. An EU humanitarian delegation visiting in May 1998 saw attempts to deal with salinity in reclaimed land in the northwest that had been overrun by flood waters that had burst the dikes. The year 1999 brought drought again.

As well as ruining farmland, the floods of 1996 and 1997 destroyed sections of the country's irrigation system and roads, bridges and railways. They also submerged a number of coalmines that have apparently still not all been pumped out, and damaged hydroelectric schemes, possibly through an accumulation of silt. Factories and public buildings such as schools were destroyed. The government of the DPRK has estimated the damage caused by natural disasters during this period at US$10–15 billion.

Patterns of flooding, drought and, in coastal regions, tidal waves are common in North Korea: a flash flood inflicted damage on the east coast in October 2001; and heavy rain in July 2004 destroyed houses and inflicted casualties in South Pyongan province and caused landslides and flooding in the far north of the country. The floods of August 1995, however, struck an agricultural sector that was already underproducing and exacerbated food shortages that had been evident from the early 1990s. A campaign in 1991–2 had encouraged people to eat only two meals a day, to which some had apparently responded, in 1991, by rioting. The distribution system that supplied the non-farming sections of the population with food and basic necessities appears to have been faltering even before 1995, and the amount that farmers could retain from the harvest was cut from the beginning of that year. Stocks of food and fuel oil seem to have always been husbanded by the government in support of its policy of continual war readiness and as general reserves. In September 1995, the loss of both harvest and emergency food stocks prompted the government of the DPRK to make a formal appeal to the UN Department of Humanitarian Affairs for assistance.

THE EFFECTS OF FAMINE

The lack of information surrounding the situation in the DPRK in the mid-1990s has led to varying interpretations of events, from doubts that there was a famine at all to claims of two to three million deaths from famine-related causes. It has so far been impossible to arrive at an agreed number of deaths. Even the two sets of figures emanating from North Korean sources are at variance: the chairman of the Flood Damage Rehabilitation Committee in May 1999 conceded that 220,000 people had died between 1995 and 1998 in excess of normal mortality; it is from this figure that commentators have extrapolated the estimate of two million dead. Hwang Jang-yop, a secretary of the Korean Workers' Party Central Committee who defected to the South in 1997, claimed to have been told by a government colleague that from 1995 to 1996, an estimated one and a half million people had died, and himself estimated a death toll of two-and-a-half million to the end of 1997. Two South Korean estimates, one an unofficial government estimate of 400,000 deaths for the period 1994–8, the other, of 300,000 deaths, from a South Korean think-tank, are closer to the 220,000 figure quoted above. Other, non-Korean estimates are higher, at 600,000–1,000,000 or even two to three million. The 1998 EU humanitarian delegation was told by a number of people on collective farms that the death rate had gone up in the three previous years, with the old, and to a lesser extent the very young, affected most.

The floods of 1995–6 touched large areas of farmland and thus the livelihoods of many farm workers, who were the first recipients of international relief together with children and their mothers and hospital patients. Thereafter, as food shortages worsened and the PDS broke down, urban populations and workers in industry and the mines, dependent on state-supplied rations, suffered increasing deprivation together with their families. These groups constitute about two-thirds of the population. Furthermore, as the general economic downturn cut salaries, factory workers were losing their purchasing power to buy in the farmers' markets. Even teachers, the military and provincial Party officials were reportedly not immune to the threat of hunger.

The worst effects of shortage of food were felt among the customarily weaker sections of any society: young children, the elderly, and pregnant women. From 1995, the sight of orphaned or abandoned children, the *kochibi* or 'fluttering swallows', became common. Evidence of the malnutrition to which children had been exposed over a considerable length of time emerged in a 1998 survey of children between the ages of six months and seven years, undertaken jointly by the DPRK government, the UN Children's Fund – UNICEF, the WFP and the EU. This showed that 16 per cent of the children examined displayed signs of acute malnutrition (which would require rehabilitative feeding), the greatest incidence coming in the second year of life; 62 per cent had stunted growth and suffered from chronic malnutrition; and 61 per cent displayed low weight for age. The North Korean government provided further indications of the toll exacted on children through insufficient food and increased vulnerability to illness in 2001, when it reported that during the years 1990–99, infant mortality had risen from 9.2 deaths per 1000 live births to 23 deaths per 1000 live births and under-five mortality from 30 deaths per 1000 to 55 deaths. Between 1990 and 1996, maternal mortality was reported to have increased from 70 per 100,000 live births to 110.

While no doubt the ruling group and top Party officials were less affected by shortages of food and the capital did not suffer as much as the rest of the country, food was, nonetheless, in short ration in Pyongyang, with people consuming on occasion as little as half a bowl of maize per day at one point. In general, however, the ravages of hunger and famine were not evenly spread throughout the country. In particular, the north and northeast provinces appear to have been badly hit. Terrain and climate have always made these regions agriculturally unproductive. The relatively high proportion of industrial workers living there, with limited resources for food production, dependent on the PDS and moreover, increasingly at risk of unemployment or underemployment, made these provinces especially vulnerable to food shortages.

OFFICIAL STRATEGIES AND ATTITUDES

The government of the DPRK adopted various strategies to cope with the famine of 1995–7. It pushed ahead with the policy of decentralization it had already been pursuing for at least a couple of decades to call for local solutions to problems, to that end devolving responsibility from 1996 on to provincial administrations to meet local needs in the food emergency and to trade on their own account. As a temporary measure, it reportedly even instructed the population to seek food where it could. It instituted selective distribution of such food supplies as there were in favour of farm workers, the military, key industrial workers and Party officials, and allowed some experimentation in agricultural production. Among the regime's basic responses to the crisis has been the support of agriculture and the farming population in a bid to increase domestic food production – a reversal of its earlier prioritization of the industrial sector. By the early 2000s, it was making larger budgetary allocations to agriculture, was implementing policies on land and crop management and irrigation and was showing some willingness to cooperate with UN agencies and NGOs on agricultural techniques.

Its apparent abandonment of various other sections of the population at the height of the crisis constitutes a far more negative response. In the absence of any explanation of its motives, it is difficult to know if the government made a hard-headed decision that certain groups should be sacrificed to allow the core elements of the regime to survive; or whether the scale of the disaster, combined with the rigid structure of North Korean society and in particular of the PDS, made it almost inevitable that many industrial workers and the poorer sections of society, already a burden on that system, would be badly hit. Government insistence that international relief should go first to the agricultural areas and only later (from 1997) to the north and northeast would seem to give some indication of official priorities.

The government's most dramatic measure to cope with the situation it confronted in August 1995, and one that is still having its effect, was to appeal the following month for international assistance. It had already, in the months shortly before the 1995 floods, negotiated with both Japan and the Republic of Korea for the delivery of large amounts of grain aid. Now it turned to the UN, of which the DPRK had become a member in 1991. (It must be a moot point whether Kim Il Sung, who had died in 1994, would have sanctioned such a démarche.) The government, having admitted to a problem and made its appeal for help, did not, however, welcome all the consequences of that move and remained determined to control investigation and reporting of the disaster and, even more, the activities of the foreign relief workers who arrived from 1995. It set up the Flood Damage Rehabilitation Committee that same year, to liaise with, and supervise, the various relief organizations. Despite constant tussles with the authorities, the WFP, which set up its office in Pyongyang in 1995–6, made headway and managed to expand its activities during 1997–8. In 1997, WFP decided to distribute its fortified food for children through kindergartens rather than the PDS. UNICEF, which had been active in the DPRK since 1985, established a resident office in 1995 to direct programmes aimed at the rehabilitation of malnourished children.

Despite the material benefits of such activities, many in the government machine, particularly the military and security services, were, and remain, extremely suspicious of the presence of foreigners in the country. Even Kim Jong Il, it is claimed, resented the need for foreign support. A speech attributed to him, delivered in December 1996 on the fiftieth anniversary of the founding of Kim Il Sung University, gives some flavour of the anxieties aroused by the crisis. In the speech, Kim Jong Il seems well aware of the problems caused for ordinary Koreans by the shortage of food; but equally deplores the possibility of 'anarchy' arising out of their need to 'wander aimlessly' in search of sustenance. He scolds Party workers for their complacency and failure to work hard to find solutions to problems. He is particularly alarmed that the military may be going short of food and thereby compromising their war efficiency. He is also aware that farmers and others were concealing food in the winter of 1996. The answer he seemed to propose at that juncture was yet more political education and exhortation to increase productivity and show a better public spirit.

POPULAR COPING MECHANISMS

As Kim Jong Il admitted, a number of people did indeed leave their homes in search of food. Movement about the country had hitherto been restricted through the issuance of passes and through checkpoints at the approach to cities. Now, clearly with official acquiescence, people could travel, often by train, to where they thought they might be able to get food through purchase or barter. Sometimes, it seems, they raided freight cars loaded with corn. Those living in the north and northeast provinces made trips across the border into China to seek relief or buy provisions. Most returned home after stocking up, some stayed on in China. The border along the Tuman river between the DPRK and the ethnic Korean region of Yanbian in China had traditionally been a porous one, with Koreans crossing over to trade. As the crisis developed, much larger numbers of people crossed the frontier into Yanbian, where they were met and cared for by voluntary aid organizations, many of them South Korean Buddhist or Christian groups.

Others stayed in their home region, but resorted to selling produce or household possessions to make money to buy rice in the farmers' markets, which grew in number and importance. Vegetables and livestock were raised wherever they could be, even in towns. Staple foodstuffs were supplemented by wild foods, such as edible grass, wild vegetables and herbs, and by seaweed and fish in coastal areas. Consumption of wild edible plants and herbs is a long-established practice in all parts of Korea and does not necessarily denote hardship; it continues to this day in South Korea; but eating grass and bark, as sometimes happened during the years of hunger, is a mark of desperation.

As the worst of the famine in the DPRK eased by mid-1998, the government moved to reimpose control on movement about the country and for a while, from 1997 to 1999, held wanderers in detention camps. Those sent back over the border from China were also detained, sometimes beaten, but it seems that severe punishment was reserved primarily for those who had tried to defect to a third country or had established contact with a religious group. The experience of having to make decisions and fend for themselves had a loosening effect on many people's thinking. They appear nonetheless to have accepted the general view that the problems confronting them were the result of natural disasters, compounded by the incompetence of officials, and not the effect of any faults in the system.

THE PRESENT SITUATION

Physical conditions

North Korean society, at the start of 2005, is clearly in better shape than it was seven to eight years before. The agricultural sector has revived somewhat, and the severe malnutrition among children noted in the 1998 survey has receded, though it has by no means been eliminated; the WFP website carries pictures of malnourished children taken in 2004. A similar survey conducted jointly in October 2002 by UNICEF, WFP and the DPRK government recorded an incidence of around 39 per cent stunting (low height for age) in the sample surveyed, by comparison with an incidence of around 62 per cent in the 1998 assessment. Underweight among children had fallen from 61 per cent in 1998 to around 20 per cent in 2002; wasting (low weight for height), which is an indication of acute malnutrition, from 16 per cent in 1998 to around 8 per cent in 2002. Failures in growth are largely generated during the first two years of life and reflect conditions during those years. The deprivation of the mid-1990s had evidently lessened by the end of the decade. The latest joint nutritional survey (October 2004) confirms the downward trend but indicates continuing nutritional problems.

The general shortage of energy that has plagued both the economy and people's livelihood over the past decade and more in the DPRK may be easing slightly. The general view in mid-2004, at least in Pyongyang, was that electricity was in somewhat better supply. This might account for the modernization and construction programme under way in the capital, aimed at the city's housing stock. Several buildings that in 2002 stood uncompleted were now ready. Over the half-century since the rebuilding of Pyongyang commenced, the capital has expanded slowly outwards into new suburbs; but these tall shining blocks, some of them twenty or thirty storeys high, must at times be hard to live in, in the frequent absence of electricity, heating and pumped water. Now, however, older residential blocks are being repainted and renovated with new balconies, some of them glassed in, and toilets are being installed inside apartments to replace the previous communal lavatories on each landing. A couple of years ago, it was clear that even this provision was insufficient in the face of power and water shortages, and residents, even in the centre of Pyongyang, were using communal privies in the grounds of their apartment blocks. These appeared to have gone by May 2004. On the perimeters of the city, older settlements exist, some of them clearly villages that the capital has reached out to, others, as in East Pyongyang, composed of single, one-storey houses in small yards, put up in the late 1950s to meet the post-war need for shelter. In 2002 in these poor districts, water had to be fetched from a well, lavatories were communal, street drainage was into open channels and the roads were largely earth. We did not revisit such areas when we went to the DPRK in 2004, so cannot say if modernization is reaching them as well.

Homelessness has never been an issue in the DPRK, though the quality of housing may be. The house-building and renovation programme witnessed in the capital is extending into provincial towns and the countryside, though with no great improvement in construction techniques: walls are generally only one brick or breezeblock thick, covered by a rough finish. A continuing problem in many parts of the country is the presence of old, broken pipe and pump installations that together with power stoppages threaten the provision of clean water and adequate sanitation. Both aid agencies and NGOs have undertaken projects aimed at improving water supplies. In the absence of piped water, women use the local rivers and streams for washing dishes, cooking utensils and clothes. Winter cold is another risk to well-being, showing itself in a high incidence of respiratory illnesses and in a general numbing that, for instance, would leave university students comatose in the classroom. Despite some small improvements in general conditions, the health of sections of society, in particular that of young children, pregnant women and the elderly, continues to be undermined by inadequate provision of basic foodstuffs and balanced diets. The worst signs of such distress are probably to be found in the provincial residential centres for children whose parents have either died or are unable to care for them. These homes are not callous places, but they are under enormous strain. Within a week of our arrival in July 2001 we visited one such centre, where we saw two sickly babies suffering from severe malnutrition, who were not expected to survive. Another cause of concern is the fate of children who may have 'slipped through the net' in that they are not being cared for at any point. The situation of those living in the closed areas of the country – about 20 per cent of the territory and perhaps 17 per cent of the population – is simply not known. The government claims that it supplies the food and medical needs of closed areas, so that they have living standards equal to those in the open areas. Generally, however, when previously closed areas have been opened to international assistance, conditions have been found not to be good.

The allocation of cereals through the PDS fluctuates between 250 grams and 350 grams per head per day during the course of a year in accordance with the availability of supplies. Such amounts meet about half the calorific needs of an individual. Farmers are said to be eligible for a substantially larger allocation of about 600 grams per day and are able to grow vegetables and maize on their private plots, which reportedly can now be as large as 1320 sq. m. (14,200 sq. ft.). To supplement their diets, urban residents with relatives living in the countryside receive such produce in exchange for manufactured goods such as clothing, furniture and tools, and foodstuffs such as seafood. In 2002, city-dwellers were continuing to resort to devices they had developed during the years of disaster. They grew crops wherever they could, raising poultry and rabbits in their apartments for sale or consumption (the rabbits sometimes came out for a walk and the cocks could be heard crowing from balconies), taking wild birds' eggs, and fishing for whatever they could get from the rivers. They are probably still doing the same, although such activities seemed less obvious in May 2004. Those with the money to do so would buy at the markets. In addition to the wild produce – herbs, fruit, mushrooms and seaweed – gathered at the appropriate season by rural populations, alternative food in the form of noodles made from cereal straw and stalks and potato powder is distributed to the needy through the PDS. WFP estimates (February 2005) that around 6.5 million people who cannot easily augment their diet continue in need of supplementary rations. This group comprises 2.7 million children in nurseries, kindergartens, primary schools and orphanages; lesser numbers of pregnant and nursing women and of elderly people; and the poorest urban families. WFP also calculates that two-thirds of the population remain dependent on the PDS because of their inability to meet the higher prices now charged in the markets.

In September 2004 and March 2005, the North Korean government set out its views to aid agencies and NGOs working in the DPRK on how it would like future international assistance to evolve. It no longer wishes to support the joint appeals process addressed to international donors, which has been used since the late 1990s. It is seeking simplified procedures for monitoring and access and a reduction in the number of international staff in the country. At the same time, it will consider bilateral cooperation and more technical assistance and development-oriented aid. (North Korean willingness in 2003 to accept the participation of UNDP and the UN Environment Programme in the preparation of a report on the state of the DPRK's environment and to commit to joint activities is presumably an example of the kind of cooperation envisaged.) WFP and the North Korean authorities are discussing more acceptable monitoring procedures. Several factors may have prompted the DPRK government's reassessment. It may be that, wary of donor fatigue, it hopes to pre-empt the uncertainties of international aid: it acknowledges that emergency humanitarian assistance has continued for over nine years. (In late 2004, WFP gave the dimensions of its aid: almost four million tonnes of food assistance, valued at US

$1.3 billion, over the period since 1995.) The DPRK may feel that its economic status is improving to the point where it can start to plan for the future in a more rational way. It is clear that security is being used as a reason for reducing the participation of foreign personnel, and the new arrangement may represent a compromise with the security services. The international aid community in the DPRK has long encouraged a move towards development projects, even though funding for UN development-oriented programmes is much less than that for emergency relief and may depend, for the DPRK, on the resolution of nuclear and military objections.

Against such hopes, the country remains vulnerable to poor harvests and clearly still has problems in providing sufficient food for all its citizens, either through cultivation or through purchases from abroad. A disaster such as the explosion at Ryongchon station south of Sinuiju in April 2004, when wagons containing ammonium nitrate and containers of fuel oil collided in a shunting accident,* can be particularly difficult to deal with. Of the 156 killed, almost half were children. Injuries to 1,300 others were sometimes extensive, in some cases possibly permanent. Much property was damaged. Relief agencies within the country were requested the following day to render assistance and have since been helping in rebuilding accommodation and assessing medical and rehabilitation needs.

Changes in society

The assessment of aid workers in recent times is that the widespread deprivation of the second half of the 1990s is being replaced by selective pockets of neediness. The implication of this, that people's experiences of hardship vary greatly and that some sections of the population are faltering where others are coping well, is almost certainly true; as is the further implication that factors other than natural disaster or general economic decline come into play. As noted in Chapter 1, North Korean society has always been characterised by categories, divided on the basis of political loyalty, occupation – farmers, industrial workers, office workers (which included Party and government officials, business people, artists and intellectuals) and military personnel –, education and family background (both closely bound up with political reliability) and specific job. For long, fixed pay scales determined salary. Now, with

* Other reports suggest that the two wagons exploded after coming into contact with electric wires from the train cables.

the economic changes of July 2002 and the gradual monetarization of the economy, cash would seem to be entering the equation and determining to some extent who can survive and who may fail.

The rigid categories of society may still be in place, but the relations between them have changed. The mutually supportive framework, for instance, within which agriculture and industry were supposed to exist, has largely broken down, with industry less able to meet the needs of farming. Agriculture is now valued as the means of alleviating national food shortages, and only selective support is given to industry to the benefit of such sectors as mining, the metal industries, weapons production, power generation and transport. Workers in other branches of industry that are running down are finding themselves out of employment or underemployed. Some factories are unable to operate at full capacity through lack of raw materials or electricity. Others are said to be unable to pay full wages because of low output or sales (for which they are now responsible). Workers thus find their salaries reduced at a time when the need to have purchasing power is becoming crucial. Those on a low income cannot easily offset the inadequacy of the PDS by buying in the markets; and prices have risen faster than wages. The areas of deprivation that are thus forming are heavier in the urban regions, among groups with few resources, such as pensioners, and appear to be concentrated to some extent in the old industrial provinces of the north and northeast. The 2002 and 2004 nutrition surveys found that the children assessed in the cities of Pyongyang and Nampo suffered considerably lower rates of stunting, underweight and wasting – in some instances almost half or one-third the rate – when compared with the children assessed in South Hamgyong and the northern province of Ryanggang, thereby reinforcing the argument that natural and social benefits are not spread evenly throughout the country.

The impression now is of a society that is becoming differentiated and unequal; or which, perhaps, is less concerned about displaying its inequalities than it once may have been. Foreigners who first knew the country in the early 1990s say that ten years on, they notice greater divergences in wealth. There are signs everywhere: purchases in hard currency, private ownership of cars, attendance on golf courses, the availability of imported foodstuffs and consumer goods, pet dogs. Other observers have pointed to a decline in concern for the collective good: for instance, snow-clearing that relied on communal efforts is no longer carried out, pilfering of state property and concentration on private plots go on, and corruption is admitted. There is an acknowledged rise in small-scale criminal activity. Public transport and markets display general warnings against pickpocketing. One section of Tongil market in Pyongyang offers heavy, double-thickness metals doors with two locks to replace or fit over an existing door. People give the appearance of being indifferent towards the needs of others; but ignorance of how the less fortunate live (young Korean officials who have spent all their lives in Pyongyang can receive unpleasant shocks when they visit impoverished parts of the country for the first time), together with an acceptance of the political and social hierarchy and a deeply engrained expectation that the state will provide for all requirements, do not encourage a more wide-ranging view on society. With the exception of the Red Cross Society of the DPRK and one or two other organizations, what might be recognized as institutions of civil society barely exist.

5

Cultural Values

LANGUAGE, EDUCATION AND SPORT

Language

AMONG THE GREAT unifying forces in which the Korean people take pride are their racial homogeneity and their language, spoken throughout the peninsula. Korean is generally classed as belonging to the Altaic group within the Ural-Altaic languages and within that group to the Tungusic branch. In its grammatical structures, it can be compared to Japanese. It has no relationship to Chinese, but has taken a large number of loan words – as many as 60 per cent of its vocabulary – from that language over the course of centuries. For a long while, Chinese characters, the preserve of scholars and officials, were used for the written form of the language, even though the syntax and morphology of Korean diverge widely from those of Chinese. Eventually, in the fifteenth century, a new alphabet, *hangul*, was devised on the instruction of the Choson-dynasty ruler, King Sejong (r.1418–50), as a means of representing accurately the sounds of the Korean language and of thus making it accessible to all. His intention was not immediately successful, but in time, all Koreans accepted the use of hangul and it is now counted as one of their outstanding cultural achievements. This shared language has persisted despite the North-South divide, in that Koreans from both sides speak a mutually comprehensible tongue; when negotiators meet for talks, they can communicate satisfactorily enough. That said, the language has developed in different ways in the two Koreas and has been the object of widely differing policies. One example of this division comes with the very name of the alphabet. In South Korea, hangul is now standard, but in the North, the older name *Choson muncha*, or Korean letters, is used.

The first set of North-South talks in 1972 revealed the extent of divergences that, despite a common base, had appeared in linguistic usage between the two states. After 1945, both Koreas carried forward measures of linguistic reform and standardization that had been initiated earlier in the century. Whereas in the ROK the process was largely in the hands of civil servants and academics and evoked much debate, particularly over the place of Chinese characters in written Korean, in the DPRK, language quickly became a tool in official policies. As might be expected, Kim Il Sung intervened and conducted two 'Conversations with Linguists', in 1964 and 1966. One outcome was the promotion from the late 1960s of *munhwa'o*, 'cultured' or 'refined' language that would allow Koreans in the North to express themselves as citizens of a new society. Munhwa'o was to incorporate, in a refined shape, forms of speech as actually spoken and written by the working people. At the same time, the most formal of the three levels of speech was to be preferred in addressing others. In practice, this standard speech was based on the language of Pyongyang. Linguistic differences between the North and the South are fairly small in such areas as phonetics, alphabetical order and morphology. Chinese characters have a very small role in the North. Vocabulary is the largest area of divergence for the DPRK: native Korean words have replaced many Sino-Korean and foreign loan words in a drive to enhance the purity of the language, and political priorities have demanded a new vocabulary. Spoken Korean in the North is said to be characterized by stronger stress and higher pitch. The television newscasters provide fine examples of this exalted style.

Education

Like health, education is another area where the DPRK has made enormous strides, to the point where it can claim near universal adult literacy. The value of education was traditionally appreciated in Korean society, but for centuries it involved mastery of the Chinese classical canon and writing system, was reserved for the aristocracy and scholars and was largely denied to commoners and women. From the end of the nineteenth century, education began to spread downwards among the people, including girls. The Japanese colonial administration permitted schooling to a certain level, but few Koreans got as far as university. On liberation in 1945, both states initiated literacy programmes and instituted increasingly comprehensive systems of education. Today, both North and South can boast of well-educated societies. The difference has been in the ends to which education has been turned.

In the DPRK, the primary purpose is to create successive generations of young people imbued with a willingness to merge their own interests with the common good. Further emphasis is put on acquiring the skills necessary for the country's economic and technological development. Learning is combined with labour, to allow the practical applications of theory to be brought home. As seen above (Chapter 1), political study, focused on the lives and teachings of Kim Il Sung and Kim Jong Il, is part of the curriculum from primary school onwards. Kim Il Sung himself urged that correct thinking should be achieved through explanation and persuasion. As the educational system developed, culminating in the eleven-year programme of free, universal, compulsory schooling introduced in 1973, the national element in teaching was strengthened. Chinese characters disappeared from textbooks when these were revised in 1949. Russian pedagogic influence was strong in the years immediately before and after the Korean War, but was discarded as a national context was increasingly demanded in all instruction. That said, many young people continued to study in China, the Soviet Union and Eastern Europe until the end of the 1980s.

Teaching starts with a pre-school year in kindergarten that leads to four years of primary school and a further six at middle school, finishing at sixteen. The curriculum obviously widens between primary and middle school, but contains core elements of Korean language, mathematics and sciences as well as political studies. Children showing talent in foreign languages, music, dance and the arts may attend specialist schools apportioned between the capital and the provinces. Mangyondae Revolutionary School, founded in 1947 to educate the 'bereaved children of revolutionaries', now prepares those from good families for careers in the Party and armed forces. Those in need of a more caring environment – disabled, deaf or blind children and those orphaned or without family support – are educated in residential institutions. Work experience may take the form of weeding the public gardens, participation in 'tree-planting' month or helping with the harvest. The economic decline of recent years has, alas, also damaged this solid structure of schooling, particularly in remote areas. Furthermore, the floods of 1995 and 1996 destroyed both buildings and teaching materials. Many school premises, especially those in remote areas, are poorly maintained and heated, equipment is not renewed and even printed textbooks and supplies of school stationery are now becoming unavailable. Attendance, once estimated at 100 per cent, is in danger of falling off, especially in the rural areas.

At the higher level, a wide range of institutions is open to older students. The most prestigious is Kim Il Sung University in Pyongyang, established in 1946 and the only multi-competent university in the DPRK. Women constitute around 30 per cent of its students. A university place is secured through a highly competitive examination, supported by a good political background. Universities are apparently sealed off during the exams, and candidates' parents meet teachers and university officials to push their offspring's chances. Once at university, students' time is not all devoted to study. They are drafted into the militia, participate in national parades and displays, and may be called upon to help with planting and harvesting. An independent job market hardly exists, and graduates wait to be assigned employment.

Since 2000, language students at a few of the capital's universities have been able to benefit from the inclusion of native German and British teachers in the staff at their colleges. France assists with French language teaching from its cultural institute in Japan. Canadian English-language teachers were scheduled to initiate courses in 2004 in Pyongyang, particularly for scientists preparing to study abroad.

Teaching is a respected profession in the DPRK. Education, moreover, is considered a lifelong activity, and adult education courses, often part-study part-work, are widely organized. The Grand People's Study House in Pyongyang is an important centre for continuing education as well as functioning as the national library and a prime resource centre.

Sport

There is undoubted enthusiasm for sport – informal games of volleyball or football are played in off-duty hours – and children go wading or swimming in rivers, even in Pyongyang. Football teams for men and women exist at many levels up to the national. Mass sport involving many thousands has for many years generally taken the form of gymnastics, which are the core of the elaborate displays of dancing, gym and music that make up a show such as the Arirang festival of 2002. Rehearsals for these events may go on for months, usually in outdoor settings and even through the winter. Children are removed from their schools for days on end, with consequent friction between the education and culture ministries; but mass activity and the accompanying socialisation of children and young people win out. A British-made film, *A State of Mind*, released in 2004, follows the participation of two Pyongyang schoolgirls in mass gymnastics.

It is doubtful how widely sports equipment is available, and the general low levels of nutrition must rule out very energetic sports except for a chosen few, many of whom are probably in the armed services. Synchronized swimming, martial arts, boxing, gymnastics, skating and wrestling are some of the sports pursued. In recent years, an international marathon has been staged annually in the capital. Pyongyang is, as ever, well equipped with training centres in its

'Sports Street' inaugurated in 1989 in the west of the city. The Pyongyang Physical Training Institute produces tall, well-built young men and women, whom it sends out for canoeing and sculling practice on the Potong river. These are the kind of young people who represent the DPRK at sports meets abroad, such as the 2000 and 2004 Summer Olympics, and the Asian Games held in Pusan in South Korea in 2002, when North Korean athletes and even more the accompanying women cheerleaders were warmly greeted. The North Korean successes at the 1966 World Football Cup series in the UK are still remembered – they were followed at the time through broadcasts – and a British film, *The Game of their Lives*, released in 2002, which assembled seven of the original team and their coach, was well received. Although the DPRK did not participate in the 2002 series jointly hosted by the ROK and Japan, recorded highlights were shown on North Korean television and South Korea's good showing was a source of satisfaction. The two circuses in Pyongyang, the state circus and the army circus, demonstrate the exceptionally high levels of strength and skill of the performers.

RELIGION

This is one of the most impenetrable areas for the outsider: how to judge the nature and authenticity of the religious activity that undoubtedly goes on and which foreigners are at liberty to observe. Freedom of belief is guaranteed in the constitution. Buddhist temples are staffed, and Christian churches have congregations. People are able to commemorate their departed family members at the Chusok festival. At the same time, reports of conditions in prison camps suggest that religious believers are among those singled out for particularly harsh treatment.

Since the late 1980s, five churches have been, or are being, constructed in Pyongyang: a church for the indigenous Chondoist sect that practises a syncretic form of worship, built in 1990; two Protestant churches, Bongsu (1989) and Chilgol (1992); the Catholic Changchong cathedral (1987); and an Orthodox church, due for completion in 2005. Around sixty Buddhist temples have survived in the country at large. Official figures for the various groups are 15,000 Chondoists; 12,000 Protestants or Christians, as they are called in both North and South Korea; 3000 Catholics; and 10,000 Buddhists. The comparative strength of the Protestant church may reflect its earlier vigour in the northern part of the peninsula during the first half of the twentieth century, while the autonomy of congregations allows them, unlike the Catholic group, to develop independently of an external structure. Religious adherence in the Christian churches seems to be a family matter; baptism is only within families, and there is no proselytizing. The Pyongyang churches have congregations of between 100 and 300 and very fine choirs, but worshippers are ageing, and few young people attend. Both in the capital and in the provinces, a system of 'house churches', groups meeting for private worship, has been in place since the Korean War and compensates for the absence of church buildings. Recent mention of a provincial Catholic church, ruined since the war, as a meeting place for the local faithful, suggests other possible arrangements.

It is not clear how well attended the Buddhist temples are, though monks speak of large congregations on the important festivals such as Buddha's birthday and in support of acceptable causes such as national unification. Buddhist monks appear to be all married, though their families do not necessarily live with them. Temples have often been restored with careful attention to traditional designs and carving and painting techniques, even if, given the long break in the transmission of such techniques, these have had to be copied from pattern books. Several contain ancient sculptures and manuscripts. What can be missing is the patina of use: wooden pillars may smell too new, lacking the permeation of incense. There is talk of assistance from the main Buddhist order in South Korea, the Chogye order, with the repair of temple buildings in the North and the restoration of wall paintings. A joint North-South exhibition on the art of Buddhist paintings was held at Mt Kumgang in July 2004.

Despite the uncertainties, training for both the Buddhist and Protestant ministries continues, a Protestant seminary exists and a second one may have opened recently. It is not apparent how all the graduates of these institutions will be employed, but references to their working in city-, provincial- and county-level administration suggest they may have some recognized role to play. The present situation, however tightly controlled it may be through the Korea Council of Religionists and the official committees that administer the various faith groups, is in contrast to the former long period of inactivity and the even earlier harassment of religious organizations and confiscation of church and temple property in the post-1945 years, compounded by the extensive destruction of temples and churches during the Korean War. Kim Il Sung had links with Protestant Christianity through his mother, Kang Pan Sok, and her family, who were believers, and he may have kept a residual interest in religion. A member of her family, Kang Yong Sop, is chairman of the North Korean Christians Federation. (And indeed, Chilgol church may have been erected as an act of filial piety, as it stands near or on the site of the former church where she used to teach Sunday school.)

By the 1970s, Kim may have decided that the religious groups could be used in the dual role of indicating plurality in the DPRK and of encouraging international interest. Delegations were sent during that decade to the World Council of Churches in support of Christian resistance to the authoritarian regime in South Korea. The spate of building and reconstruction from the late 1980s clearly gave an impetus to international contacts, and visitors and support from South Korea have multiplied. The evangelical pastor Billy Graham, whose wife attended school in Pyongyang in the 1930s when her parents were missionaries in China, has preached at Bongsu church and met Kim Il Sung. The Catholic cathedral depends on visiting priests, generally from Japan and the ROK, to celebrate mass, since it lacks its own ordained ministry. (The loss of ordained priests by the end of the Korean War left a gap in the apostolic succession.) Priests visiting from South Korea introduced the congregation to new practices, such as use of the vernacular and the positioning of the officiant facing the faithful. Unlike the Catholic church in China, which the Vatican regards as schismatic, the Catholic church in the DPRK receives regular visits from Vatican officials.

In trying to assess the true state of belief in the DPRK, the temptation is to reject the overt signs of religious practice as bogus, even, some have claimed, the work of actors; yet it does not seem wholly so. One clue may lie in the family-generated nature of Christian participation. Just as various occupations, such as pottery-making, were historically reserved in Korea for identified social groups, so the profession of Christian, whether Protestant, Catholic or Orthodox, may be regarded as the prerogative of those families that have been believers for generations. As recognized church-goers they are allowed to function. The difficulty comes for those who, without a religious family background, may wish to join a church or temple, or those who seek a religious life or religious contacts outside of the officially sanctioned congregations. Their wish for independence will be seen as a challenge to authority.

The initiative, attributed to Kim Jong Il, to construct an Orthodox church in Pyongyang and to provide it with a congregation illustrates the decisive part the state plays in religious affairs. Kim is said to have been struck by what he saw of a Russian orthodox church when he visited the Russian Far East in 2002; pictures published in the DPRK media showed him carefully questioning the priest about his church. Completion of the Pyongyang church is expected for spring 2005. It is to function as the Korean Orthodox church, for Koreans, and is to be independent of the Russian hierarchy, although training of several priests has begun in Moscow. It is not clear how the congregation will be found, but from 1929 to 1939, a small Russian Orthodox congregation existed in Pyongyang; and earlier still, Korean emigrants to Siberia and Manchuria, who had been baptized into the Russian Orthodox church, brought their new faith back with them when they returned to Korea in 1895. Following the concept of a 'family occupation', it may be that their descendants will be invited to rediscover their beliefs. The news, in October 2003, that a third Protestant church would be built in central Pyongyang with the active participation of South Korean Christians may at this stage primarily reflect North Korean willingness to cooperate with the ROK.

At the popular level, traditional festivals such as lunar new year, the spring Tano festival and the autumn harvest festival of Chusok are being celebrated again. Chusok is marked by family picnics to which the deceased may be 'invited'. Lack of transport can be an obstacle to travelling to the ancestral graves. In the cities, where cremation is encouraged, the ashes of the deceased are stored at a central point in the neighbourhood and may be taken out by the family for a few days over Chusok or at an important anniversary. The riverside is a favoured spot. Family members, usually the middle-aged or old, lay out food, rice liquor and flowers on a cloth or piece of cardboard stretched on the ground, in front of a photograph of the dead relative, which is propped against the urn containing the ashes. The urns themselves are often made of porcelain, wood or metal and are transported carefully in large wooden carrying cases. Occasionally an elderly member of the family may make reverences before the photograph, but for most it is a question of gathering as a group around the urn.

THE ARTS

It does not take long to realize the high value placed on the arts in the DPRK and the importance of the nation's cultural life. In a country almost entirely devoid of commercial advertising until 2004, film and theatre billboards catch the eye. Television is filled with song-and-dance shows and with domestically produced 'soap operas' and films; schoolchildren on their long treks through the streets sing as they walk and are always ready to perform for visitors to their school. On group outings, people end up singing and dancing or entertain each other with a talent contest.

Official positions . . .

In the DPRK, the arts in all their branches flourish in a very particular climate. They are encouraged, not for their own sake or as an outlet for individual ability and sentiment, but primarily as an element in official policies, and artists are co-opted into the task of educating the people in a truly revolutionary outlook. To complain that North Korean culture is nothing but propaganda is, in a sense, to miss the target. That is precisely the main point of cultural activity: there is no alternative culture, although it seems possible to speak of public and private strands within cultural life. The other inescapable aspect of cultural activity in the DPRK is the intervention of first Kim Il Sung, then of Kim Jong Il, both as ideologues guiding the course of creative endeavour and as subjects of creativity. Kim Jong Il's leading role in cultural affairs may have served the purpose of consolidating his position in a manner that would not openly threaten other interests, such as the military or the Party. But both father and son have understood very clearly the part that culture could play in affirming their philosophy and rule and have spoken and written forcefully on artistic priorities; both have been complicit in the at times extravagant use of their images.

The propaganda role imposed on the arts is of enduring importance in the maintenance of the regime. While the operation of the economy may represent the implementation of juche precepts, and family life and social structures may reflect a particular concept of national life, it is the constant repetition of chosen themes through the medium of the arts that impinges most directly on the population, filling minds and thoughts with reiterated images and sentiments and reminding people of the permissible boundaries of reaction and emotion. Particular subjects – any depiction of or allusion to the two Kims or their immediate family, celebrations of the benefits of socialism and of the collective spirit, expressions of national pride, calls to step up production – demand a positive response. Defiance is called for in face of the representation of foreign aggression and hostility; the miseries of past exploitation by landowners and capitalists and by colonial masters are the signal for a proper show of anger and sorrow; warm feelings may be aroused by scenes of affection between family members or friends. Preoccupation with purely personal issues or relationships, especially of a sexual nature, is not, however, a suitable subject for artistic treatment; although a rather kitschy taste for prints of attractively, even expensively dressed, pretty young women is indulged. The response to certain triggers is automatic: applause during a film as soon as the actor playing Kim Il Sung makes his first appearance on the screen, enthusiasm when a foreign company ends its performance with the 'Song of General Kim Jong Il'. These responses have all been learned at some point, but they nonetheless often come across as moments of genuine pleasure. By contrast, villains are routinely exposed, and paintings and stage impersonations of 'ugly' or foolish Americans, Japanese and South Koreans are quite acceptable. Drawings of US and Japanese soldiers are targets at shooting galleries, and you can tell the state of US-DPRK relations from the appearance or non-appearance of clowns dressed as Americans at the army circus. This well-understood scheme of emotions and responses, together with thorough training, may account in part for the confidence with which artists, even small children, tackle their repertoire. They know in advance the kind of response they can expect to elicit and can play to that.

Within this range of emotions, the most important, perhaps, is enthusiasm. Art should encourage and exhort, it should raise morale and devotion. This can lead to an unrelenting pitch of performance. More *is* better, as are louder and bigger, inasmuch as each magnification of size and volume betokens an intensification of feeling. (It may also be that Koreans love a measure of exaggeration: the percussion that accompanies the farmers' dances performed in South Korea can also be ear-shattering.) But when loyalty should be boundless, there can be no constraints on its expression: thus the amplification of a brass band to ear-splitting painfulness, the mass gymnastics and shows with casts of thousands, the towering monuments, the heroic sculptures, the vast paintings of Kim Il Sung and his son, even the exalted style in which television news is delivered. Repetition of words, music and gestures is also an expression of devotion and participation, as with the reciting of a rosary. Eventually, listeners' and viewers' responses to the stimuli they are presented with may become so engrained that they can achieve the paradox of anticipating and producing a burst of 'spontaneous' reaction.

Some of the particular features of North Korean painting, song, dance, film and so on are the outcome of deliberate decisions on the part of the cultural establishment and of the two Kims to eliminate certain artistic elements and enhance others. From the outset, influences remaining from the Japanese colonial period were to be eradicated or neutralized; many themes, styles, even instruments that had been associated with the court and the aristocracy were discarded as being too élitist. Not all old subject-matter and practices were rejected, since the intention was not to repudiate traditional art in all its forms, but to select those elements that appealed to the people and could at the same time be accommodated to the prevailing ideology (and also, it must be assumed, to Kim Il Sung's and Kim Jong Il's personal tastes). One result has been the elimination of extremes of pitch and tone and of art forms that offended the ear or eye or proved too difficult to 'understand'. The regime's anti-élitist norms would probably please many people far beyond the boundaries of the DPRK!

The half-century since the foundation of the DPRK has seen a slow evolution of the arts. In a period of re-evaluation of the past and of rectification that lasted up to the late 1950s, artists and writers adapted themselves to new requirements. Some were forcibly removed in political trials on charges of sabotaging policies on art and literature. The stylistic model in both fields was Soviet social realism. From the end of the 1950s and the onset of the Chollima movement to speed production, art workers provided their support by encouraging the revolutionary zeal of their fellow workers. As the spirit of juche, first proclaimed by Kim Il Sung at the end of 1955, was applied to more and more areas of activity, so the task for cultural workers became that of emphasizing and illuminating juche's central tenet of man's self-determination and from there the independence of the nation and the leadership's role in guiding society. Increasingly, the site for creative inspiration was to be located in the anti-Japanese guerrilla activities of Kim Il Sung rather than in the life of the proletariat. Responsibility for a work's creation came to be taken collectively, especially for large-scale projects. Kim Jong Il's influence in cultural life was increasingly noted from the early 1970s and with it the concentration of vision on his and his father's teachings and ideas. They did not confine themselves to theory and both Kims are credited with intervening in the production of dramas, operas and films. Within their prescriptive approach to culture, the concepts of 'seed theory' and 'speed war' are important: 'The seed', in Kim Jong Il's own words, 'is the basis and the kernel of a literary work. It integrates material, theme and thought in an organic relationship' (*On the Art of the Cinema*, p.14). Once the ideological heart of a new work has been secured, subject-matter and the treatment of character will follow. Creation has to proceed at high speed, aiming at a large output, as if in a battle for artistic production.

Since 1961, artistic and literary activity in the DPRK has been monitored by the Korean Literature and Arts Confederation, placed above three specialized federations for writers, artists and composers. The Ministry of Culture also has supervisory powers. Cultural workers operate in the provinces, generally in support of work campaigns. All artists, writers, performers and other cultural workers are trained, employed and paid by the state, sometimes quite handsomely. In return, they are expected to contribute in the 'speed war', maintain a good rate of production and submit to regular evaluation. They are in short just another type of worker. A system of national awards, progressing from the title of 'Merit Artist' up to that of 'Hero', provides the individual with incentives and rewards in the absence of any independent structure of competitions and exhibitions.

... and private ones

A closer look at cultural activity, however, suggests a more nuanced reality. The rejection of foreign influences, for instance, was directed primarily at Japanese and Chinese sources: the imposition of Japanese colonial culture, Chinese characters in writing, certain Chinese models of classical painting, and so on. Soviet styles in architecture, literature, painting and music, on the other hand, were tolerated in the early years, even absorbed. Soviet models were, perhaps, familiar to Kim Il Sung from his stay in the Soviet Union, and their transmission was further eased by the presence of many Soviet advisers in the DPRK from 1945 to 1948 and Soviet assistance in physical and social reconstruction. The Soviet influence started to wane from the late 1950s but has persisted selectively to meet particular needs and tastes: propaganda posters, for example, and Red Army choir and sub-Tchaikovsky compositions rather than Shostakovich. The brass bands that sound out on public occasions and can be heard in practice all over Pyongyang were first brought to Korea by Europeans at the end of the nineteenth century and were later taken up by the Japanese colonial administration. Another Western influence that has become rooted in both North and South is a fine style of choral singing, inherited from the hymn-singing introduced by Christian missionaries, again in the late nineteenth century. Indeed, as one listens to the well-known tunes that accompany public events in the DPRK, a sequence of notes familiar from an evangelical hymn may start up, to be quickly diverted into another melodic line. In short, foreign influences are all around. The Korean reaction will almost certainly be to insist that even if these influences have infiltrated, they have been refined and developed to meet Korean needs and are no longer alien. Not much is required to 'Koreanize' a foreign model. To assist in the preparation of a joint celebration with Korean colleagues, we lent an instruction video of Scottish country dancing. At the party, four expert Korean women dancers performed an Eightsome Reel (*sic*) to a synthesized and jazzed-up version of the music; reworked, they said, because they judged the original style of music too dull, but more certainly to render the dance acceptable as something they had created.

After a while in Pyongyang, one comes to glimpse the existence of an almost private cultural life in parallel to the public displays. Individual Koreans with the means to buy equipment have computers, on which they largely play games in the absence of access to the Internet, music centres for playing recordings of Western classical music and Korean pop music, and video machines for watching such evergreen favourites as *The Sound of Music*, *Mary Poppins* and *Titanic*. We listened to Korean singers give an excellent rendition of

Abba songs in English at a private show. The Ministry of Foreign Affairs is full of talented singers, whose repertoire ranges from Western pop to grand opera. Karaoke videos are produced for the Japanese-Korean market that project an almost fantasy picture of life for young Koreans in Pyongyang, with flirting and leisure time filled with swimming and outings in sunny settings.

At a more serious level, an annual festival of the music of Yun Isang (1917–95) has been held since 1983, performed by a dedicated ensemble who mix their presentations of Yun's music with pieces by other Korean composers and by nineteenth and twentieth-century Western composers. Only a small number of people hear Yun's music, stimulating, experimental, at times demanding, and marked by the double influences of Western musical innovation and traditional Korean treatment, yet he is held in high esteem in the DPRK. It is doubtless his difficult life caught up in the conflicts between North and South Korea that commands official support. Born in the south of the peninsula, Yun studied in Japan, then, in the mid-1950s, received a Seoul City Award to study composition in Western Europe. In 1963 he visited the DPRK, then settled in Berlin. Because of his North Korean trip, he came under suspicion from the South Korean government and in 1967 was abducted in Berlin together with his wife and other South Koreans and with them flown back to Seoul, where he was accused of spying for the North. His sentence of life imprisonment was rescinded after two years in the face of international outcry and he returned to Berlin. He visited the DPRK several times thereafter, where a research institute for the study of his music was established in 1984 and a concert hall named after him, but he never returned to the South, where his music was banned for a number of years. His music is judged to be too difficult for popular taste, and only music students and invited audiences may listen to it. Nonetheless, whatever the reasons, it is performed, and the festival and other concerts ensure that Korean musicians in the DPRK remain familiar with developments in the international music world.

The musicians who perform in the bands and orchestras that one hears, whether on public occasions or at invited concerts, have all been assigned to their positions on graduation from training. Their formation, as we found on a visit to the University of Music and Dance, seems only to reinforce the idea of parallel strands in cultural life. Students in their teens and early twenties performed arias from Italian opera for us, in Italian, and played Russian and European classical music. Others gave us beautiful presentations of traditional Korean song and traditional Korean instrumental music (*kayagum* – zither and *chottae* – transverse flute). These training sessions stood in contrast to the concert performed for us by the younger students from the feeder school who, though expert and enthusiastic, produced a coarser effect with their electric kayagum and accordions. We know from our own experience that officially sponsored or sanctioned 'private' entertainment is laid on for visitors, who can listen to arias by Massenet and Bizet and Western classical music; but these do not seem to be the stuff of everyday musical experience.

Painting, sculpture and pottery

PAINTING

The North, as did the South, inherited a dual legacy of the ink-and-wash painting long practised throughout Korea, and Western oil painting. Some aspects of Western art, such as perspective and dimension, had been familiar to Korean artists for over a century before the first Korean painters began to practise in oils in the early years of the twentieth century under the influence of Japanese teaching. A smaller number of artists began to study and produce Western-style sculpture. Under the impact of the new style of painting, traditional art came to extend its subject-matter to cover scenes of everyday life, and to incorporate a palette of colours.

Developing out of the same conditions, painting and sculpture have followed very different routes in the South and the North. Oils have everywhere been accepted as a medium alongside ink and wash, although a painter tends to specialize in one or the other; and a range of other art media have developed. Thereafter, there is considerable divergence between the experimentation of the art scene in the South and the explicit requirements laid upon painting in the North. Only a realist style is permitted in the DPRK: abstract or conceptual art is not tolerated since it cannot convey realism and moreover, obscures the meaning of a painting. Official preference is for 'Korean', that is, ink painting, known as *Chosonhwa,* on the grounds that it best expresses national taste and sentiment and best incorporates the three basic elements of juche art: realism, ideology and tradition. Even Chosonhwa, however, has had to enlarge its subject-matter and the very scope of its paintings to depict large-scale industrial scenes and heroic or exemplary human subjects, which moreover are portrayed in a realistic, colour-rich style. It is a long remove from the monochrome ink paintings of classical Korean art with their subjects drawn predominantly from nature and their tiny figures. Oil painting, print-making and woodcuts are encouraged alongside ink painting and have produced some striking results. Since the 1970s, the range of permitted subjects has been widened from depictions of socialist construction, army-people relations (always close), nationalistic themes and paintings of Kim Il Sung, to include landscape, and oil is a favourite medium for this last type of painting. The scene shown is often a 'real' one, in the tradition of Choson-dynasty 'true view' landscape painting; numerous schoolchildren may thus be seen in sites that combine both nature and history, such as Kaesong, all working away in the open air at the same scene. Other landscapes gain significance from the 'value-added' element of a place newly opened up to agricultural or industrial development. Oil is also popular for portraits and scenes of construction.

Other important areas are film art, theatre art and television art. Large mural paintings, often displayed free-standing at the entrance to a village or in an urban public place, depict Kim Il Sung, sometimes immersed in guerrilla activity or engaged in giving on-the-spot guidance; the best examples are undoubtedly the murals at several of the Pyongyang metro stations. Another vivid form of art is the propaganda poster, hand-painted in large numbers from some centrally approved model. Calligraphy in both Chinese characters and the Korean alphabet is still practised. Examples can be seen engraved on steles and monuments, including inscriptions attributed to Kim Il Sung's own hand, in Chinese characters at the tomb of King Tongmyong, in Korean lettering at Panmunjom. The applied arts also receive considerable attention, and some beautiful handicrafts and embroidery are produced.

SCULPTURE

Sculpture, based on the human form (though sometimes, as in the simple street sculpture that fills parks and public places, on animal, bird and fish forms), ranges from memorial busts and the small, almost intimate studies of single figures in the shadow of the War Memorial in Pyongyang, through the soaring Chollima statue, to the large groups of militant figures that make up the War Memorial itself and the revolutionary groupings that flank the truly gigantic statue of Kim Il Sung on Mansu hill. Equally, vast sculptural ensembles of guerrilla fighters led by Kim Il Sung are presented at Lake Samji in the Mt Paektu region in the far north of Ryanggang province. These large groups, all in bronze, are generally the product of collective design and execution. Their scale rules out any great delicacy of detail. More satisfying are the bronze reliefs that decorate some other monuments, such as the Party Foundation Monument otherwise crudely worked in granite. Granite is also used for the Juche Tower itself and for the sculpted figures to its rear and for the vigorously delineated carvings at the recently restored tombs around the capital. The harder media of bronze and stone are clearly intended to communicate a forceful message, whether it be of revolutionary exhortation or nationalist zeal.

POTTERY

Pottery, by contrast, retains the delicacy associated with the best Korean specimens, even if some vast and overblown vases are produced. The Koryo capital of Kaesong was primarily a centre of consumption for the celadons produced mainly from kilns in the southwest of the peninsula (although North Koreans insist that Koryo celadons came from kilns around Kaesong, not from further afield), and thus original examples are to hand to serve as models. Their historical associations with the court and the élite do not appear to hinder their production in the modern DPRK. North Korean potters produce both traditional and contemporary celadon designs, as well as vases and other pieces in porcelain. Some of it is decorated with very contemporary themes, such as the Pyongyang skyline.

TRAINING

Training in the fine and applied arts is centred on the Pyongyang University of Fine Arts, founded in 1947. Acceptance on to the five-year courses is by examination. All the branches of art discussed in this section are taught at the university, as well as others. Students numbered one thousand in 2002, staff around 350. Training in all the arts in the DPRK is very thorough, and the technical superiority of North Korean artists is admitted even by the Chinese, who send students every year to train in ceramics. Artists are all members of the Korean Artists Federation and are state employed. Many of them work in or for one of the 'creation centres' or at art studios, a system that permits a degree of specialization; others may belong to regional creative companies. The largest such organization is the Mansudae Creation Centre in Pyongyang, which numbers a thousand 'creators' among its workforce. The centre produces about four thousand paintings a year, about half of them ordered for public institutions. Many others go to buyers from Japan, China and South Korea. Paintings, prints and sculptures by North Korean artists have been displayed in exhibitions in Japan in 1985 and 1989 and at the Kwangju Biennale in the ROK in 2000. North Korean work may be seen at the British Museum's Korean Gallery, which presents changing displays of contemporary art from both North and South.

LITERATURE

Literature has in the past been a scene of some turbulence, as measures by Kim Il Sung in the 1950s to eradicate opponents spilled over into the literary world. Somewhat over one hundred writers had left the South for the North by the early 1950s, many voluntarily, some against their will. Others had returned to the DPRK from China and the Soviet Union. Among a number of groups of alleged spies and traitors who, by the second half of the 1950s, had been eliminated, sometimes by execution, were several whose offences were claimed to include opposition to the Party's policies on literature. A number of intellectuals were among those removed. Three writers were implicated in the plot that Pak Hon Yong, a vice-premier and foreign minister in 1948, was accused of launching against Kim Il Sung towards the end of the Korean War. Two other men, who had both headed the Party newspaper and journal in turn, were charged later with plotting with others to move against Kim while he was out of the country in June-July 1956. Some of the charges were very specific: the poet Yim Hwa, eliminated as a spy and traitor in 1953, had been arrested for a poem he had written in 1952 lamenting the Korean War's destruction of the country, thereby harming morale. One of the journalists removed had denigrated the Korean Artists Proletarian Federation (KAPF) of left-wing writers and artists that had been active in Korea in colonial times. Whatever the truth of these claims, the greater threat of these erstwhile colleagues in Kim's eyes was to his own authority. They were members of rival factions to his own group of former partisans: those in Pak Hon Yong's group had come, as had Pak, from the South; the two journalists were among the Soviet-Korean faction.

From the outset literature was to be a tool in the struggle to develop new cultural norms for a new socialist society. In particular, it could not hope to escape from political control nor from political in-fighting. Writers were registered in their own federation, which publishes a journal, *Choson Munhak* (Korean Literature). The prescriptions laid on literature were spelled out: it was to strictly apply Marxist-Leninist aesthetic principles, above all that of socialist realism, and was to reject 'non-ideological and non-political' writing; it was to inculcate warm feelings for the new society among readers; writers were to learn from the people the truth of 'real life' by living among them and studying them; and they were to accept that what they wrote could not be regarded as an individual effort, but belonged to the party and state. Various pernicious literary trends were condemned, such as naturalism, formalism, decadence and nihilism. Other more wholesome influences were permitted, such as the example of the KAPF from the mid-1920s, classical Korean literature, Soviet and 'advanced' culture from abroad and a number of world classics, including Shakespeare. The period up to the mid-1960s brought a re-evaluation and sifting through of earlier literature. It was marked by further purges of writers and other artists, but did nonetheless accommodate discussion and some diversity, perhaps because factional differences still unsettled the political scene.

Already by the early 1960s, however, a new source of artistic inspiration was being acclaimed alongside the significance of the Chollima movement for socialist reconstruction: the exploits of the partisans who had fought against Japanese colonial rule in the 1930s. Their leader, of course, had been Kim Il Sung. The assertion was also made that these same guerrilla fighters had themselves produced fine literature and art even during the years of struggle. As the decade progressed, Kim, his activities, teachings and philosophical theories, above all that of juche, came to occupy the central, if not only place in creative endeavour, just as they formed the content of political activity. This shift in focus to Kim's achievements in liberating the country and guiding it forwards led to the discrediting of earlier models and influences. There was a halt to the publication of translated works. The KAPF, once praised as a worthy precursor of post-liberation literature, was denounced. Even the principle of socialist realism, with its truthful depiction of life, lost its value if not interpreted in the light of Kim's thought. Kim Jong Il, who from the late 1960s emerged as a powerful figure in his own right, was at pains to support his father's image.

Kim Il Sung's confidence in his own authority may have encouraged him in the 1980s to permit some small relaxation in literary matters. Literary works were reviewed afresh and some authors who had been earlier eliminated were restored. Translations from foreign children's books were permitted and the publication of foreign literature was resumed, though not necessarily of new works. Some classical literature was released. The DPRK felt sharply the shocks of disintegration and change in the Communist world in 1990–91 and its reaction was to recall students studying abroad, to reimpose tight ideological control and to reaffirm the country's belief in its own form of socialism. The further blows of Kim Il Sung's death in 1994 and the years of disaster that followed caused society to withdraw into itself. Only recently has the country felt able to relax somewhat. The KAPF, for instance, has been restored to favour. The cultural scene is opening up to some foreign influences, in literature as in other branches of the arts. We were delighted to watch an abridged version, in translation, of 'Mickey's Christmas Carol' shown on Sunday afternoon television late in 2001. As 'pages' from Disney's film passed across the screen, a woman story-teller read the tale with all the humour and warmth one could wish for.

Novelists, short-story writers and poets thrive on access to a wide range of human emotions. In the DPRK, a children's programme may be able to show warmth, but for fiction writers some emotional avenues appear to be closed off. Sentiments of romantic love, fear, suffering, grief and loss run the risk of being condemned as 'side issues' that dwell too much on personal reactions. This interdiction seems to be particularly strong in treatment of the Korean War and the division of Korea. Writers may describe the sufferings of the South Korean people at the hands of the US aggressors as they are lambasting these aggressors; but they should not touch on the despair and yearning that North Koreans may feel in the face of separation. Hatred and hostility towards the enemy appear to be the only acceptable sentiments. Similarly, the hardships and disappointments of the 1990s may be acknowledged but are to serve as proof that the Korean people can overcome all difficulties under correct guidance. Hope is to gain resurgence over pain. Literature may nonetheless reveal in passing some of the anxieties that perplex ordinary people in the DPRK.

Cinema, theatre and dance

CINEMA

Film is probably the medium that demonstrates most clearly the demands placed on cultural activity in the DPRK. Its capacity for direct visual impact and strong development of theme and character makes it a valuable tool for propaganda. Kim Jong Il's close involvement in the cinema further ensures it status and adequate resources. The rate of film viewing appears to be exceedingly high, with audiences that appear to be several times the size of the population. The adult North Korean must therefore see a lot of films each year, not primarily for entertainment but as part of his or her political education. Film-showings are largely at workplaces and communal facilities rather than in cinemas, and attendance cannot therefore be assumed to be entirely a personal choice.

The film industry is a state-controlled enterprise and there is no commercial film-making. Its forerunner, according to North Korean sources, was again the KAPF, which started making silent films in the mid-1920s. A number of KAPF film-makers came north after liberation, bringing their skills with them. Political control was quickly established over the nascent film industry, and a state film studio was established early on, in 1947, with technical assistance and equipment from China. Output has been considerable, at an annual average of 130 of all types of films (feature, documentary and scientific) over the decades 1980s–1990s. Cartoon films are produced at the Animation Film Studios, which are also said to undertake work for a French television station. There is a fondness for films running over many parts, the outstanding example being the fifty-part *The Nation and Destiny*, made between the years 1992–99. The most important of the studios that have been responsible for production are the Korean Film Studios (the state studios) on the outskirts of Pyongyang, which make twenty-five feature films a year. The site, maintained by 1,400 staff, has an impressive display of lots. The army has its own film studios, now located in a new building close to the Unification Arch. For a while, a further studio provided facilities for the South Korean producer Shin Sang-ok and his wife, the actress Choi Eun-hee, during the years 1983–6 that they spent working for Kim Jong Il on film projects.

That episode, described by Shin and many others as abduction, by the DPRK as defection, lasted from 1978, when Shin and Choi found themselves in the North, to 1986, when the couple escaped from North Korean surveillance during a trip to Vienna. Whatever the exact circumstances, the story illustrates the intense nature of Kim Jong Il's involvement in North Korean cinema and the lengths he may have been prepared to go to in order to perfect it as an art. He is said to have a vast collection of films, many of them foreign. His intervention in the creation and development of a new film is acknowledged, and in 2002 we were told he had visited the Korean Film Studios over 350 times (since the late 1960s). His thoughts on film-making and on other branches of the arts are contained in his 1973 treatise *On the Art of the Cinema*. Here he argues for the focused, logical development in a film of a carefully chosen story towards a clearly understood conclusion. The purpose of each film, indeed, of all art, is to create examples of 'a fine and ennobling way of life' and to help towards 'the revolutionary transformation of the whole of society' (p.45). Such themes as redemption, conflict and love – staples of much creative work – have to be handled through the prism of the demands of socialist thought, national and class identity and the relationship of the individual to the collective. Everything, down to the style of language used and the tone of a film – a 'bright, cheerful and hopeful light' for the lives of working people – is spelt out. It is small wonder that in the face of such regulation and close supervision from above, North Korean film-makers find it difficult to maintain the originality of approach that Kim Jong Il demands.

The DPRK has held an annual international film festival in Pyongyang since 1987, which has permitted it to screen a number of foreign films as well as presenting its own productions. In an indirect fashion, it has thus been able to indulge in some experimentation and to keep abreast of the international film field.

THEATRE

Korean traditions of drama are very different to Western forms, being rooted in the masked dances and the style of solo story-telling, accompanied by a drum, known as *pansori*, which requires a rigorous control of the voice and breathing. Pansori was given no public place in North Korean dramatic art; indeed, on the grounds that it was insufficient to express revolutionary spirit, Kim Il Sung took the decision not to allow others to hear it. The theatre now performed in the DPRK has evolved from plays first presented in the 1920s and early 1930s by groups of left-wing actors who drew on contemporary social and labour issues for subject-matter. Their particular art was in itself an innovation in Korea and had been brought in from the West via Japan. After 1945, the state quickly brought the theatre companies that sprang up in the North under its control and their productions were used, and continue to be used, in support of whatever campaign was in hand. A number of popular classical tales were adapted to the stage, such as the *Tale of Chunhyang*, the story of a low-born young woman who, after many tribulations, is reunited with her noble-born husband. There is considerable circularity of material in the performing arts: thus the Chunhyang story exists also in opera and film form, while the drama of *Pi pada* (The Sea of Blood), telling how a mother passes through trials to become a true revolutionary and supposedly written by Kim Il Sung himself during his partisan years, has been rendered as a film and an opera and has been reworked as a symphony. It is clear that actors move between film work and the stage. The high didactic content of both cinema and theatre, which relies heavily on the spoken word to put its message across, probably blurs distinctions in acting style between the two genres.

DANCE

One of the most spectacular forms of entertainment in the DPRK is the mass display of combined dancing, gymnastics, acrobatics, music and singing, such as the 2002 Arirang festival. Thousands upon thousands of children and young people, including detachments from the armed services, are drilled exhaustively until they flow as one. That is, indeed, one of the purposes of such extravaganzas: to mould individual bodies into a collective whole, so that they ripple as water or surge as flames. Large dancing parties are held on Kim Il Sung Square on the evenings of national celebrations in which young men and women perform simple circle dances and invite visitors to join them. The effect at both types of entertainment is always colourful, even if the individual movements have to be repetitive and simple, given that few of the dancers are professionals. What hold the attention are the organization and discipline. More accomplished dancing features in dance dramas, in the dance sequences in operas and in variety concert shows. As might be expected, technical standards are very high, the outcome of long and rigorous training.

In developing its own styles, the DPRK has drawn on one strand of traditional dance, the folk or peasant dance. It rejected the other two strands, court dance and ritual Buddhist dance, as inappropriate. The movements of traditional dance, in particular the positioning of the arms and pulsing of the shoulders, are still discernible but have been combined with 'modern', largely balletic, elements such as repetitive foot movements, an elevated carriage and corps de ballet groupings. (Classical ballet as such is taught, but is not performed publicly.) In the mid-1970s, Kim Il Jong made his own contribution to the establishment of modern Korean dance with the Chamo system of notation that drew on a variety of elements including music staff notation and the principles of the Korean alphabet. The claim made for it is that it is easily understood and is applicable to other national dances and to callisthenics and mass games. Away from organized activities, Koreans on social outings, as they do in the South, will readily dance to the beat of a drum and cymbals, holding themselves in the traditional way and moving through the familiar steps.

In dance, as in all other forms of art, innovation can only come from the top. Thus, when an otherwise routine army concert was broken by a formation of pilots in flying jackets and helmets, moving in a straight-line, arms-by-the-side, rhythmic-footwork tap dance, to the amazement of the Koreans in the audience and the joy of many of the foreigners, we knew that Kim Jong Il had been watching a great many *Riverdance* videos.

Music, song and opera

MUSIC

The patterns of musical development in North and South have diverged considerably. In the South, what might be termed a 'conservationist' approach has applied to traditional Korean music both folk and classical. In parallel, the whole apparatus of Western classical music has been adopted and cultivated. Pop music, which grew out of Japanese popular music of the 1920s and 1930s, has taken many experimental turns in the South and has experienced varied foreign influences.

In the North, there has been some attempt at a synthesis of Korean and Western musical elements, particularly in the instrumental field. Given the louder volume and wider range of many

Western instruments, this has meant that many Korean musical instruments, such as string and wind instruments, which traditionally utilized such soft materials as silk and bamboo and consequently produced an uncertain pitch, have been 'improved' through the introduction of harder materials and the remodelling and enlargement of their frames to allow them to be tuned to and compete with corresponding Western instruments. An orchestral group thus often comprises both Korean and Western instruments. Purely Western-style orchestras and groups, such as the Yun Isang ensemble (see above), also perform. There are three state orchestras.

Sources of themes for new orchestral music are restricted, since it is a question of touching an appropriate emotion and conveying an acceptable mood rather than exploring a personal inspiration (although a composer may insist that the latter is subsumed in the former). Revolutionary songs and folk melodies provide the basis for orchestral and instrumental compositions; and 'recycling' goes on of scores written for one genre, such as opera, and reworked for another, such as a symphony. The presence of Korean instruments in an orchestra gives a distinctive flavour to music that sometimes seems very dependent on late nineteenth-century Western models.

For variety concerts, an electric version of the Korean zither or kayagum, electric keyboards and the ubiquitous accordion appear. Light music, or pop, based on songs, has become acceptable since the late 1980s and incorporates synthesizers and electric guitars, yet for all that retains an old-fashioned, foxtrot-based tempo reminiscent of its antecedents in Japanese popular music of the colonial era. The recurring experiments that have swept the international pop scene have bypassed the DPRK. There is nonetheless great demand for music for live concerts, radio and television shows and recorded listening, a need met by three popular music ensembles. In the absence of a club scene, people listen to a lot of music at home on cassettes, CDs and karaoke tapes. The many films produced also need scores.

As noted above, the highest institution for musical training is the Pyongyang University of Music and Dance, established in 1949. Its five departments offer tuition in vocal and instrumental music, composition, Korean music and education. State troupes function at provincial level, generally as an adjunct to political campaigns.

SONG

Song probably enjoys the highest affection among the performing arts in the DPRK. Koreans of all ages seem to have good voices and the confidence to sing solos and duets in public at cultural and social events. Visitors to a school or children's home are invited to listen to the children singing. Television closes down each evening with a rousing rendering of the 'Song of General Kim Jong Il' by a military choir. Radio is often filled with song; and karaoke videos encourage you to join in. The music is tuneful and undemanding, the words follow familiar themes, since singing is a powerful way of internalizing a message. Indeed, singing in the DPRK can be said to be a word-driven, not a music-led, activity. (The same insistence on the value of the written and spoken word might be said to characterize a lot of North Korean culture.)

The first Western-style songs were introduced through Japanese models in the 1920s and 1930s. Composers with socialist sympathies worked on songs with patriotic and revolutionary content and, after liberation, many of them carried this tradition into the North, where it was reinforced by Soviet styles of song-writing. In the late 1950s, as society shook off Soviet influences, composers were directed towards native Korean folksong as a source of inspiration. As ever, however, it was a critical and selective approach, and original songs were 'enriched' by new words and the replacement of the pentatonic (five note) scale in which many of them had been composed with the diatonic (seven note) scale. Among the various regional styles of Korean folk-song, the choice was for the more lyrical and flowing; and a smoother tone replaced the nasal resonance typical of the delivery of folk-songs. The reflective, even melancholy tone of many folk-songs was lost. Now, indigenous elements blend together with the Western style filtered through Japanese colonial imports in songs that praise the Kims, father and son, or roam over a wide range of topics that all, nonetheless, stress the collective and national interest over the personal. Indeed, you do not hear songs with a subjective content. Emotion can only be expressed, in anger or in rejoicing, over issues that affect the whole of society. To underline the importance of song, Kim Jong Il is said to be the composer of certain 'classical' songs. In spring 2004, a number of collections of songs said to represent the taste of earlier periods were published for a general usership. They included songs of protest sung during the era of Japanese colonial rule, folk songs both new and old (the latter with their notations) and even songs said to date from medieval times. The intention is presumably to present readers with an up-to-date summation of what is acceptable.

OPERA

Those who enjoy Western opera, particularly in its more florid nineteenth-century tradition, should find opera in the DPRK to their taste. It is not, of course, a close imitation of the Western product, and many elements, from the choice of subject to the style of direction, show the mark of the model operas of the Chinese Cultural Revolution (usually dated to 1966–76). The first Korean opera, The Sea of Blood (*Pi pada*), appeared only in 1971, which would seem to reinforce the validity of Chinese influence. Kim Il Sung was said to have been involved in its genesis, and it set the style for succeeding works. As with other species of opera, various artistic forms combine into a dramatic whole: orchestral music, solo and choral singing, acting, dancing, stage fights, special effects. At times, there is even something a little cinematic about the staging, an effect, perhaps, of the close cross-influences between the cinema and the dramatic arts. A gamut of strong emotions works its way through such themes as patriotism, loyalty to leader and party, and past bitterness. The struggle against class oppression is never far away, even in the folktale of Chunhyang.

The musical score is always vivid and expressive, giving scope to both Western and 'improved' Korean instruments, the melodic line, sometimes based on folk tunes, is flowing, never incorporates too extreme a range of notes and is not broken by arias in the Western operatic style. Indeed, arias are explicitly rejected as going against 'normal' singing style. A further practice, ascribed to Kim Jong Il, is the extra chorus, sometimes with its own conductor, known as *pangchang*. This may be placed to each side of the proscenium arch, lower than the stage but above the orchestra pit. Its role is to comment on events on the stage and to describe the mental state of the principal singers, thereby allowing them to concentrate on the action. It is also meant to represent the audience's reaction to the drama and as such guides the spectators towards a 'correct' understanding of what they are watching and listening to. Songs from a number of operas have become very popular as free-standing concert items.

CREATIVE AND INTELLECTUAL FREEDOM

The present state of the arts in the DPRK, as they are publicly presented and performed, is flourishing, in the sense that many people have access to them as audiences and participants; but, despite superb staging and execution, there is a stifled feeling about much artistic activity, as if it cannot move on. In the absence of independent experimentation and diversity, the arts are losing their vitality. So much of what is happening right now in North Korea – the effects of the hardships of the 1990s, economic changes and their impact on family life, social divergences and social misfortune, technological innovation, gradual exposure to foreigners and foreign tastes, the sense of confrontation with the outside world – would provide excellent material for new paintings, novels, plays, songs, films, operas, but the moment for them has not come.

Even more pressing are doubts about the impact of the constant and all-encompassing indoctrination and state pre-emption of thought on intellectual originality. On the face of it, there is no problem. The DPRK sees itself as a refined society composed of well-educated citizens who enjoy an abundant cultural and spiritual life. In its essentials, this is a not indefensible description: schooling is free and universal, cultural and social activities offer many chances of participation, a powerful philosophy of national independence and self-determination sustains the spirit, while a benign leadership provides emotional security. For many people this network of support *appears* to be sufficient, and we met many Koreans whose loyalty to the system and belief in its promises seemed firm enough. Their reasons for enthusiasm may have included considerable self-interest, but they seemed fairly content. Eventually, however, we began to sense that even the most subtle among our acquaintances were operating a cut-off in their thinking, were refusing to take some arguments past a certain point, were putting a cap on their questioning. Some of them may have been aware of what they were doing, but for many, it may have been an unconscious process. Where access to knowledge and information can only be justified on a 'need to know' basis and where speculation is discouraged, there may be much risk in inquiring into subjects outside of one's area, whether it is life in another society or the work of a neighbouring office department. In our own case, most contact with universities was limited to practical questions about English-language teaching. It took almost a year for us to be permitted to address a group of university staff and students. Certainly, public interrogation of the status quo is not tolerated, and we had almost no means of knowing what individuals may have thought in private.

Those whose activities are primarily intellectual, whether as scholars or ideologues, come up against a further challenge demanding not just passive acceptance but active participation, that of being required to profess certain views and theories. Party theoreticians have passed beyond Marxism to concentrate solely on the merits of juche; university philosophers, although knowledgeable in other branches, likewise have to make juche the core of their reflections. As seen above (chapter 2), historians are expected to subscribe to particular chronologies and interpretations of the Korean past, and archaeologists find that interpretation and presentation of material evidence may be taken out of their hands. Isolation from current trends and theories being discussed elsewhere in the world, which the country's inability to afford publications and exchanges has exacerbated, does not help their situation. Much sound work, unaffected by politics, is done in North Korean universities, but it is nonetheless true that in few places has the subordination of intellectual activity to ideological and political considerations (which can happen in any society) become so entrenched as in the DPRK. Academics appear to acquiesce in this relationship from which they may see no easy way out. But perhaps some comparison can be made with the sphere of cultural activities, where, as already observed, personal tastes and external influences are in practice tolerated, whatever the official line. Although we did not see any signs of a similar relaxation among our academic contacts, it may be that away from public situations, they discuss a far wider range of subjects and come to individual conclusions.

6

The Outside World

BACKGROUND

FOR NORTH KOREA, the outside world beyond the immediate area of the Korean peninsula has not been a matter of great interest until recent years. In this, its leaders have reflected one of the great traditions in Korean history. Koreans boast of the peninsula's role as a channel for the transmission of religion, art forms and political structures between China and the Japanese islands; but that was long ago, and since the unification of the peninsula in the seventh century AD, the desire of most of its inhabitants has been to be left alone. The sheer political weight of China on one side, and the power of Japan to inflict damage on the other, left Koreans with a sense of vulnerability. The arrival of the West in East Asia in the middle of the nineteenth century heralded nothing but trouble. Here were forces able to bring China to the verge of collapse and to lead Japan into barbarian ways. The Koreans resisted these new pressures without success. They then tried to exploit and use the Western powers to help cope with the pressures created as China and Japan struggled for control over Korea. That policy too failed and Korea was defenceless in the face of Japan's determination. The result was annexation and thirty-five years as a Japanese colony.

Those who came to power in the Korean peninsula after liberation in 1945 looked back on the last years of the old Korean kingdom with a sense of shame. In different ways, both Kim Il Sung in the North, and Syngman Rhee in the South, had impeccable records as independence leaders. But in the circumstances in which they found themselves in 1945, neither could admit the other's claims without compromising his own position. The result was that both Koreas would place strong emphasis on their independence, and each condemns the other for alleged reliance on outside powers. No matter that they were both in fact highly dependent on powerful external supporters.

The other great defining factor for both Koreas was, and remains, the division of the peninsula and the existence of the other.

Although both have fudged the issue from time to time, especially when they have decided to negotiate, for most of their history each has denied the other's right to exist and each has claimed to be the lawful government of the whole peninsula. Much of their energy in international affairs, therefore, has been in one form or another devoted to the struggle to deny legitimacy to the other, rather than in pursuit of normal international relations.

In presenting its own view of its history, North Korea has largely chosen to ignore the circumstances of its foundation. Rather than acknowledge that Kim Il Sung came in on the coat-tails of the Soviet forces in 1945, the North Korean historical account implies that it was Kim Il Sung's sole efforts against the Japanese from the time that he was twelve that led to victory in 1945. It is perhaps understandable that the North Korean version of 1945 should exclude the US contribution to victory, given the subsequent history of DPRK-US relations. But this hardly explains or excuses the grudging acknowledgement of the Soviet and Chinese role in defeating the Japanese. The contribution of these outside forces has never been totally neglected. In the past, there were regular references to their role, and even today, it receives the occasional mention. Each May, the Russian embassy in Pyongyang holds ceremonies at the Soviet/Russian memorial on Moranbong hill in the heart of the city, and more simple ceremonies at the carefully tended Russian cemetery to the east. The North Koreans are punctilious in their attendance, though perhaps this is easy since the ceremonies essentially mark the end of the Second World War in Europe. If challenged, North Korean officials admit that Kim Il Sung did not achieve it all unaided, but the general claim is that the North Koreans did it all themselves.

EARLY DIRECTIONS

Dependence on the Soviet Union and its allies

The manner in which Kim Il Sung came to power was important in other ways. It ensured that in the initial stages the new North Korean state would be heavily dependent on the Soviet Union. In 1945–6, there was a practical need for assistance in rebuilding an economy heavily damaged by years of supporting the Japanese war effort. The new state, motivated more than its counterpart in the South by a strong wish to do away with the outward forms of the Japanese colonial structure, needed a new framework. The old Korean monarchical system appeared to provide no model, there was yet no Chinese pattern to follow, and Western-style democracy was unknown to most Koreans. Inevitably, therefore, Kim and his followers turned to the Soviet Union, the strongest state they knew best, for models. The onset of the Cold War isolated the DPRK from the West. With the Soviet Union and its Korean supporters rejecting the role of the UN in the future of the Korean peninsula, the North was effectively cut off from that body and its support organizations. It remained so until the 1970s. Ideology played a part in the DPRK's gravitation towards the Soviet Union and the Eastern European socialist states; but added to the North Korean leadership's desire to be left alone was the Soviet Union's policy of keeping its client states away from outside influences.

The founding of the People's Republic of China in October 1949 at first seemed to do no more than extend the number of socialist states. The new state and the DPRK established diplomatic relations in the same month, but apart from the signing of a posts and telecommunications agreement in December 1949, the PRC seemed to be in no hurry to multiply its links with the DPRK. It was to be several years before the PRC would offer an alternative centre of support and sustenance for North Korea.

A lack of interest in the outside world is reflected in the paucity of foreign affairs-related subjects in Kim Il Sung's early writings and speeches. The limited room to manoeuvre in diplomatic matters is clear from the restricted range of the DPRK's formal diplomatic contacts before the mid-1950s, confined as they were to the Soviet Union and its East European allies, Mongolia, the PRC and North Vietnam. In those days of an apparent Communist worldwide United Front, the North Koreans took the tone of their comments and their official concerns from the Soviet Union. Thus, when the Soviet Union attacked Tito's Yugoslavia, Kim Il Sung did so too.

One long-term consequence of this restricted pattern of international relations was the creation of a generation of North Korean diplomats who had little experience of international standards of diplomacy. Some of North Korea's continued difficulties in international relations spring from the very limited exposure to the world of its diplomats. The older ones invariably learnt the Soviet or the pre-1978 Chinese style of diplomacy. The younger ones are different but the older style has not disappeared. Even when students studied abroad, they were under very tight control and usually banned from contact with other students. This produced a generation with great suspicion of outsiders and a dour and unyielding approach to negotiations. DPRK officials avoided mixing with their opposite numbers, and saw every negotiation as a matter of win or lose. Until the 1990s, North Korean embassies tended to be sealed against the outside world: staff did not go out alone and there was little attempt to mix with the host country. Embassies saw their main function as the promulgation of Kim Il Sung's merits rather than learning about the society in which they found themselves. Exhibitions of Kim Il Sung's works or the placing of his speeches in the local press often occupied much of their time until the mid-1980s. Since then, North Korean diplomats have come to behave in a more normal fashion, but they are still somewhat reclusive members of any diplomatic community.

The North Korean tradition of somewhat unorthodox diplomacy has operated in other channels too. Because of the growing economic problems at home, DPRK diplomats found that their financial support from Pyongyang dried up in the 1970s. They were to make their missions self-supporting wherever possible. In some cases, it seems that gaining legitimate business and, presumably, either receiving a commission or being credited with a proportion of the funds created, might do this. In other instances, however, DPRK diplomats have gone in for less regular methods of financing themselves. The result has been a sustained stream of reports of North Korean diplomats trading in duty-free liquor and similar goods and, more worryingly, narcotics. This running of embassies as rather shady business units has not endeared North Korean diplomats to their host governments and has helped to further increase their local isolation. (Without in any way justifying these breaches of diplomatic protocol, it is only fair to note that other diplomats have also engaged in shady practices. These have usually been individual initiatives, however. What makes the DPRK practice unusual is that it appears to have at least some measure of official sanction behind it – although this has never been admitted.)

The Korean War and its effects

The Korean War confirmed that the DPRK was firmly in the socialist camp. It survived only because the PRC intervened to prevent its total destruction in late 1950. Inevitably, the outcome of the war and the unsuccessful attempts to find a solution to the division of Korea at Geneva Conference in 1954 left the North Koreans with even less room for manoeuvre than before. The war had shown up the North Koreans as difficult partners. The Chinese in particular had found it hard dealing with DPRK suspicions and brutality and had consequently insisted on taking control of the foreign civilian prisoners captured in Seoul and elsewhere in 1950, as well as of many of the prisoner-of-war camps.

The war's immense destruction meant that even the proud North Koreans had to seek assistance. It was forthcoming, but the North Koreans proved tough negotiators on the terms on which they expected it to be supplied. We lack a full account, but from evidence emerging in Moscow and Beijing, and especially from the Eastern European countries, it is clear the North Koreans made heavy demands on all the socialist countries, and often did so with a singular lack of grace. Such behaviour did not stop with post-war reconstruction. By the mid-1950s, both the Chinese and the Russians were having problems with the North Koreans' wish to follow their own political and economic paths, and their tendency not to pay their bills. The East European countries, which were generous with aid at Soviet insistence, also found that giving to North Korea was no easy task.

Finally, the North's need to concentrate on rebuilding the economy, and political infighting among the leadership, both to apportion blame for the failure to reunite the peninsula and to remove rivals to Kim Il Sung, left little energy for other activities. Even the issue of unification was very much a low priority.

Opening up: the 1960s and 1970s

The 1950s, however, brought changes on the international scene that gave the DPRK a rather freer hand. The struggle over the nationalization of the Suez canal and similar issues that pitched East against West in the late 1950s turned many countries away from the United States and Western Europe. Decolonization brought into existence new countries, often with rulers anxious to emphasize independence from former colonial masters. Many were looking for new roads to both economic and political development. The DPRK now found itself welcomed into a world that was soon to become the 'Third World' or later, the 'Non-Aligned', and seen by some as an alternative model for development to the Soviet and Chinese ways.

There was no rapid change in the DPRK's position. Publications and speeches from the late 1950s still laid most stress on links with the socialist world. At the same time, North Koreans began to travel in search of support and trade, and foreign visitors were welcomed to the DPRK. The withdrawal of Chinese troops in 1958 was portrayed as further evidence of North Korea's independence, in contrast to the South's continued links with the United States and the presence of US troops on South Korean soil. Gradually, the DPRK began to expand its network of external contacts. For the first time since 1948, its foreign policy became multi-directional. Trade, friendship and cultural delegations travelled widely. The opening of diplomatic relations with Guinea in 1958 marked the first move away from sole dependence on the socialist states for diplomatic support. The pace increased after 1970 for several reasons. One was the rapid spread of decolonization. Another was a series of shifts in the ROK's position. In the wake of the general air of détente following improved Sino-US relations in 1971–72 and the North-South talks of 1972 (see below), the ROK officially abandoned its version of the West German 'Hallstein doctrine', which had meant that the ROK automatically broke off relations with any country that established them with the North. President Park Chung-hee announced that henceforth he would not oppose the spread of North Korea's diplomatic links or the joint entry of both Koreas into the United Nations (even if, in practice, as late as the mid-1980s, ROK ambassadors to countries that established diplomatic relations with the DPRK were likely to be recalled to Seoul in semi-disgrace).

These moves were also reflected in the UN. Although the 'United Nations Command', which dates from the Korean War, continued to exist (and still does), UN disengagement from the Korean question began in 1973, with the abolition of the United Nations Commission for the Unification and Rehabilitation of Korea (UNCURK). Originally set up during the Korean War, UNCURK's efforts had been thwarted at every stage. Nonetheless, most Western countries had considered UNCURK's existence and its commitment to the principle of Korean unification as a legal obstacle preventing them from recognition of, or any involvement with, the DPRK. This hesitation (and a powerful ROK campaign), for example, was behind Britain's reluctance, eventually overcome, to allow a DPRK football team to take part in the 1966 World Cup. With the final dissolution of UNCURK, therefore, a longstanding barrier to diplomatic relations disappeared.

There now began intense competition between the two Korean states for recognition. The ROK led the way, riding on its membership of the 'free world' but the gap was significantly closed. In 1961, twenty-seven countries had diplomatic relations with the ROK and fifteen with the DPRK. By 1975, the figures were ninety-two and eighty-seven. In 1973–4, Western countries such as Sweden, Denmark and Australia established relations with the DPRK, and Portugal followed soon after. Even Britain contemplated such a move in 1975–6. There was also some hope in the West that the DPRK's expressed interest in Western technology as the older Soviet equipment began to wear out meant that new markets would open up.

These developments were the effective acceptance by both Korean states that the other was destined to stay around for some time, even if neither acknowledged such a position publicly. The war had dashed Kim Il Sung's hope for reunification on his terms, and the continued presence of the US forces in the South meant that to try again would be a costly undertaking. Attempts to stir up revolution in the South by exhortation or by infiltration failed. By 1972, when

15

15. Kindergarten, Haeju, October 2001.

16

16. Welcoming the immunization team, South Hwanghae province, October 2001.

12

13

12. Family group, collective farm near Hamhung 1998.
13. Nutrition survey October 2002 (© UNICEF).
14. 'We'll be soldiers of the Great General' – outside the children's hospital, Hamhung 2001.

14

9

9. Wedding party, Mansu hill, Pyongyang 2002.

10

10. Pohyon temple, Mt Myohyang.

11

11. Catholic cathedral, Pyongyang.

5

6

5. In the snow (©) UNICEF).
6. The nation's grandfather – Kim Il Sung with children, painting Pyongyang 2002.

7

8

7. Children's playground Kaesong, 2002 (© Jenny Pares).
8. Salvaging the rice, East Coast, October 2001.

3

3. 'Let's become human bombs like Ri Su Bok and suicide warriors like Kil Yong Jo, who guarded the leaders of the revolution in a do-or-die struggle' – Poster Pyongyang 2002.

4

4. Kim Il Sung's picture leads the parade: Army Day (25 April 2002), Pyongyang.

1

2

1. Calendar showing Nampo port and slogan on the 'Eternity of Kim Il Sung' – see – pp. 15 and 27 (© Foreign Trade Publishing House Pyongyang). **2.** Computer assembly (© Foreign Trade Publishing House Pyongyang).

17

17. High-rise apartments, central Pyongyang.

18

18. Traditional-style housing, Chilgol village, Pyongyang.

19

19. Modern-style village apartments, near Pyongyang.

20

20. Making *yontan* (coal briquettes) for heating and cooking, Hamhung, autumn 2001.

21

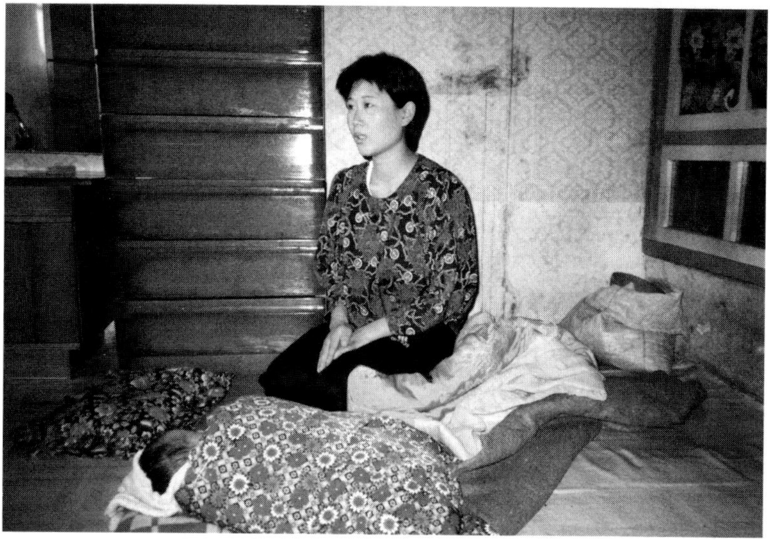

21. Mother and new-born baby in their apartment, Hamhung, October 2001.

22

23

24

22. 23. 24. Street scenes, central Pyongyang.

25

26

25. 26. May Day, Pyongyang 2002.

27

28

29

30

27. Outdoor art class, Kaesong – faithfully reproducing the same scene – see p. 98. **28.** String quartet with piano, Queen's Birthday Party on board the Pyongyang No. 1 riverboat, June 2002 – see p. 223. **29.** Theatre posters, Pyongyang. **30.** Modern dragon mural: tomb of King Tongmyong – see pp. 32–33.

31

32

33

31. Typical collective farm housing, with domestic plot.
32. Country life: woman farm worker with heavily laden *jige* (A-frame).
33. Close-planted rice fields, North Pyongan province, with slogan praising '*juche nongbop*, or the concept of 'farming in our way' – see pp. 6 and 43 (© Susan Pares)

34

35

36

37

34. The Korean red ox – once again indispensable for transport in the countryside. **35.** Military officer and family in front of Unification Arch, Pyongyang, Winter 2001 (© Thomas Imo – Phototek). **36. 37.** Posters praising mechanization in the countryside.

38

39

38. Old technology in modern guise – recently built hydroelectric turbines near Hamhung autumn 2001.
39. Packing vitamin-fortified biscuits for WFP distribution to school-children.
40. A food for labour project – dam building near Hamhung 2001.

40

41

42

43

44

41. Waiting for the ferry – country bicycles for men and women – see p. 10. **42.** Heavy-duty lorry, probably a copy of a Russian or Chinese model, perhaps based on a 1930s Chevrolet. **43.** Mainline locomotive, Pyongyang railway station. **44.** Saltpans near Nampo, west coast.

45

45. 'The Arch of Triumph'. Monument to Kim Il Sung, located at the foot of Moran hill, Pyongyang. Completed in 1982, to mark Kim's 60th birthday, at 60m high and 50.1m wide, it is bigger than the Arc de Triomphe in Paris. The dates 1925–1945 supposedly mark Kim's 'struggle for national liberation' from his departure for China to his triumphant return (© Foreign Languages Publishing House).

the DPRK's new constitution made Pyongyang rather than Seoul the DPRK capital, the DPRK leadership had tacitly accepted that unification was not going to happen in the short term. The ROK appears to have come to a similar position. While Syngman Rhee had remained president of the ROK, there was little chance that any ROK government would abandon or modify its claim to be the sole legal government on the peninsula, or accept that the DPRK could exist. The overthrow of Rhee and the coming to power of the military regime under Park Chung-hee in 1961 changed that. Park had few illusions about reunification. Rather than worry about that issue, the ROK should build itself up as an independent state, seeking a broad measure of international support and creating a modern economy that would match or overtake that of the DPRK, which would also supply the means of defence.

The Sino-Soviet dispute

The Sino-Soviet dispute, which filled much of the 1960s and 1970s, brought a change to the international scene that worked to the North Koreans' benefit, though it required a difficult balancing act. Kim Il Sung was well placed to exploit the differences that began to dominate Sino-Soviet relations in the late 1950s, for he knew both sides; not many people had both fought with the Chinese communist forces and been a Soviet Red Army officer. During the Korean War, the DPRK drew on the Soviet Union and the People's Republic of China in different ways. Both had aided post-war reconstruction. Following the United States' introduction of nuclear weapons into South Korea in the late 1950s, Kim sought and obtained additional security reassurances from both countries, in the form of mutual defence treaties signed in 1961.

Almost straightaway, however, the DPRK experienced doubts over the degree of protection it could expect, especially from the Soviet Union. The DPRK did not draw attention to the 1962 USSR-USA Cuban missile crisis in which the USSR backed down. But clearly this action – or inaction – in the face of a US threat raised doubts about the Soviet Union's willingness to defend the DPRK in the event of an attack. It seems highly probable that the North Korean decision to explore developing its own nuclear weapons' capability dates from this period. Certainly, the North Koreans began their first civilian nuclear experiments about this time. It was no coincidence either that the ROK appears also to have begun exploring such a possibility at the same moment, until pulled up short by the Americans.

Some question whether the North Koreans gained or lost by the Sino-Soviet dispute. For the North Koreans, as for other socialist states, the tensions in Sino-Soviet relations from 1957 onwards were not easy to handle. For those whose closest neighbour was the Soviet Union, there was little choice but to side with that power. For others, such as Cuba, there was more to be gained from the superior military power and the advanced economic development of the Soviet Union than there was from the Chinese, particularly when China embarked on the 'ten wasted years' of the Cultural Revolution in 1966.

North Korea was in a different position. It was both close and far away. Its economic model was undoubtedly the Soviet Union, with its emphasis on heavy industry. Yet in other ways, the DPRK drew its inspiration from the PRC. Partly this was a product of the strong cultural and historical links between China and the Korean peninsula. There were also more immediate reasons for preferring China. Kim had spent longer in China than he had in the Soviet Union and the 'Asiatic' style of the PRC's approach to economic issues was more appealing than the European model of the USSR. He also seems to have admired Mao Zedong's approach to rapid social and economic transformation, especially as shown in the 'Great Leap Forward' of the late 1950s. Here was no long passage through the various stages of social development, but a rapid move to something like the final goal while bypassing most of the intermediate steps. Like many others, however, Kim did not realize the full extent of the failure of the Chinese policy until much later; even then, it may not have mattered. This was still the model to be emulated.

The split undoubtedly caused problems for the DPRK. Siding with one of the two great socialist powers ran the risk of alienating the other. Ideologically, as we have seen, Kim Il Sung was closer to China, and as the beneficiary of a cult of personality himself, he disliked Khrushchev's attack on Stalin's reputation. Economically, however, in the early 1960s, his regime was far more dependent on the support of the Soviet Union and Eastern Europe than on the PRC. Its industrialization linked it to the Council for Mutual Economic Assistance, or COMECON, both in terms of the supply of raw materials and for outlets for its products. In military terms, only the Soviet Union had the means to stand up to the United States. This remained true even after the Chinese exploded their first atomic bomb in 1965. On the whole, therefore, the DPRK tended towards neutrality in the Sino-Soviet dispute, sometimes leaning one way, sometimes the other. One positive aspect of the dispute for Kim Il Sung was that it left him a free hand to dispose finally of those in the North Korean leadership who were associated with either the Soviet Union or China. This process, begun in the aftermath of the Korean War, was now completed with vigour.

Overall, North Korea probably benefited from the Sino-Soviet split. Kim was periodically able, from about 1960 to the mid-1980s, to exploit the tensions between them. When the Russians and the Chinese were collaborating, the former were content to let the latter take most of the burden of supporting the DPRK. For sophisticated weapons and modern industrial equipment, however, the Soviet Union was the only real source available. For most of the DPRK's history, China has been a supplier of raw materials, foodstuffs and less sophisticated equipment, generally at low prices or as gifts. Later, as the PRC's own weapons industry developed, the Chinese were able to replace the Soviet Union as North Korea's suppliers. Neither the Soviet Union nor China did this for altruistic reasons, although there was some socialist solidarity, especially in the early years.

The reasons for courting the DPRK lay in the strategic position of the Korean peninsula. Both Russia and China were concerned, from 1953 onwards, that unless Kim Il Sung was restrained, there was a danger of further conflict on the Korean peninsula. Such conflict might not be containable, given US support for the ROK. It was important therefore to keep the North Korean regime from 'breaking out' and to exercise restraint in the face of such confrontations as the 'Pueblo incident' in 1968, when North Korea captured an American spy ship, allegedly in Korean waters, or the killing of two US officers at Panmunjom in 1976. At the same time, the DPRK could also be used to bring pressure on the US. Thus the Soviet decision to supply new and advanced aircraft to North Korea in the mid-1980s showed the other side of the coin. The trick was in getting the balance right to create enough pressure, without making the DPRK over-confident and therefore dangerous.

The difficulties of depending on its big neighbours regularly came home to the DPRK. The Cuban missile crisis and the willingness of the Soviet Union to practise peaceful coexistence with the United States were worrying. A Soviet decision in 1962–3 to reduce aid to express displeasure at the DPRK's independent line hit the economy badly. For a time, the China of the Cultural Revolution seemed safe and reliable – even if it also hurled a few insults at North Korea; young Chinese Red Guards on the Amnok and Tuman rivers apparently made derogatory references to 'fat Kim Il Sung' at one stage. Then came the reports that Dr Kissinger had been to Beijing. If United States talks with the PRC struck a major blow at South Korean self-confidence, it did the same for the North. Each set of Koreans found that their closest ally was talking to their worst enemy – and in both cases, with the minimum of consultation. This development would lead to major changes in the two Koreas' relationship with each other and in their diplomacy.

THE 1970S: CONTACTS AND COMPETITION BETWEEN THE TWO KOREAS

One of the early effects of Sino-US rapprochement was that North and South Korea began talking to each other for the first time since the Korean War. Red Cross meetings in 1971–2 led to by government talks and eventually by the signing of agreements. Despite high hopes, there was little evidence of a meeting of minds between the two sides and the exercise fizzled out in mutual recriminations. The longest lasting result was that South Korea's leader, Park Chung-hee, used the pretext of the talks and the supposedly increased risk from the North to stage what has been described as a coup against himself, in order to establish a more authoritarian government.

The 1970s were nonetheless to prove a watershed for the international affairs of the two Koreas. If the North entered the diplomatic race behind the South, it had caught up by the end of the decade. It also appeared to be the more politically stable of the two Koreas. Not only had Park staged his 'internal coup' in 1973 and then established a progressively more autocratic regime, but his assassination in October 1979 and the events that followed, seemed to prove that the ROK regime was inherently flawed.

The DPRK, by contrast, continued under the dominant influence of Kim Il Sung, who seemed ready to contemplate a possible transfer of power only within his own family. In the 1960s, it seemed that one of his brothers was being prepared for this role, but from at least 1973, it was rumoured that he was grooming Kim Jong Il, his eldest son by his first wife, to succeed him. South Korean sources also claimed that this process was leading to opposition among the more conservative groups in the DPRK. The younger Kim was credited in ROK sources with responsibility for a series of infiltrations and terrorist attacks on the South from the late 1960s onwards (an attempted commando raid on the South Korean presidential residence in 1968 and an attempt in 1974 to assassinate President Park that killed his wife). Nonetheless, whatever the uncertainties about the succession, the regime itself seemed strong and united.

Yet, while the ROK's political world became increasingly turbulent in the 1970s, economically it began to surge forward. Park's economic policies, pursued in as draconian a fashion as his political aims, were paying off and the South was moving to overtake the North. By the mid-1970s, if not earlier, ROK Gross National Product per capita began to pull ahead of that in the DPRK. South Korea found that it could woo third world countries with cash and expertise. Where the money went, political recognition followed. The DPRK, faced with declining production at home, found it harder to compete. It faced additional problems as well. To replace worn-out industrial plant from the Soviet Union and Eastern Europe, it had begun a policy of buying new and updated equipment on the world markets. Advanced technology began to flow into North Korea. Some was paid for outright, but much was bought on credit. The South also began a programme of military modernization, which the North felt compelled to match, either by purchase or by the development of its own capacity. The two were soon locked into an expensive arms race. The ROK paid for its share out of an expanding economy, the DPRK out of one that was contracting.

Then came the oil crisis of 1973. The South, with a stronger base, managed to ride out the situation, though not without sacrifices. The North found that its claimed independence from the international economic order was illusory. It could not sell its raw materials on the world market. However, the sales of these commodities were essential to pay for the new equipment. When the burden of repaying proved too difficult, the DPRK defaulted on its payments, the first socialist country to do so. In 1987, North Korea's Western creditors declared it to be formally in default. Following the expansion of diplomatic links with the European Union after 2000, the DPRK approached a number of countries to try to settle the issue of these old debts. While admitting that the DPRK had accumulated the debts, they made no offer of even a token repayment, but rather suggested that the debts be written off as a gesture of goodwill; unsurprisingly, the proposals got nowhere.

The awareness that it was falling behind economically may have fostered a North Korean belief that it could no longer afford the conventional arms race with the South. ROK and US figures show the North ahead in numbers and much equipment by the mid-1970s. By the early 1980s, the conventional wisdom was that North Korea had about one million men under arms and had a larger air force and larger mobile units than the South. The latter had only some 500,000 men in its armed forces, and on paper, was inferior to the North Koreans. The reality was that South Korean forces were better equipped and better trained than their North Korean counterparts. All the DPRK's crop-spraying aircraft, for example, were counted as though they were frontline fighting aircraft. In terms of actual spending, moreover, the ROK laid out more than double in real money on defence. There was also a tendency to ignore the 37,000 US forces in the ROK, which remained a firm indication of the US commitment to South Korea. The North Koreans, faced by the enemy that had destroyed most of their cities in 1950–51, had no similar assurance. The Chinese and the Russians maintained no physical presence in the DPRK and were both, in their different ways, anxious to remain on good terms with the United States. Certainly, it must have seemed to the DPRK as the 1980s progressed that while the theoretical ability of the USSR in particular to oppose the US grew steadily, the will to do so seemed to be eroding. This was particularly the case after Gorbachev came to power in the Soviet Union. In such circumstances, Kim Il Sung or Kim Jong Il – both have been credited with the policy, on dubious grounds – may well have decided that nuclear weapons might redress the balance, or at least reduce the expense of the arms race. Exactly when the DPRK began to look at a nuclear weapons' capability is not known, but by the late 1980s international suspicions were being aroused by the Yongbyon complex north of Pyongyang in the central-west section of the country.

With Soviet assistance, the DPRK had been developing a nuclear programme for civilian use from the 1950s. DPRK nuclear scientists trained in the Soviet Union. There they became well known for their diligence and ability, though it was noted that once they had graduated from their institutions and returned to the DPRK, their Soviet mentors rarely had further contact with them. Neither were Soviet scientists allowed into DPRK nuclear facilities. Yet only after the DPRK, at Soviet persuasion, signed the Nuclear Non-proliferation Treaty (NPT) in 1985, as the price for further assistance with its civilian nuclear programme, was the possibility of a North Korean nuclear weapons programme raised internationally. Thereafter, international scrutiny of the DPRK's known nuclear installations intensified. By the early 1990s, there was a growing belief in the United States and in some other Western countries that what was visible at the installations at Yongbyon went well beyond the civilian programme and related experimental work that the DPRK claimed to be undertaking.

The greater concern, however, at the time was about the DPRK's ability to produce missiles and its willingness to sell these. During the 1980s, the DPRK found that it could benefit from the tensions prevalent in the world and in particular from the Middle East's search for new sources of arms. The Iran-Iraq War proved particularly useful as the demand for missiles increased. The DPRK, supplied with Soviet missiles, had worked hard to reverse engineer these so that they could be produced more cheaply than buying them. These now found a market in Iran, desperate for weapons. The DPRK, once payment was guaranteed, was happy to supply all the missiles required.

A CHANGING WORLD

By the mid-1980s, the DPRK was in trouble, whether taken on its own terms or other people's. Its economy could not deliver as the

South's clearly could. The ROK had shown that it could come through political upheavals such as the death of Park Chung-hee and the consequent disruptions, and survive, and when the North reverted to terror tactics in 1983 with a bomb attack in Yangon that missed President Chun Doo-hwan but killed several of his ministers, the ROK rode out that crisis too. The DPRK's stability was beginning to look like sclerosis rather than something positive. The prospect of the first communist dynasty, as Kim Il Sung's eldest son, Kim Jong Il, was groomed to take over from his father, added to the sense of the bizarre.

Internationally, the North was also losing out to the South. Dramatic proof of this came when the latter won the right to stage both the 1986 Asian Games and the 1988 Olympic Games. The DPRK tried to persuade its friends and supporters not to take part in either games and further argued that the games should not be held in one half of the divided peninsula, but to little effect. The PRC attended the Asian Games, and the Soviet Union and the PRC the 1988 Olympics. North Korea once more engaged in terrorism in late 1987 to achieve its ends, planting a bomb on a South Korean airliner that blew up over the Andaman Sea, killing all on board. Such tactics, despite widespread condemnation, were not entirely unsuccessful. The fear of a continued terror campaign led the United States into direct talks with North Korea for the first time since the armistice negotiations of 1950–53. These talks, held in the International Club in Beijing, achieved little except to break through the longstanding US refusal to participate in direct talks. It was a small victory in a world that was increasingly ignoring the DPRK's wishes.

In attending the games, neither of the DPRK's allies had suffered a sudden change of heart towards the ROK. Each had been developing cautious contacts with the ROK from the late 1970s, stepping back if the DPRK questioned their behaviour. Yet, each time the contacts began again and were edged forward. Cultural and sporting links gave way to economic exchanges. For the Soviet Union (and its East European allies, which tended to lead the way) and the PRC, the ROK had much to offer economically, and in management and other techniques. Political contacts followed the economic links. Hungary established diplomatic relations with the ROK in 1988 and by 1990, the Soviet Union as well as the other Eastern Europeans had followed suit. The Chinese were more cautious, but they too established diplomatic relations with South Korea in 1992.

The DPRK's reaction to the Hungarian decision was one of fury, though stopping short of breaking diplomatic relations. As other Eastern Europeans, the Soviet Union and the PRC followed the Hungarian lead, its ability to do anything diminished. There were further blows, as the North Koreans found that the economic advantages they had once enjoyed *vis-à-vis* the socialist countries were no longer available. The 'friendship prices', which the DPRK had long enjoyed, ended – though eventually, in the case of the PRC this seemed more a theoretical than an actual position. With the collapse of the Soviet Union and the changes in Eastern Europe, much of what the DPRK had seen as the established world order disappeared. The PRC now became, and has remained ever since, the DPRK's main source of political and economic support. This gives the PRC a certain degree of leverage over the DPRK, which it has used from time to time, though the Chinese always remain cautious about the degree of pressure they will exert on the DPRK.

The DPRK was not oblivious to the developments around it. From the beginning of the 1980s, some in the leadership had seen the need for new approaches to the outside world. Perhaps inspired by the Chinese example of opening up special economic zones, the DPRK set out from 1984 onwards to woo foreign investors (see Chapter 3). Despite its record of past defaults, it did manage to attract some interest, often small-scale and with major participation from overseas Koreans resident in Japan. New legislation provided foreign investors with the right climate. The problem was to produce goods under the DPRK economic system that would find a place in the world market.

In order to learn more about capitalist trading methods, North Korea took advantage of the assistance offered by United Nations organizations such as the United Nations Development Programme (UNDP). From the late 1980s onwards, UNDP ran courses for North Koreans to learn about international trade and related matters. The DPRK was also involved in the proposed development of the Tumen river basin, intended to turn the river delta into the Rotterdam of the 21st century. The DPRK's first special economic zone, at Rajin-Sonbong, begun in 1991, was within the area of the proposed Tumen Development Zone. While the Rajin-Sonbong zone seemed to indicate new thinking, it was equally important in DPRK eyes that it was almost as far as one can get from Pyongyang. In addition to these economic development projects, the DPRK expressed interest in regional bodies such as the 'ASEAN Regional Forum' (ARF) of the Association of South East Asian Nations. Increasingly, the emphasis seemed to be on the DPRK as an Asian or even a Pacific country, rather than an outpost of socialism.

In the early 1990s, the DPRK pursued two lines. One was to improve relations with the ROK. Talks at prime ministerial level eventually produced the December 1991 'Agreement on Reconciliation, Non-aggression and Exchanges and Cooperation between the North and the South'. The agreement laid down that each side would respect the other's right to follow its own political system, and until the achievement of unification, both would respect the 1953 armistice agreement. There were provisions for a wide range of economic and cultural exchanges, and for reconnection of road and rail links between the two. Later in December 1991, the two sides initialled the 'North-South Joint Declaration on Non-nuclearization of the Korean Peninsula'.

The DPRK also pursued a new campaign to improve its diplomatic position. The diplomatic offensive in the 1970s had brought little benefit. Relations had quickly gone sour with the Australians. The Scandinavian countries wanted repayment of debts or trade. When neither materialised, those that had missions either reduced or closed them. Now, the DPRK tried to renew contacts with a number of countries and to establish new connections in Europe. At the same time, however, its economic problems were reflected in the steady closure of DPRK embassies. Some were in the poorer countries of Africa, but they also included posts in Portugal, Norway and Albania.

THE NUCLEAR ISSUE RETURNS

From a small cloud in the late 1980s, the nuclear issue grew to a major crisis by 1992. The DPRK regularly denied it intended to develop nuclear weapons. Kim Il Sung himself said so on several occasions before his death. According to DPRK accounts until 2002, the country's development of a nuclear capability was solely to meet its well-known shortages of energy. While the DPRK has hydroelectric power, this is unreliable, especially in winter, and its coal supplies are inadequate for its energy needs. (The country's inefficient use of such electricity as it generates has compounded these deficiencies.)

To outside observers, nuclear weapons have never made much sense on the Korean peninsula, whoever held them. Given the relatively small size of the peninsula and the proximity of important towns on both sides of the armistice line, it is hard to see in what context the DPRK might use a nuclear weapon, unless it was a final suicidal act of defiance. Despite all the rhetoric, the DPRK has a record of stepping back from the brink, and a desire to commit regime suicide seems unlikely. But by 1992, when it finally signed the safeguards' agreement required by the NPT, there were growing international doubts about its nuclear programme. The DPRK's cavalier attitude towards its obligations under the NPT and the discrepancies between what it claimed to have at Yongbyon and what satellites showed, fuelled such doubts. One of the consequences of the DPRK's relative isolation from the world was its leaders' failure to appreciate just how sophisticated international surveillance methods had become by 1990. What once might have been concealed could be concealed no more. The lists submitted as part of the safeguards' agreement confirmed that there were discrepancies in the North Korean record.

One of the plants caused particular concern. The DPRK claimed that it was a radiochemical laboratory for research purposes, but satellite photographs indicated that it was a spent nuclear fuel reprocessing plant. Such a plant would allow the extraction of plutonium, used in making atomic weapons and for no other purpose, from spent fuel rods. The International Atomic Energy Authority (IAEA), charged with ensuring international compliance with the NPT, insisted that it should be able to investigate the Yongbyon facilities. Unfortunately for the DPRK, the IAEA now decided, after its failure to detect an Iraqi nuclear weapons' programme that had come to light in the 1991 Gulf War, to invoke its right to conduct intrusive inspections at Yongbyon and at all the DPRK's other nuclear-related facilities. The DPRK reacted in a predictable manner, denouncing the IAEA as a US puppet. As the pressure for inspections continued, the DPRK announced in March 1993 that it would withdraw from the NPT. That the NPT does not provide for a state's withdrawal, and that no other state had done so, did not shift the North Koreans from their position.

This action had major implications for the whole non-proliferation system and led to widespread international concern. The ROK suspended all economic aid, but the United States took the lead in condemning the DPRK. International pressure on the North Koreans included the threat of UN sanctions. The DPRK's reaction was to assert that such sanctions would be 'an act of war'. The DPRK also warned the ROK that the outcome of any conflict on the peninsula would be catastrophic, with Seoul turned into 'a sea of fire'. These were hardly new threats, and in later years, the DPRK would use the same rhetoric about Japan, but the government of ROK President Kim Young-sam professed to take the threats seriously. It later emerged that the United States had come near to attacking the DPRK, including some form of military 'surgical strike' on Yongbyon. The difficulties of guaranteeing success and the fear of starting a wider conflict, with the possibility of immense damage to the ROK, led to wiser counsels prevailing.

Instead, the United States consented to talk to the DPRK. Each side eventually agreed not to threaten the other, and the DPRK suspended its withdrawal from the NPT. The ROK indicated that, if the nuclear issue was settled, a North-South summit might be possible. Early 1994 saw a series of talks that failed to solve the issue, but provided an opportunity for the US and the DPRK negotiators to discuss the problems in detail. Negotiations on a Korean North-South summit also continued. In the summer of 1994, former US President Jimmy Carter took up a long-standing invitation to visit the DPRK. The North Koreans viewed Carter as a potential friend, who at the beginning of his presidency had advocated the withdrawal of US ground forces' from Korea. His initiative was not so popular with the Clinton administration in Washington. In fact, Carter's visit in June 1994 proved to be a catalyst for ending the immediate nuclear standoff. During talks with Kim Il Sung, Carter found him ready to examine a way out of the impasse, adapting an idea being discussed in some think-tanks in the United States. If the DPRK agreed to freeze its current nuclear programme, re-join the NPT and accept some, if limited, inspection of its facilities, the United States would respond. The US would lift part of the economic sanctions' regime that dated back to the Korea War, would establish a diplomatic presence in Pyongyang, and would assist North Korea to construct nuclear Light Water Reactors (LWRS), which are much less suitable for producing weapons' grade plutonium.

Although Kim Il Sung died in July 1994, his seal on the Carter visit was enough to make these proposals the basis of the first-ever direct US-DPRK agreement. Negotiations on the detail culminated in the signing of an 'Agreed Framework' between the two sides at Geneva in October 1994. The Agreed Framework accepted that the issue of whether or not the DPRK was actually pursuing a potential nuclear weapons' programme should be postponed until the LWRS would be on the point of going critical, several years down the line. In 1995, the Korea Peninsula Energy Development Organization (KEDO) came into existence, to carry out the practical terms of the Agreed Framework. Soon after, work began on the KEDO project. In addition, until the LWRs would come on stream, KEDO would supply heavy fuel oil to the DPRK, to compensate for the loss of energy from Yongbyon. Despite criticisms and doubts, euphoria over the ending of the standoff, the saving of the NPT regime, and the lack of any alternative strategy that did not involve the possibility of war, carried the day. For the North Koreans, the Agreed Framework was a major triumph. For the first time in forty years, they had persuaded the United States to the negotiating table, with some success.

Some of this euphoria continued until the end of the decade. The United States lifted a number of economic sanctions, though others remained. The US continued to list the DPRK as a state supporting terrorism and therefore barred from access to the Asian Development Bank and other financial institutions – not because of its very real terrorist attacks on the ROK but because it continued to give asylum to a group of Japanese aircraft hijackers from 1970. In other ways, too, the 1994 Agreement was never more than partially implemented. The United States got as far as identifying suitable premises for a small diplomatic mission in Pyongyang, but the question of actually opening the offices stalled on such matters as embassy supplies and how they might be provided. The DPRK ruled out Panmunjom as a crossing point. By 2001, when the British were looking for premises in Pyongyang, the US had given up and the former East German offices once earmarked for the Americans became the new British Embassy. The implementation of the KEDO agreement was not without its problems either. The DPRK tried to drive hard bargains over ships' clearances and wages; in the latter case, KEDO shipped in Uzbek workers at less cost than the Koreans. Much time was spent on preparing the site for the reactors, and it was several years before work began on the reactors themselves.

Meanwhile, DPRK-US relations developed on other fronts, albeit slowly and cautiously. Various US delegations went to the DPRK, including humanitarian delegations as news filtered out about severe food shortages. In the early 1990s, after years of ignoring requests passed through the Military Armistice Commission at Panmunjom about US forces missing since the Korean War, the DPRK began returning what it said were US remains. These early approaches developed into a full-scale Missing in Action (MIA) programme, which continues to this day. In addition to its humanitarian purpose, this programme has brought the US military and the Korean People's Army into their first-ever non-confrontational experience and has enabled US military personnel to visit areas normally off limits to foreigners. Despite persistent suspicions in some quarters that the DPRK was cheating on the Agreed Framework, and the retention of many major US sanctions, relations had so developed that the then US Secretary of State, Madeleine Albright, could visit in autumn 2000. There was even talk of a visit by President Clinton. Other positive developments, such as a proposal to remove the DPRK from the terrorist supporters' list, petered out in the last days of the Clinton administration. This was not entirely the United States' doing. The DPRK moved very slowly and suspiciously, perhaps on the assumption that the Democrats would retain the presidency and they had plenty of time. Instead, a new president in the White House in January 2001 betokened a more hostile US approach to the DPRK.

President George W. Bush is said to 'loathe' Kim Jong Il, though exactly why is not clear. Whatever he may have thought of the DPRK, President George Bush senior authorized direct US-DPRK contacts in the late 1980s, and the experience of dealing with the DPRK in the 1990s indicated that deals could be done. Perhaps it was, as some have speculated, another example of the ABC, or 'anything but Clinton' doctrine that Bush was supposed to pursue.

Whatever the cause, the new administration came with a hostile attitude towards the DPRK. Almost at once, it announced that it would examine the Agreed Framework in the light of alleged DPRK breaches. The stage was set for confrontation.

This was unfortunate. The DPRK had since the mid-1990s gradually come more on to the international scene. Economic problems following the collapse of the Soviet Union and of the old COMECON trading system had hit the DPRK badly. Worse was to come with a series of natural disasters in the mid-1990s. In desperation, the DPRK did not, as President Bush claimed, let its people starve, but made an unprecedented appeal for international assistance. This was forthcoming from UNDP, the World Food Programme and other international sources, but relief groups soon ran into difficulties. They found that they confronted, not a disintegrating administrative structure, but a strong state that wanted to control outside assistance. In the face of Korean rigidity, a number of international bodies including OXFAM withdrew from the DPRK. Others stayed, and gradually worked out a *modus operandi*.

Another factor bringing the DPRK into the world followed on from the 2000 summit (see below) between the leaders of the two Koreas. To this impetus, the ROK added strong pleas for more international involvement with the DPRK. Even before the summit, Italy had established diplomatic relations in January 2000. Australia resumed relations in May 2000, although this time without a resident mission. Others followed in establishing relations: Britain in December 2000 and Germany in March 2001. Before long, all European Union countries except France and Ireland had diplomatic relations (and Ireland followed in 2003). The EU not only established relations but also sent a high-level delegation to Pyongyang in May 2001. This obtained a pledge directly from Kim Jong Il that the DPRK would observe a moratorium on missile tests until 2003. The DPRK may have hoped that the EU and its member states would pursue a different line from the Americans on issues such as nuclear developments, but such hopes were ill-founded. The DPRK also found that the EU had its own concerns, including human rights' issues, which would preclude any major breakthrough in dealings.

The Bush administration opposed none of these developments but continued to hold the DPRK at arm's length, even when the DPRK reacted promptly to condemn terrorism and express condolences at the loss of life after the bombing of the New York World Trade Centre on 11 September 2001. For those trying to persuade the DPRK that the US was not hostile, the task became more difficult as 2001 moved into 2002. KEDO's existence was questioned. In his State of the Union message in January 2002, President Bush listed the DPRK as part of 'an axis of evil', together with Iraq and Iran. This was striking rhetoric but it ignored the hostility between Iraq and the DPRK since the latter had assisted Iran in the Iran-Iraq war. The DPRK's first reactions were low-key but it quickly came to present the speech as another example of unremitting US hostility.

Meanwhile, KEDO fell steadily behind schedule. The US declined to provide a formal explanation for this, to the exasperation of DPRK officials, who began to say that they might have to restart their earlier nuclear programme to compensate for the loss of energy that KEDO's non-functioning represented. The LWRs were to have come on stream in 2003, but the first concrete-laying ceremony was held only in August 2002. At the ceremony, the chief US representative warned that the reactors could not come on stream unless the DPRK complied with the Agreed Framework's provisions for an examination of Yongbyon's past history. The DPRK complained that the US military continued to target the country with nuclear weapons.

The Bush administration had argued that it would not engage in a dialogue with the DPRK based on the previous administration's policy, and that it would review relations. By mid-2002, the administration had carried out this review, concluding that there should be discussions with the DPRK. By the autumn of 2002, the US was ready to talk and found the DPRK very receptive. James Kelly, US Assistant Secretary of State, arrived with his party in Pyongyang in early October 2002. The DPRK, which had worked hard to accommodate the demands of Kelly's party, claimed later that it had expected a wide-ranging discussion, examining both sides' concerns. Kelly, however, confronted the North Koreans with one issue: the US had evidence that the DPRK had broken the terms of the Agreed Framework and was engaged in a clandestine programme involving highly enriched uranium (HEU). According to leaks in Washington later in October, the DPRK at first denied the claim, but later admitted it. The DPRK for its part began to claim from the moment of Kelly's departure that he had misunderstood their position. Eventually, they would say that they had not admitted to an HEU programme but had said that they were not prohibited from undertaking such a programme. At the same time, they expressed a willingness to discuss nuclear and other issues of concern to the US, if the latter would sign a non-aggression treaty and agree not to interfere in the DPRK's internal affairs. By the end of 2002, the Agreed Framework was in ruins and the DPRK was well on the way to withdrawing from the NPT. The DPRK expelled the IAEA inspectors, and the process of starting up the Yongbyon reactors was put in hand. KEDO's deliveries of heavy fuel oil stopped. Since then, the KEDO project has been suspended, although not formally abandoned. The one part of the DPRK's known nuclear programme that had been under international control has been totally uncontrolled since the end of 2002.

Since early 2003, the DPRK has made various statements implying that it might have some form of 'nuclear deterrence'. The most explicit came in February 2005, when a Foreign Ministry statement said that the DPRK had 'manufactured nukes [*sic*] for self-defence'. Exactly what this meant is still unclear, and it is not certain that the DPRK has nuclear weapons. No North Korean nuclear test has so far been detected. In other ways, the signals from the DPRK have been ambiguous. It has stuck to its various promises about not testing missiles, though it has fired off one or two short-range missiles, presumably to show what it could do if it wanted.

The United States, for its part, has tried to bring international pressure to bear on the DPRK. While some in or near to the administration continue to talk in tough terms about what might happen to the DPRK if it does not abandon its nuclear programme, other voices have been more mollifying. The US has organized an international grouping to handle the issue, involving the PRC and Russia, Japan and the ROK in addition to the US and the DPRK. This six-nation group, hosted by the PRC, had a number of meetings in 2003–04, without any progress, but in the run-up to the November 2004 US presidential elections, the DPRK appeared to be even less interested in talking than usual, as it awaited the outcome of the contest. Any hope the North Koreans were nursing of a Democratic president who might prove more amenable than a second George W. Bush administration has been dashed by the result. In February 2005, when the DPRK announced that it had nuclear weapons, it also announced that it was suspending participation in the six-party talks indefinitely. In March, however, it was less dogmatic.

Recent years have seen growing concern expressed in the United States about human rights' conditions in the DPRK, fuelled by graphic reports of ill-treatment and claims of large losses of life because of famine during the 1990s. The EU and other countries have also raised the issue both in private and in public. This concern has led to pressure for a linkage between any US humanitarian assistance to the DPRK and improvements in human rights, culminating in the presidential signing of a North Korea Human Rights Act in October 2004. Although this seeks to force the administration into a more vigorous pursuit of human rights' infringements, the executive can choose how far to press the issue. The US Congress has appointed a special ambassador to monitor human rights in the DPRK and has allocated a budget of over US $24 million to assist with implementation of the act. The act has been widely welcomed among religious and activist groups, and rejected by the DPRK, but it is unlikely to make a great deal of difference in practice.

An additional element in the concern over human rights' injustices in the DPRK is the issue of refugees/defectors. As already seen (chapter 1), there are fears over the treatment of those returned from the PRC to North Korea. The porous nature of the Sino-DPRK border made it possible for large numbers of people to cross over during the years of food shortages in search of provisions. On the Chinese side, humanitarian groups, many of which came from South Korea, often looked after such groups. In the past few years, the refugee issue has become politicized as activists have helped to organize invasions of foreign embassies and schools in Beijing by small groups of North Koreans aiming to force the Chinese and South Korean authorities to allow them to travel to the ROK. Other North Korean escapees turn up in Mongolia and Southeast Asia, similarly seeking to reach South Korea. Nearly 4,000 North Koreans made their way to the ROK by various routes in the period 2002 to November 2004, a major increase on earlier escapees. The South, which once rewarded handsomely the few who managed to defect from the DPRK, has now scaled back payments as it seeks to integrate the larger numbers arriving and is screening new entrants against spies, criminals and Chinese Koreans. Would-be North Korean defectors working in the Russian Far East are now being discouraged from trying to get to the ROK by staff in the ROK consulate in Vladivostok. In late 2004, the PRC revealed it had appealed to the DPRK to restrict the numbers of North Korean citizens entering China and to South Korea to curb their flow through the PRC to the ROK.

THE NORTH-SOUTH DIALOGUE TAKES OFF

The election of Kim Young-sam, the ROK's first civilian president for over thirty years, in 1992 brought hopes of an improvement in North-South relations, especially given the agreements signed at the end of 1991. In the event, Kim Young-sam displayed little imagination in dealing with the DPRK, and the North responded accordingly. Relations were complicated by the nuclear issue and by the US wish to prevent nuclear proliferation. After years in which the United States had declined to talk directly to the DPRK, now the imperative was different and Kim Young-sam found himself being left behind, discouraged by the tough tone of the DPRK's rhetoric. The 1991 Agreements, for all practical purposes, remained a dead letter. Nevertheless, contacts were never entirely broken off, and relations developed to the point where in June 1994, Kim Young-sam was willing to meet Kim Il Sung at a summit meeting. Then Kim Il Sung died. Kim Young-sam, who had been prepared to meet the North Korean leader one day, was not prepared the next to express any form of condolences on his death, in contrast to US President Clinton. The DPRK, which had lost the only leader it had ever known, professed outrage at this breach of good manners, and broke off contacts with the ROK.

Kim Il Sung's death also aroused concern in the South. There was fear of what a new regime in the North, likely to be led by Kim Jong Il, who had been demonized for years by the ROK security forces, might be like. There was also fear that, as often predicted, Kim Il Sung's death might herald the collapse of the DPRK, with unknown but probably very costly consequences for the ROK. There was also shock and worry because of the unexpected reaction from students at many universities. Rather than rejoicing at the death of the man widely seen as the country's greatest enemy, many students went into mourning and set up memorial altars on campuses throughout the ROK. The police moved swiftly to break up both the altars and the mourning groups, a reaction that provoked further outrage from the North. Relations cooled even further when a North Korean submarine, apparently engaged in an infiltration attempt, went aground on South Korea's east coast in 1996. The crew either died in the crash or were killed by ROK forces. The North eventually apologized for the incident, which it claimed was the result of engine failure, and the cremated remains of the crew were returned at the very end of 1996. North Korea, which had not been told of the cremations, claimed to be shocked at this treatment.

When Kim Dae-jung became president in early 1998, he announced a new policy towards the DPRK, described as the 'sunshine policy'. Rather than confrontation, Kim said that, while attacks or intrusions would be firmly handled, there would be no ROK attempt at takeover of the North, and that the ROK was ready to provide assistance to help the DPRK both feed its people and rebuild its economy. Despite periodic upsets, including a further submarine incident in 1998, occasional tension along the demilitarized zone, and regular naval clashes in the West Sea during the May-June crab fishing season, this policy of engagement has been maintained ever since.

In an even more positive development, Kim Dae-jung and Kim Jong Il held a summit meeting in June 2000 in Pyongyang. The meeting gave new impetus to the 1991 Agreements and led to growing contacts between North and South. Private efforts such as those of the Hyundai Group and of a host of South Korean non-governmental organizations forged additional links. Whereas in the past, few if any South Koreans saw more of North Korea than the view across the demilitarized zone, since 1998, thousands have visited the North either as tourists on tours to the Kumgang Mountains, or in other capacities. Even if subsequent revelations about the financial inducements, brokered through the Hyundai Group, which persuaded the DPRK to the summit have removed some of the original glory, it nevertheless marked a major step forward. Roh Moo-hyun, Kim Dae-jung's successor in 2002, has continued the 'sunshine policy', as the 'peace and prosperity' policy.

Engagement has not won support on all sides, however. Many older people remain suspicious of the DPRK and its motives. Others are concerned that most of the benefits from the new relationship lie with the North, which seems happy to take ROK money and assistance and to give little in return. Even in official circles, there remains a reluctance to accept the DPRK's legitimacy. Displays of the North Korean flag and other state symbols are not normally allowed. Since January 2005, the armed forces no longer officially view the DPRK as their principal enemy, but suspicions of the North remain strong among the military and veterans. Despite recent progress, reconciliation remains a long way off.

JAPAN

Concern over the nuclear issue and the possible threat from the DPRK also led Japan into formal contacts with the North. As with the ROK, the colonial inheritance has plagued Japan's relations with the DPRK. Given Kim Il Sung's anti-Japanese guerrilla background, it could hardly be otherwise. However, although there were no formal contacts between Japan after it regained its independence in 1952 and North Korea, there were many links. Red Cross negotiations, for example, led to the repatriation of many Koreans from Japan to North Korea in the late 1950s and even later.

The Korean community in Japan, at some 650,000, is even today the largest single body of foreigners in that country. It has long been divided into pro-North and pro-South groups. The former, Chongryon, or *Chosensoren* in Japanese, has been an important source of hard currency for the DPRK. The amounts remitted to the North in recent years have declined, however, and there are signs that the current generation is less enthusiastic in its support. Chongryon has also maintained a network of schools and other institutions, which have stressed the need for loyalty to the North Korean leadership. Here, too, there are signs of generational differences as younger Koreans see the DPRK-orientated education available in these institutions as of marginal use in modern Japan.

Until well into the 1970s, most ordinary Japanese looked more favourably upon North Korea than upon the South. By contrast, the formal Japanese attitude towards the DPRK reflected the United States and ROK positions. Only when the latter indicated in the late

1980s that there would be no objection to contacts with the North was there any real Japanese momentum towards the DPRK. A series of visits by politicians in 1989–90 and a number of conciliatory gestures by the Japanese government led to inter-governmental talks in 1990. The Japanese found themselves faced with massive demands for compensation for past and current wrongs, and a blistering negotiating style. In 1992, the talks ended with mutual recriminations and no agreement, when the North Koreans walked out after the Japanese raised the issue of the alleged abduction by DPRK special forces of several Japanese citizens over the years. By that time, the wider question of the DPRK nuclear programme had become an added complication. Japan, the only country to have suffered a nuclear attack, did not look favourably on a potentially hostile neighbour's acquisition of a nuclear capability. Even the advent of a Socialist prime minister in Japan and the willingness of the Japanese government to express official condolences on the death of Kim Il Sung in July 1994 failed to restart the talks. When they did resume in 1997–98, they once again stalled on the issue of the abductees, but the two sides did manage to reach agreement on visits to Japan by some of the Japanese women who had accompanied their Korean husbands to the North as part of the earlier repatriation process.

In August 1998, North Korea announced that it had launched a satellite from a rocket fired over Japan, though in the event, no satellite was ever detected. Various incidents involving suspected North Korean ships in Japanese waters increased popular sentiment against the North, already much roused by the abduction and nuclear issues. Outrage at the missile firing, seen as heightening the security threat to the country, led to a series of sanctions, including the suspension of food aid and a ban on charter flights. The sanctions were lifted in December 1999, since there had been no more missile tests, and diplomatic contacts resumed. The election of Koizumi Junichiro as Japan's prime minister in April 2001 seemed to bring a better turn to the relationship. Contacts were clearly going on behind the scenes, for at the end of August 2002, it was announced that Koizumi would visit the DPRK.

This was a major breakthrough; no previous Japanese prime minister seems even to have contemplated visiting North Korea, and Koizumi, widely seen as on the right of the political spectrum, a man willing to visit the Yasakuni Shrine in Tokyo, which commemorates Japan's war dead including convicted war criminals, appeared an unlikely breaker of this particular mould. The DPRK treated Koizumi's one-day visit to the DPRK on 17 September 2002 in a low-key way: no Japanese flags, no public appearances, workmanlike proceedings, without even a formal lunch. But there was no doubt that this was a major meeting. It had been assumed that the DPRK had promised something to the Japanese to entice Koizumi to Pyongyang, but there was no advance indication on what that something might be. Up to the last moment, DPRK officials denied firmly that any Japanese had ever been kidnapped or that DPRK ships had either intruded into Japanese waters or in other ways engaged in improper activities.

The exact details of what transpired between Koizumi and Kim Jong Il have not been made public, but as with Madeleine Albright's visit, the two leaders seem to have got on better than anybody could have expected. Kim admitted to Koizumi that the abductions had indeed taken place, carried out by an agency of the DPRK government. There had been thirteen kidnappings. Some of those abducted were alive, but the others had died. He had ordered that all such actions should stop and said that he would investigate further what had happened. There would be no repetitions. Kim also confirmed incidents involving ships in Japanese waters; these incidents, he thought, involved the military, and they, too, would stop. He promised that the DPRK would abide by its international commitments on nuclear matters, and that missile tests would be suspended indefinitely. Finally, the two leaders signed the 'Pyongyang Agreement', which laid down a broad framework for the improvement of relations. Koizumi returned to Japan with a sense of euphoria. The log-jam on relations with the DPRK seemed broken at last, and the Japanese Ministry of Foreign Affairs (MFA) began negotiations with the DPRK on the process of normalization. When the DPRK allowed some of the surviving abductees to visit Japan in October 2002, a new relationship still seemed possible.

This proved not to be the case. Koizumi's 'surprise diplomacy' backfired, and the MFA, hitherto the keenest advocate of an improved relationship with the DPRK, found that it was no longer in control of policy. Where the Japanese had previously seemed only to want confirmation of past DPRK actions and contact with those kidnapped, now the demands increased. Immense public pressure prevented the government from allowing the returnees to go back to the DPRK. Soon demands arose that their families should come to Japan as well. On top of this came the US revelations that the DPRK appeared to have broken the terms of the Agreed Framework. When this story leaked in Washington in October 2002, it further inflamed Japanese public opinion and added to the case against an attempt at improving relations with the DPRK. So effective was the impact of this news on Japanese rapprochement that many believe that the leak was timed precisely to undermine what many in the US administration thought was a dangerous Japanese move, and one that would certainly have reduced American leverage.

A two-year standoff developed, though some contacts continued behind the scenes. Domestic pressure in Japan for a resolution to the problem waxed and waned, but never disappeared. Then in a further surprise mood, Koizumi returned to the DPRK in May 2004. This time, he secured the release of a number of the former detainees' children, and an undertaking to look again at what had happened to the other known detainees, but he was unable to shift the DPRK on other matters of international concern.

A further humanitarian problem remained. One of those released in 2002, Hitomi Soga, had married an American, Charles Robert Jenkins, while in Pyongyang. Jenkins was one of a small group of former US soldiers who had defected or, some claimed, been kidnapped in the 1960s. The couple had two daughters, and Mrs Soga wished them and her husband to come to Japan. The US authorities regarded Jenkins as a deserter liable for court-martial, should he go to Japan, under the terms of the Japan-United States Status of Forces Agreement. Eventually, in the summer of 2004, Jenkins and his daughters travelled to Indonesia, where they joined Mrs Soga. The whole family then went to Japan, where Jenkins appeared before a US court-martial in November 2004 and was sentenced to 30 days' imprisonment and given a dishonourable discharge.

Then in autumn 2004, the DPRK sent to Japan what it claimed were the ashes of one of the abductees, Ms Yokata Megumi, who died in the early 1990s. Japanese DNA tests, however, did not confirm the DPRK claim. This development caused further outrage in Japan, while the North Koreans, for their part, denounced the Japanese tests and eventually demanded the return of the ashes.

Japanese relations with the DPRK therefore remain strained. The abductees' families are unhappy at the Japanese government's failure to make progress on the issue. Dislike of the DPRK has intensified rather than diminished in recent years, fuelled by continued concern over the DPRK's nuclear and missile programmes. While some Japanese ministers and officials, including the prime minister, still seem keen to wipe the slate clean with a settlement with the DPRK, public opinion will make such an outcome difficult. The United States, too, will be wary of any Japanese attempt at a settlement that might weaken leverage on the DPRK.

CONCLUSION

The world has changed much for the DPRK over the last twenty years, as has the way it interacts with that world. The old dependence on the Communist countries has gone. Even those remaining, except for the PRC, matter less to it. After thirty years of hostility, North Korea is now a full member of the United Nations. The UN system provides points of contact with governments with which the DPRK still does not have normal relations, as well as other benefits.

Yet for the DPRK, the world is still basically hostile. The continued division of the peninsula, the existence of two Korean states, and the great transformations in the circumstances of its former guarantors mean that its right to exist is still not fully acknowledged. There is a widespread belief that it is destined for extinction; the mirror image for the North Koreans is that much of the world is, in fact, plotting just such a course. Perhaps the DPRK's attitude to the outside world is because it is, as President George W. Bush and some of his supporters appear to believe, a fundamentally evil society. It may be that the DPRK should never have been created. The fact is that it is there and the world has to deal with it. More sensible than a confrontational and hostile approach is one that draws the DPRK ever more into the wider world, and one that accepts that the North does fear a genuine threat from the massive armed forces of the United States. Indeed, if not to threaten or contain the DPRK, why are US forces still on the Korean peninsula so long after the end of the Korean War?

Some will argue that it is wrong to allow the DPRK to get away with defiance of international opinion, others that, doomed by economic failure and international isolation, it has no choice but to accept that it is going to disappear. It may well be that the division of Korea will fade, given the peninsula's long historical, cultural and political unity. There is no guarantee, however, that the process will be either quick or easy, no matter how strong or weak the parties concerned. There are advantages for everybody if the DPRK's continued involvement in the world and its possible future disappearance take place with the least possible upheaval. To this end, reassurance and undertakings not to hasten the process may be more prudent and productive than threats.

▶ Part II

Visiting and Living in the DPRK

7

Practical Aspects

SOME OF THE MOST beautiful scenery in East Asia is contained within the Korean peninsula: mountain ranges rising to needle-sharp pinnacles that enfold clear streams and waterfalls, valleys watered by meandering rivers, long sandy beaches, an island-fringed south and west coastline. Not many historical sites remain in their original state, since the medium of construction was generally wood, always vulnerable to fire. The Japanese invasions at the end of the sixteenth century destroyed much, as did later conflicts, and the Korean War often devastated what had been rebuilt. Many 'old' buildings, castles, pavilions and temples are thus reconstructions, but for all that are attractive. The picturesque sight of thatched roofs has almost entirely vanished from the countryside, dismissed by leaders in both the North and the South as evidence of backward ways. Up until the 1970s, both halves of the peninsula, particularly in the rural areas, probably produced much the same impression on a visitor. Over the past twenty years, the ROK's industrialization and urbanization have imposed a new landscape on the southern part of the peninsula, sometimes harsh to the point of brutality, in tune with new global design, always dynamic. The DPRK has created something different, also undoubtedly modern, particularly in Pyongyang, and imbued with an equally strong purpose, to present the achievements of a policy – *juche*, a regime and a leader. Poverty and politics have hindered the country's development into a popular tourist destination, but have at the same time permitted the continued existence of much of what makes the DPRK such an attractive place: untouched countryside, clear skies and enormous calm. The largest tourist groups consist of Japanese Koreans, who come out of sentiment and family ties, and of Chinese, who like to visit the DPRK to remind themselves of how life used to be in China. A small number of tour groups are even coming from South Korea.

TRAVEL FOR WORK AND TOURISM

Although foreign tourists are welcomed, with the exception of US visitors, and foreign residents treated courteously, if cautiously, foreigners are a 'problem area' in the DPRK, since they represent at the very least a break in the smooth surface of society, and may appear disruptive or even subversive. Paradoxically, tourists are kept on a tighter rein than foreign residents, who can be monitored in a more discreet and leisurely fashion. Careful arrangements are made to direct tourists in particular towards achievements and what are considered significant elements in the history of the country. Visitors would be ill-advised to seek to criticize what they see, but even some lines of questioning may be viewed as unfriendly and unexpected requests, such as wanting to visit one's embassy, seen as difficult behaviour. It is best to try to bring any particular interests or wishes to attention at an early stage in your travel arrangements, as there is generally great reluctance to alter a programme once you have arrived in the DPRK.

Travel to and in the DPRK is not easy, even for those who may be going to work there. Entry requirements are strict, controls can be irksome, and the infrastructure has deficiencies. There is, however, a great deal to do and see. Tourists, even single people and small groups, might find it easiest to travel with a company that has experience of dealing with the Korean system. In any case, they will be accompanied throughout their trip by a tourist guide provided by the Korea International Travel Corporation (KITC), which arranges visits, transport and accommodation. There is no question of roaming independently about the country.

For the majority of visitors, Beijing is the starting point for the journey to Pyongyang, whether by air or by train, and it is there that they must pick up their onward tickets. Air Koryo operates regular flights from Beijing into Pyongyang twice a week; these are often heavily booked; return flights from Pyongyang should always be reconfirmed well in advance before travel. Other flights are to and from Shenyang in northeast China, and Vladivostok and Khabarovsk in Russia. There are currently three permitted points of entry into and exit from the DPRK: Pyongyang, Sinuiju and the Tuman river crossing. Visas normally list all three. The train service between Pyongyang and Beijing crosses the border at Sinuiju/Dandong. An international bus service is reported to have been introduced between Pyongyang and Dandong in June 2004.

The best seasons of the year for visiting any part of northeast Asia are the spring and autumn, and so it is for the DPRK. Spring comes later in the north of the peninsula, around the end of April. Fine warm weather lasts into June, but the following two months can be unpleasantly hot and humid. From September through to the end of October, sunny, dry days are matched by cooler evenings; then from November, the first snows fall in the extreme north of the country, and the whole of the DPRK becomes progressively colder. The cold weather can last until March.

Closed counties

Not all parts of the DPRK are open to visitors. Of the 206 counties within the country, somewhat over one-fifth are closed to access at any one time, and foreigners are generally prevented from visiting. Some of these counties lie in border regions. Thus, access to the Kumgang mountains on the east coast is difficult from the north, but this is because the area has been sealed off to ease the operation of tours from the south. Other counties in coastal or frontier regions are clearly closed for security reasons; yet many others are open, and the frontier with China appears to be a fairly easy one to cross for Koreans. Yongbyon county, a closed inland county in North Pyongan province, is known to house nuclear facilities. The largest tranche of closed counties lie in a block running down from the central section of the Sino-Korean border to the south of South Hamgyong province. About half of Jagang and Ryanggang provinces are thus closed off. The reasons for this inaccessibility can only be conjectured: defence installations, army camps, possibly further nuclear facilities, location of the country's labour and prison camps. These remote regions appear to be regarded as suitable areas for the safe-keeping of national treasures such as documents from earlier dynasties. Foreign relief agencies do not run supplies and services into the closed counties, given their inability to monitor distribution and use.

Visas

Travel to the DPRK necessitates the possession of a visa, the only exemption being for Chinese nationals. A visa must be obtained before arrival, outside of the DPRK, as visas are not issued on arrival. The number of DPRK diplomatic missions abroad is limited, and most travellers end up collecting their visa at the country's embassy in Beijing – another reason that makes a stop in Beijing almost inevitable. Britons can now collect visas at the DPRK embassy in London. Visas are often issued only at the very last minute.

Those entering the DPRK through China must also apply for a Chinese visa. A multiple-entry visa, if granted, removes the necessity for repeated applications. A double-entry or double-transit visa allows the traveller to go back into China without having to apply at the Chinese embassy in Pyongyang for a new entry visa. Those travelling in from Russia will need a visa, again preferably double-entry, for that country.

A DPRK diplomatic mission may be the point at which a visa is actually issued on receipt of a completed application form, two passport photographs and payment of a fee. However, application for a visa should be made at least a month in advance to the appropriate section of the Korean bureaucracy, which will then fax authorisation to the embassy in question. Those coming to work in an established office or to visit as consultants will find their office will handle visa and ID requirements. They should send full passport details a good month in advance to their organization. Those coming on business may like to use the services of a consultancy company at least for their first trip (see section below on Doing business in the DPRK). Private visitors will need a letter of invitation from their host (who will already be working in the DPRK).

Visas fall into categories according to the type of work or activity one wishes to pursue in the DPRK: UN agency, NGO, diplomatic mission, business, journalism, tourism, study, etc. Different regimes apply to these various groups, ranging from multiple-entry to single-entry visas. Visas are frequently denied to holders of US, Japanese or ROK passports. UN 'Laissez Passer' (UNLP) documents are recognized. Visa fees vary, but not in accordance with a standard scale; rather, visitors are charged approximately what it costs a DPRK national to get a visa for the visitor's country. Those travelling on diplomatic and UN passports are not charged for visas.

The Beijing embassy of the DPRK is open Monday, Wednesday and Friday, 9.30–11.30 a.m., 2–5.30 p.m.; Tuesday, Thursday and Saturday, 9.30–11.30 a.m.

Address: Embassy of the DPRK
Ritan Beilu
Jianguomenwai
Beijing

(Entrance to the visa section is at the northern end of the east wall of the embassy compound)

The DPRK's London embassy is open Monday to Friday, 9 a.m.–5 p.m.

Address: Embassy of the DPRK
73 Gunnersbury Avenue
London W5 4LP
Telephone: 44 (0)20 8992 4965
Fax: 44 (0)20 8992 2053

Registration and ID cards

Travellers arriving in the DPRK must register with the immigration authorities within forty-eight hours. Those staying in a hotel should leave their passports at the reception on arrival; they will be returned within a reasonable time, though you may have to ask for them. Those coming to work for an organization should ask their administrative staff to handle registration. Many, but not all, foreigners taking up residence in the DPRK are required to apply for an ID card. Again, various categories exist: diplomatic, service, etc. Visitors staying with an embassy or other organizations should ensure that the organization arranges for them to be registered.

Currency

The currency of the DPRK is the won, divided into one hundred *jon*. The won is not convertible, may not be used by foreigners, and may not be taken out of or into the country. Since the early 2000s, a parallel, hard-currency system has existed alongside the domestic won. At first the US dollar was the favoured currency, but since December 2002, it has been replaced by the euro; although there are rumours that the dollar may be coming back. Shops and restaurants frequented by foreigners demand payment in hard currency or convert their prices into euros. From being fixed for many years at an exchange rate of 2.16 won to one US dollar, the North Korean currency, as of spring 2004, had an official exchange rate of 139.9 won to one US dollar and of 172.8 won to one euro. Other rates, as at Tongil market in May 2004, may be more favourable. One of the effects of the economic changes introduced in July 2002 was to release the won from its earlier straitjacket.

Cash is the preferred method of payment, even for large items such as travel tickets, and, however reluctant they feel about doing so, visitors should bring sufficient amounts of euros with them to fund their trip. There are no restrictions on the volume of foreign currency that may be brought into or taken out of the DPRK. Visa and MasterCard credit and debit cards (but not American Express) are accepted at the big international hotels. There are no cash dispensers. It is difficult to use travellers' cheques and they are best avoided. Money can be changed at the big hotels and at the Korea Foreign Trade Bank near Kim Il Sung Square; the rates are the same.

Comprehensive insurance against loss, theft, cancelled flights, etc., should be taken out.

Regulations

Travellers may not bring mobile telephones or GPS systems into the DPRK. If they do, they will be required to relinquish them at the point of entry and collect them again on departure. It is probably best to leave mobiles at home or at some safe place along your route. Books and newspapers in Korean will be viewed with suspicion by immigration officials, as will bibles, even in English. (Bible pages may be counted with a view to determining if any have been removed and handed on before departure from the DPRK.) Always carry some form of identification with you during your stay in the country and to that end make sure you reclaim your passport from hotel reception after registration.

Photography is permitted within certain bounds: subjects with a military connection must be avoided unless permission is given, officials may not like to be snapped, and your guide, if you are accompanied, may try to direct you towards 'good' subjects and away from the picturesque, if dilapidated, group of cottages you might have your eye on, or the uncompleted Ryugyong Hotel, which is a subject of great sensitivity. It is always advisable to seek permission before taking a photo, especially if people are involved.

The DPRK, despite its reputed bellicosity, has one of the highest levels of personal security in the world, and it is extremely unlikely that a visitor will be threatened. Nonetheless, petty crime does exist, and you should protect your belongings as you would anywhere else.

Health

With the decline in universal health provision in the DPRK, some illnesses once under control have re-emerged, such as malaria and tuberculosis (see section on health in Chapter 4). If you expect to spend most of your time in or around Pyongyang you are probably at little risk, but if you are travelling in other parts of the country you should be aware of the situation. Cholera is also said to be a risk. Equip yourself with up-to-date information and seek medical advice on what precautions you should take to protect yourself against these illnesses. Although there are no specific vaccination requirements for international travellers to the DPRK, it is wise to keep standard vaccinations, including hepatitis A, up to date and to check whether vaccination against other illnesses such as hepatitis B and encephalitis might be advisable. During the SARS epidemic in 2003, which hit China and in particular Beijing, the DPRK imposed strict quarantine and isolation requirements and can be expected to re-impose these in the event of any such epidemic recurring. As your journey will almost certainly be through China, check for any new incidence of SARS or of other epidemics on the World Health Organization's website at www.who.int/csr/don/en. Standards of hospital care in the DPRK have also deteriorated in the face of inadequate funding, shortage of drugs and equipment and outdated knowledge among hospital staff.

Bring with you sufficient supplies of both prescribed medication and ordinary remedies and of any equipment such as syringes and needles that you might expect to need. Even something like aspirin may not be easy to find. Once in the DPRK, use only boiled or bottled water for drinking and brushing teeth, as local sources of water may no longer be safe. Bottled water is generally provided in hotel bedrooms and can be easily purchased. Local milk is likely to be unpasteurized, but imported cartons of pasteurized milk are generally, though not always, available in supermarkets used by foreigners. It is best to eat well-cooked food and to wash vegetables and fruit before consumption.

The seasonal extremes of winter cold and summer heat and humidity do not in themselves impose health risks, but those who feel the cold should bring adequate clothing in winter – thermal underwear and outer wear are recommended – and supplies of lip salve, etc. Hotels may be inadequately heated in winter, and visits to offices, ministries, museums and other show places can be very cold. For travel in the wet summer season, bring light, cotton clothing, an umbrella, and adequate supplies of insect repellent.

It is wise to take out comprehensive medical insurance before you leave home.

Accommodation

Not all hotels are authorized to receive international guests. In Pyongyang, the three main hotels in which foreigners are currently accommodated are the Pyongyang Koryo, the Potonggang and the Yanggakdo. The Koryo, a twin-towered structure in the central district, opened for business in 1985. The Potonggang operates under Japanese management and has links with the Unification Church. The Yanggakdo, completed in 1995, stands on Yanggak island in the Taedong river. Pyongyang has a number of middle-range hotels, some of which do take foreign visitors, particularly students or long-stay guests who need less expensive accommodation. Visitors whose presence or services are valued by the state may be lodged in one of several state guest houses.

A complicated structure of room rates applies in hotels, dependent on the floor level, size and standard of accommodation. Cheaper rooms are available; but hotel rates are generally high, and what might be recognized as a backpackers hostel hardly exists for foreigners. Whatever the standard of the hotel, it cannot always escape the effects of power cuts, with consequent rationing of hot water. Bedrooms may be kept warm in winter, but hotel public areas may be unheated. The big hotels all offer a range of facilities: restaurants, bars, sometimes a swimming pool, a hairdressing salon and barber's shop, postal services, a shop selling Korean souvenirs and imported goods and foodstuffs, a book shop, film processing and so on; but do not expect foreign newspapers – they are not available. Each hotel has advantages and disadvantages. The Pyongyang Koryo is very central, but does not maintain the highest standards of service and only installed locks on its bedroom doors in 2004. It has now joined the Potonggang in offering foreign TV channels – BBC, CCTV and NHK. The Potonggang's location by the Potong river is attractive, though rather isolated. The Yanggakdo's basement, off limits to Koreans, is under Chinese management and offers one of the two known casinos in the DPRK (largely patronized by Chinese), a nightclub and sauna. The Yanggakdo's chief drawback is its island setting. Some visitors have found they have been prevented by security guards from walking off the island, and for that reason, one of the other hotels may be preferable, if there is any choice in the matter.

The main provincial cities also have hotels that receive foreign guests. Their standards and prices correspond to the lower end of the big international hotels in the capital. They can be expected to provide meals, but in winter may have almost no heating at all and very restricted provision of running water, particularly hot water. Some resorts and tourist spots have very attractive hotels. The Folk hotel in Kaesong forms a kind of street of twenty-one single-storey buildings constructed and furnished in traditional Korean style, with underfloor ondol heating. Guests sit and sleep on the floor. The Hotel serves delicious food; but even it cannot escape frequent power cuts. On the east coast, southeast of Hamhung and Hungnam, the Majon resort offers accommodation in small beachside villas. In the mountain valley of Mt Myohyang, the Hyangsan Hotel, shaped like a ziggurat, is well appointed.

Transport

Tourists under the wing of KITC will have all transport arranged for them and will be discouraged from making their own arrangements. Those freer to make their own plans, but who lack private means of transport, can try using the taxis, distinguishable by the prefix '50' on the licence plate, that are available for hire by foreign visitors from outside the big hotels and department stores. Be warned that taxis do not seem to operate on Sundays! A car and driver can be hired by the day, but this is expensive: around sixty euros per day plus an extra mileage charge outside Pyongyang. Such drivers expect to convey passengers to meetings at fixed points, with a guide in tow. Whether they are willing to undertake sightseeing tours is not so certain. Standards of driving are not always good, and motorists have scant regard for pedestrians. Pyongyang has an extensive public transport system of buses, trolley buses, trams and metro. Fares are cheap, but payable only in won, which foreigners are not supposed to have. For this reason, and in the unspoken but clear intention of preventing contact between the local population and foreigners, the latter are strongly discouraged from using the transport network unless accompanied by a Korean. Nonetheless, it can be done. One of our visitors managed, within a day of his arrival, to buy an ice-cream, acquire some won in change and travel on a bus. Nothing happened to him and we received no complaint about his behaviour!

Some provincial cities have their own transport system, but no national long-distance bus service exists as it does in the ROK to link towns, and the rail network, often starved of power, offers an at times erratic service. Foreigners cannot hitch lifts on passing lorries to get home at night, as local people do. Travel out of the capital is thus generally by car or minibus, either one provided by your Korean hosts or one to which you have access. Resident foreigners are allowed to drive themselves unaccompanied in and around Pyongyang and even to agreed places further afield such as Mt Myohyang, Wonsan, and Majon resort, but must first pass a local driving test, since an international driving licence is not recognized. Driving tests are waived for heads of diplomatic missions. Air links exist between Pyongyang and some provincial destinations.

Travel agents

A small group of travel agents offers tours to the DPRK. At least one has been operating into the country since the second half of the 1980s, when first group travel, then individual travel was permitted. These agents have considerable experience, but even they have had occasional difficulties with the authorities. However, given that independent travel to and within North Korea is not possible, those who wish to visit as tourists should investigate these companies. Tours tailored to individual interests are on offer from these travel agents. The Internet is the best place to go looking. In Britain, Regent Holidays (a trailblazer) seems still to be the principal player. VNC Travel is based in the Netherlands, Koryo Tours in Beijing. Websites for these three are as follows:

UK
Regent Holidays: www.regent-holidays.co.uk

Netherlands
VNC Travel: www.vnc.nl/korea

China
Koryo Tours: www.koryogroup.com

DOING BUSINESS IN THE DPRK

When it comes to doing business, the DPRK is often no different from other East Asian countries. North Koreans' negotiating techniques and expectations do not vary so much from those of their ROK brethren or Chinese cousins. Given the past history, and especially the shared cultural inheritance of these countries, this is only to be expected. But because of the isolation of the DPRK until relatively recently from the capitalist market, there will be some twists and turns that are unexpected.

The fundamental principle is *caveat emptor*. The DPRK defaulted on a number of debts in the 1960s and early 1970s, which has left the country with a bad international reputation and with considerable problems in securing credit. The North Koreans are aware of this, but those who deal with foreign business are not in a position to do anything about the matter, so there is little point in raising it with them. The foreign debt has in a number of cases now become government debt as export credit guarantees have been taken up, and the DPRK authorities have proposed to a number of governments that the debts should just be written off, as a gesture of goodwill. So far, no government has done this. Even Russia, as successor state to the former Soviet Union, is now attempting to persuade the North Koreans to repay some of their old debts, again, with little progress. One or two stories of sharp practice in recent years – cargoes sold twice, or offers of the same mining concession to different foreign consortia – have added to the DPRK's negative reputation.

At the same time, some companies have managed to do business with the DPRK on a successful basis. The reason there are thirty-year old Volvos driving around Pyongyang, but brand-new Mercedes, is that the latter company made sure that it was paid in advance; the unlucky Swedes never saw their money, though the vehicles have continued long on the road. Other companies who have insisted on advance payment may have met some initial complaining but in the end have managed to do business to both sides' satisfaction. One small company worked very successfully to update sound-recording facilities in Pyongyang on a cash-up-front basis. The number of foreign business people in Pyongyang's hotels at any one time indicates that there are opportunities.

As explained in Chapters 2 and 3, the DPRK's economy has always been somewhat outside the mainstream of the world's trade. It declined to become a formal member of COMECON, though was prepared to operate under its auspices. It was not, however, quite as isolated from the capitalist world as it liked to think; the 1973 oil crisis and the subsequent worldwide fall in commodity prices contributed to its decision to default on its debts in the 1970s. Even before the collapse of the Soviet Union, the DPRK had been making overtures during the 1980s to attract capital to the country. The Rajin-Sonbong Special Economic Zone was established, but has yet to contribute significantly to the economy. A series of natural disasters in the 1990s further damaged an already weakened economy.

The result is that today the DPRK needs all forms of economic assistance. Until the political problems arising from its nuclear and missile programmes, and its relationship with the United States and Japan, are solved, there is unlikely to be any massive inflow of international funds to the country. However, there is still trade to be done, especially as relations between the two Koreas have slowly and steadily increased since the early 1990s. Foreign business is welcome, and providing you are careful, there are profits.

In theory, all economic activity, including foreign trade, was once under firm state control. While the state remains important, much, however, has changed since the mid-1980s, and business visitors will find that that they can now deal with a wide variety of enterprises. Be aware nonetheless that the power of the state to intervene is still strong and that some of what may be presented as private enterprises are, in fact, state organizations.

Making contact

Prospective visitors should make clear from the start that the purpose of a visit is business rather than tourism; it can be very hard to change programmes once in the DPRK. A number of companies, mainly established in Beijing or Seoul, will assist with initial contacts with DPRK trading organizations. None is very large and their degree of access varies from time to time. Some have had short-lived offices in Pyongyang, but their presence in the city cannot be relied upon. Their services are not essential, especially not for British firms now that there is a DPRK embassy in London and a British embassy in Pyongyang, or for most Europeans, since they too have relatively easy access to DPRK offices. Some businesses have established contacts in the DPRK without such assistance. But these companies can help smooth the way. As well as introductions and assistance with visas and travel, they may offer language assistance, which can be helpful in making sure that documents are in order or properly translated. Because DPRK officials are suspicious of foreigners who know Korean, their involvement may not be so welcome once the initial contact is made. Each business will need to decide for itself if and how to use the services of such consultants. Several travel agents, some based in Europe and others in China, can also advise the business traveller both on the practicalities of getting to the DPRK and on how to conduct matters once there. Another useful source of information is the European Chamber of Commerce in Seoul. This group has led trade delegations to the DPRK and has also published guidance on doing business there, both in conventional and electronic forms.

To get your visa for the DPRK, you will need a sponsor in the country. You can do this by contacting DPRK organizations directly. Postal and fax addresses are given in North Korean magazines such as *Foreign Trade*, and there are directories available in English. However, this is rather a hit-and-miss way of making contact, with no guarantee that there will be a response. Much better is to approach a DPRK embassy or other office, or indeed, one of the various consultancy companies mentioned above, and seek their advice on a likely partner. At least one DPRK embassy, in Vienna, has a website offering details of what is on offer and contact points – see www.dprkorea-trade.co

Whether using a consultancy company or dealing directly with the North Koreans, a visit to the DPRK at an early stage is essential in conducting negotiations. Indeed, it is wise from the beginning to assume that a number of visits will be required. Like other East Asian countries, the DPRK professes to value 'old friends', by which its officials mean those who come back at least once. The biggest mistake is to think in terms of wrapping up a quick deal. Such deals can be done, but they have a habit of unravelling.

Visits will not only be about business. Because of the air schedules, even the shortest visit to the DPRK is likely to be three nights. For the same reason, many people go for a full week. As a result, because few DPRK organizations work on Sundays, and because a measure of sightseeing is deemed essential to improve visitors' knowledge of the country, even business people will find that part of their time is devoted to such pursuits. They are also likely to find that their hosts expect them to lay a wreath or flowers at the statue of Kim Il Sung on Mansu hill, or at one of the other sites associated with him. Individuals will need to decide for themselves whether they wish to do this. If they accept, there is a risk that their actions may be used for propaganda purposes. If they refuse, their guides are likely to express disappointment but not to insist. Although it is possible that a refusal could have an effect on subsequent business dealings, there are also signs that some North Korean officials can accept that others have a different way of doing things.

It is wise to keep views on politics, and especially on the political structures of the DPRK, out of any discussions. The visitor is unlikely to learn much, and there is a strong risk of causing offence, often unwittingly. Beware also of any remarks or actions that seem to treat Kim Il Sung or Kim Jong Il in a disparaging way. While it may be tempting to imitate the stance of the great statue of Kim Il Sung, for example, such actions are likely to be seen as very offensive by your hosts. Similarly, copies of North Korean publications with pictures of either leader are best handled with care. There are reports of foreigners getting into trouble for apparently disrespectful behaviour such as sitting on a newspaper bearing a leader's picture, or even defacing such pictures with additions. Even if nothing is said, what has happened will be noted and could tell against the perpetrator on another occasion. Those who intend to write or broadcast about the country should be aware that the DPRK monitors both foreign publications and broadcasts closely for items about the country; hostile or facetious comments are likely to lead to a refusal of further visas.

Practical factors

DRESS

This tends to the formal. Most North Korean men will appear in suits and ties, and women's dress will be sober in style and colour. In the summer, which is hot and sticky, open-necked shirts are acceptable, even among senior officials, but colours will still be relatively muted. Foreigners doing business tend to follow the Korean example.

MOBILE TELEPHONES

There is little point in bringing a mobile telephone to the DPRK. At one time over the past couple of years it appeared that a mobile telephone network was being installed in the country to which foreigners might be admitted, but the project seems to have been halted during 2004. In any case, such a network would be unlikely to have links to points outside the country. As noted above, visitors' mobile phones are removed at point of entry, as is GSP equipment, and are returned on departure – do not forget to collect yours!

TELEPHONE, FAX AND COMPUTERS

The DPRK operates a number of telephone systems, which are not interconnected. All those with whom you are likely to deal will have a connection to a '381', or international, exchange number, though, unless you are a Korean speaker, it may not always be easy tracking people down through this number, which will be a central point rather than an individual desk. Telephone directories are not available. Embassies and other foreign organizations also have 381 numbers. As said, these numbers allow international direct dialling. This is efficient, with none of the long delays that visitors experienced in the past when attempting to make international calls. However, it is also expensive from hotels and the system does not always work well for incoming calls. The cause of this is mainly the poor command of English of hotel operatives, rather than any deliberate attempt to prevent outsiders having contact with you. It is wise to assume that all calls are monitored.

Fax facilities are also available, though these too tend to be expensive and liable to interruption because of poor power supplies. They will also be monitored. Although embassies, UN organizations and resident foreigners have email, originally provided through servers in China but now increasingly via satellite, attempts to use email from hotels in the DPRK seem doomed to failure. It is probably better to work on the principle that you will be largely out of touch with your head office or other outside contacts while visiting the DPRK.

It is sensible to bring a laptop computer, portable printer and paper, and supplies of ink cartridges. This will enable you to produce drafts and letters quickly and efficiently, and laptops can cope with the power cuts. Some hotels may have a 'business facilities office' but it will be very simple and may not always have paper, for example, or will charge per sheet. Copy paper can sometimes be bought in hotel shops – the Potonggang Hotel, where a number of Japanese companies have offices, is good on business-related stationery – but supplies can be erratic. A number of outlets sell computers and computer-related materials but again, supplies can be unpredictable. Should you need it, the postal service is effective, with letters taking about a week to reach Europe and the United States, less for China. Many foreigners believe that the mail is closely examined before it leaves the country.

CURRENCY

Banking facilities are somewhat restricted. Credit cards are in use in hotels and to some extent in hotel restaurants, but it is not possible to draw cash with them, and travellers' cheques may be difficult to cash. Against that, the North Koreans prefer cash, and it is a good idea to have this in large quantities, preferably euros (see section on Currency above under Travel for work and tourism). Other currencies can be exchanged at the banks or in the hotels. You may well get an assortment of currencies in your small change, including Japanese *yen* and Chinese *renminbi*.

BUSINESS CARDS

Business cards are as popular in the DPRK as elsewhere in Asia, and it is a good idea to bring plenty. It helps if you can arrange for them to be printed in Korean as well as English. You can obtain cards in Pyongyang but in general the quality is not good. North Koreans may not be so keen to give you their cards, as they are to collect yours. In any case, their cards may not be very informative. Some only have a name and an organization. Even when the cards give telephone and fax numbers, they will not be for an individual but for the organization as a whole.

CONDUCTING NEGOTIATIONS

Negotiations will probably take place in a hotel or possibly in another public building such as the People's Palace of Culture. DPRK organizations are often reluctant to take visitors to their offices or factories. This can be frustrating if you want to make an assessment of, say, a coalmine. At the same time, your interlocutors will be interested in specific proposals rather than any generalized agreement. They will also bargain hard. The best approach is to be firm, sure of your position, but always polite. Loss of temper puts you on the wrong footing. Standards of English vary. If it is clear that you are not being understood, it is best to wait until the end of a session, and then try to get this message across quietly, without causing embarrassment to any of those taking part. Do not sign anything of which you are not absolutely sure.

Documents are likely to be analysed in great detail. This does not mean that on signature, negotiations are over. Koreans are not alone in seeing a 'final document' as anything but that. Regard the signature of documents as an important stage, signifying intent but not necessarily the final stage. At the same time, should there be a dispute, expect a highly legalistic and literal approach to the interpretation of documents.

PRESENTS AND ENTERTAINING

At some point, the question of presents may be raised. DPRK negotiators have become used to accepting gifts as part of the process of doing business; some have been known to ask when the presents will be handed over. Do not be surprised if there is some degree of reciprocity. This is fine, as long as the gifts are on a small scale, such as a bottle of whisky or perhaps a box of chocolates for the never-seen wives or children. Such gifts should be properly wrapped, not just handed over naked. But some business visitors have found that the demands are much greater. In really big deals, it is sometimes suggested that an up-to-date car or truck might be acceptable, and requests for computers, especially laptop computers, are very common. Each person or company must decide what to do when faced with such demands. In some cases, where big and long-lasting contracts have involved the provision of equipment or vehicles, companies may decide to leave these behind at the end of the contract. Others may decide that they are not in the business to provide goods in this way. A refusal will not necessarily mean the end of the deal, though an acceptance of one set of demands may not preclude others.

Less demanding is the tradition of dinner giving. Quite early on, perhaps even on the first night in the country, your Korean counterparts will offer you a banquet. Do not worry, the term merely means dinner, but probably in a private room and almost certainly at your hotel. You will be expected to reciprocate. If you are happy to do so at the hotel, that is fine, but it is often more interesting to ask those looking after you to arrange for another venue. Make sure that prices for food and drink and the number of participants are agreed in advance.

FOLLOWING UP

Having reached agreement on a deal, remember that it is a good idea to follow up with repeat visits. If exporting goods or materials from the DPRK, be careful also that what you order is what you get – inferior products have been known to arrive rather than the good quality seen. Air Koryo operates a cargo service from Beijing, and possibly from Macao and Bangkok from time to time. The Beijing service is heavily oversubscribed and delays are possible. The DPRK maintains a shipping fleet and goods can be shipped to and from a number of ports. The port for Pyongyang is at Nampo, some fifty-five kilometres away. It can handle small containers but there are often problems with onward transport. A regular container service plies between Nampo and the South Korean port of Inchon, although DPRK officials sometimes deny its existence. South Korean companies and international shipping organisations know differently, however. Road and rail facilities within the DPRK are poor, and the rail system in particular is often congested.

Embassy and consular assistance

It is a good practice to get the details of which embassy is responsible for you in advance; this may not be the same one that might look after you elsewhere. Although most Western countries have now established diplomatic relations with the DPRK, few have representation in Pyongyang, and the number of Western embassies in the city is low. Apart from the former Communist countries, Sweden is the longest established, having had a presence in Pyongyang since 1973. Since 2001, it has been joined by British and German embassies. All three are conveniently located in the same office block on the old East German embassy compound in the eastern suburb of Munsu-dong. Britain and Germany of course see to their own nationals, but most other Western countries have always looked to the Swedes for protection, and this continues to this day. Although Commonwealth countries usually turn to British representatives in an emergency, this is not, for example, the case for Australians and Canadians in Pyongyang, where the Swedes still look after their interests. Because the Western embassies are small, they do not have the range of commercial or economic experts to be found in larger establishments. However, all make an effort to acquire information about commercial possibilities, which they will share with visitors.

The embassies' role is somewhat complicated, however, by the attitude of the DPRK towards links between them and visitors. Essentially, they are against such contacts. This may be a reflection of the compartmentalism within the Koreans' own organizations, or a more general attitude of divide and rule. For whatever reason, DPRK officials have shown great reluctance in facilitating contacts between visitors and their embassies. This is as true of business travellers as it is of tourists. Firmness pays off, at least sometimes, but it is sensible to have embassy contact numbers with you, so that you can make a direct approach on your own.

If there is a problem for a Westerner and it is not possible to contact the correct embassy, any of the embassies, or other members of the foreign community, would try to help. Pyongyang's foreign community is very small and generally quite close-knit.

EATING OUT

Among the questions we were asked about our stay in the DPRK were anxious inquiries, particularly from our South Korean and Chinese acquaintances, for reassurance that we got enough to eat. We could always answer that we did. Visitors to the DPRK can be certain that they will not go hungry. Whether they welcome it or not, they are towards the top of the chain and will always be served sufficient food. Whatever the undoubted problems of distribution in the country, they are unlikely ever to affect guests and visitors. Menus may not vary much, but are always adequate. Foreigners still may not purchase in the markets, except for a new one in Tongil Street, and even that privilege is still uncertain, but the foreign currency shops have a reasonable range of foodstuffs, much of it imported. The greatest difficulty there may be coping with unpredictable supplies.

The North Koreans have the same basic dietary needs and preferences as the South Koreans: rice as a staple food, with side dishes of meat, fish, vegetables and condiments. It has always been the case that the better off you are, the more numerous and richer your side dishes. Many poor families eat little animal protein and exist largely on rice and vegetables. Soy and sesame oil are essential cooking ingredients. *Kimchi,* a spicy preparation of fermented Chinese cabbage leaves, is common in both North and South, but for whatever reason is generally less good in the North. Beef is the preferred meat and is often served as *bulgogi,* literally 'fire meat'; strips of raw meat are laid over a kind of barbecue, often set up on the diners' table, and turned with chopsticks until done. Soups are popular, and a luxury meal is *sinsollo,* a meat and vegetable hotpot cooked in a special dish that consists basically of a brass bowl transfixed by a funnel full of hot charcoal or heated by a spirit lamp. The trough thus formed is filled with boiling water in which the ingredients are simmered. The resulting soup is very superior. The dish that North Koreans profess to enjoy most is *naemyong,* or cold noodles. These are served all year round, whatever the temperature, in a raised flat dish from which the noodles may be sucked into the mouth. The rice produced in Korea is a glutinous 'sticky' rice, which forms clumps in the bowl and which should be eaten with the long-handled spoon that together with chopsticks make up the Korean table set. Forks are not used, and knives are confined to the kitchen.

The DPRK produces a range of drinks, largely alcoholic. Spirits, *sul,* are distilled from rice and vary from the refined *chongju* to vile, brightly coloured concoctions. Additions inside the bottle may be ginseng or even a snake! Imported spirits are available in shops. Beer is brewed, some of it very dark and almost like stout. A few places have installed micro-breweries yielding quite good draught beers. A new (old) brewery, re-erected in Pyongyang from its original site in the UK, produces a new brand, Taedonggang beer, under the auspices of German technicians. Wine may be bought in foreign currency shops, but is not always offered in restaurants. Mineral water, some of it bottled in a North-South joint venture plant, is readily available. 'Red' tea, that is, Chinese black tea, can usually be had; but the summer staple of South Korean teashops, barley tea (*boricha*) does not seem to feature on the menu.

With the exception of the Mokran restaurant (see below), Western-style food is perhaps not the best choice in the DPRK. The foreign cuisine that has been absorbed and copied is Russian cooking. Where an attempt is made at a beef burger, the results can be downright unpalatable. The pizza chefs reputed to have worked for Kim Jong Il do not appear to have made an impression on the general repertoire of Korean restaurants.

Many restaurants are in indoor, sometimes windowless, premises; but in recent years, the practice of temporary tented snack bars and eating-places in the summer months has been permitted. Koreans enjoy eating out. Some benefit from restaurant vouchers provided by their work unit. Others, who are better funded, pay their way. Eating in a local restaurant is a good way for a foreigner to be alongside Koreans, even if opportunities for closer acquaintance do not arise. Little effort is made to separate foreigners from local people in a restaurant. The chief criterion seems to be ability to pay in whatever currency is demanded.

WHERE TO EAT

Pyongyang

As ever, the biggest range of restaurants is found in the capital, although Kaesong probably offers one of the best culinary experiences (see below), and seaside towns such as Wonsan (see Chapter 8) have good seafood menus. New restaurants are opening up all the time in Pyongyang, and new arrivals should seek the advice of the resident foreign community on what is good. The selection below represents some of those we have used and enjoyed.

HOTELS

The three principal hotels catering to foreign visitors all have restaurants serving Korean, Japanese or Chinese food. The Koryo's coffee shop is now open throughout twenty-four hours. Both the Pyongyang Koryo and the Yanggakdo have revolving rooftop restaurants that on a fine day allow you to see, if not forever, at least a long way. Unless there are other guests already installed when you arrive, the revolving mechanism will only be switched on when you appear. To reach the Koryo's revolving restaurant (on the forty-fourth floor), use the lifts on the left-hand side of the lobby. These convey guests to rooms in the further tower, which are not normally accessible to foreign visitors, and you may have to make it clear to the lift attendant you wish to go to the rooftop restaurant.

The Pyongyang Koryo, Potonggang and Yanggakdo seem to have shared out the good foreign-cuisine restaurants between them. The Koryo has a Japanese basement restaurant entered from the street, to the left of the main entrance to the hotel. It serves good Japanese food, but is expensive, and the menu is only in Japanese and Korean.

At the Potonggang, the Mokran restaurant on the ground floor, to the right at the further end of the lobby, appears to be the only restaurant in Pyongyang offering a truly European menu, and even that has been modified gently to meet Japanese tastes in Western food. It certainly has the best wine cellar of any restaurant in the capital and knows how to keep and serve wine, though at a price. Its Japanese dishes and Korean restaurant are also good.

The Yanggakdo runs a good Chinese restaurant, the Macao, again in the basement. It is reached by a descending spiral staircase at the far end of the lobby, past the lifts and shop. The food is prepared and served by a wholly Chinese staff. The fruit platter at the end of the meal is always delicious. Beer and tea are the best drinks. Wine is available sometimes, but is of variable quality. The Macao claims to be open through twenty-four hours and can accommodate large parties of diners.

RESTAURANTS ON THE WEST SIDE OF THE TAEDONG

Several restaurants can be recommended in the Central district, around the Pyongyang Koryo Hotel. To the right of the Koryo as you exit, a new, highly satisfactory restaurant has been incorporated into the ground floor of the relocated and rebuilt philately bureau. The spacious dining-room downstairs is decorated with large-scale reproductions of stamps. The menu offers such traditional dishes as *kujol pan,* the eight savoury preparations served in a special tray, to be eaten with small pancakes. A visit afterwards to the 'stamp shop' upstairs will allow you to choose your postcards from a wide selection.

A couple of longer-established restaurants situated a short way down the side-street diagonally across to the right from the main hotel entrance are still worth going to, even if they have somewhat lost their edge. They are just past a sauna establishment, in a compound entered through a large gateway. One restaurant, apparently bearing no name, is immediately to the left of this gateway, the other, the Changgwang, is at the further end of the compound. This small neighbourhood is said to be a centre for the Japanese Korean community in Pyongyang. The two restaurants have certainly served in the past as meeting points for family reunions between local Koreans and relatives visiting from Japan. Both these restaurants have menus in Korean and English. They serve a good selection of Korean and Japanese dishes. Beer is always available, wine, sake and chongju sometimes so. The establishment immediately to the left as you enter the courtyard serves soft ice-cream as its speciality, usually in cornets. This can be carried in to the Changgwang restaurant if you are looking for a sweet end to the meal.

Not far from these two restaurants is the Minjok (signifying 'nation', 'people'; it is often known in translation as the National restaurant). The Minjok is one element in a cluster of institutions dedicated to the national culture, and indeed is said to be owned by the Ministry of Culture. It is situated between the rear facade of the Yun Isang concert hall and the Chollima Cultural Club. Both of these buildings are attached to the International House of Culture, a tall building that fronts on to Yonggwang Street. To reach the Minjok from the Pyongyang Koryo Hotel, strike left to the corner, cross the street at a right angle and walk down the road ahead towards the tall group of buildings ahead. The restaurant entrance, up a short flight of steps, is imposing, but once inside diners have to plunge down a spiral staircase past a counter selling sweets and dried seafood to reach the restaurant in the basement. It is a large, colourfully decorated place with a small stage. Seating in the central part of the restaurant is on upright chairs, but elevated sections and a long room to one side provide traditional low dining tables and floor seating. Entertainment used to be in the hands of women singers and musicians in Korean dress, who worked through a repertoire of popular songs; but it has now been entrusted to the waitresses, who perform to a much higher standard and in some instances on traditional instruments. Guests are encouraged to join the performers on stage to make their own contributions. The menu offers a good choice of well-prepared Korean dishes and drinks. An English-language menu card is usually available, and the waitresses speak some English. Prices are quite high. A good place for a special dinner and a sense of a night out.

The stretch along the west bank of the Taedong river between the Taedong and Okryu bridges is particularly pleasant, lined with a narrow park at street level and a broad riverside walk along the quay below. The principal riverboat moored there is Pyongyang No.1. It offers summertime river cruises with dinner, combining good food and service. The whole boat may be hired for the afternoon or evening, or several small parties can be held there at once. A smaller boat with pink net curtains offers drinks, including the black beer, and meals, and is a nice place for lunch. The menu is in Korean and the staff speak no English.

At the west end of Okryu bridge going towards Moranbong is the Okryu restaurant, a vast establishment distinguished by its green curving roofs and traditional architecture. It serves thousands of meals a day. The speciality is Pyongyang cold noodles, which will be the centre of any meal, but other dishes are available. Foreigners are not segregated but will be shown into one of the smaller dining-rooms. In summer, guests can eat outside on the riverside balcony. The restaurant is unheated in winter, so wrap up well!

In the Potong district, the Pyongyang Programme Centre, in the shadow of the uncompleted Ryugyong Hotel, houses a restaurant serving good food. To reach it you should walk or drive around three sides of the plot of land supporting the hotel, starting left from a point in front of the hotel, then turning right and working your way from there. The trip will give you excellent views of this particular landmark.

RESTAURANTS EAST OF THE TAEDONG

The Taedong Diplomatic Club, known also as the 'Old Diplomatic Club', is at the east end of the Taedong bridge. It probably owes its location to the original siting of most foreign embassies across the bridge in the Central district. The club is still much used by the international community for receptions and parties. The principal room is equipped with a stage and sound system and can be adapted for film shows. The style of catering is not very imaginative, but the management is prepared to accept clients' requests to cook special dishes, even haggis, and also does outdoor catering. A further restaurant, known as the 'Dancing room', does indeed have a small dance floor and a bar and offers a somewhat restricted daily menu. Service can be slow.

North of the east end of Okryu bridge, the Gold Lane bowling alley has a bar serving beer and snacks on the ground floor and a restaurant on the first floor.

Moving away from the river towards the Munsu-dong diplomatic quarter, you come to the Taedongang Ryogwan. This is a Korean-style hotel or 'ryogwan' at the point formed by the junction of Taehak Street and Tapje Street, almost opposite the maternity hospital. The hotel is not open to foreigners, but its two restaurants are and have become popular with those living in the nearby diplomatic area, since it is within walking distance. Entrance to the restaurants is through a narrow door at the base of the round building. The first-floor restaurant offers a fairly wide menu of well-cooked food. Those wishing bulgogi must go to the floor above. The establishment has a micro-brewery, and draught beer is available in both restaurants.

Within the Munsu-dong diplomatic quarter, the New Diplomatic Club and its nearby shop, known as the 'Diplo', sooner or later become familiar to all foreigners living in the area. The two buildings are in a separate compound between the Vietnamese embassy and the German compound. The Club has a ground-floor bar and a first-floor restaurant and bar-cum-karaoke room. The restaurant is much frequented at lunchtime by expatriate office workers, who come to know the menu intimately and order without even looking at it. Korean, Chinese and 'Western' dishes are offered. Beer and sul are available. The restaurant stays open until quite late into the evening. For some reason, the food is generally better then.

The Pyongyang Friendship International Health Centre, also in the diplomatic quarter, offers massage, but its promotion of health does not seem to go beyond that, and instead it provides a couple of restaurants, one of which, on the terrace, is open in the summer only. The Centre's best feature is its bar and dance floor, which offer a pleasantly intimate atmosphere. This room is sometimes used for receptions. Now and again a Korean group provide live music and singing, both very good.

A pleasant place to visit in the summer is the restaurant immediately outside the entrance to the Botanical Gardens at the foot of Mt Taesong.

Kaesong

If you are booking into the Folk Hotel in Kaesong, you may be asked if you want to eat there. Unless you are on a very tight budget, say yes, since the hotel offers the experience of seeing and tasting the traditional pattern of high-class eating. Each guest, seated on the ondol floor, is brought a small, low polished table laden with dishes, which is placed in front of him or her. This is the complete set meal: rice and soup in larger bowls form the essential elements, but are augmented by a selection of small side dishes of amazing versatility. Main dishes, such as chicken with ginseng, may be ordered as well. Kaesong is said to produce the best ginseng in the peninsula. The plant finds its way into spirits as well as into cooked dishes.

Sitting on the floor is not easy on Western leg and back muscles. If possible, take your meal in one of the small dining-rooms, where you will be able to prop yourself up against the wall.

SHOPPING

The DPRK cannot be called a shoppers' paradise. Hard currency shops offer imported consumer goods, but their eye is on wealthy Koreans and resident foreigners. The main department stores, if you can find them open, will let you look and buy, but the range and quality of goods are limited. The most interesting and unusual things to bring back from a visit are various craft goods, paintings, posters, CDs, postage stamps and books.

Art and souvenir shops

A number of outlets exist for purchasing arts and crafts made in the DPRK. The hotel in which you are staying may be a good place to start looking. In Pyongyang, the three big hotels all have shops which will have a souvenir section, with embroidery, clothes, lacquer and basket-work, musical instruments, ginseng and local liqueurs. There will also be a bookshop that may have pictures and scrolls, both showing traditional themes, posters and possibly stamps for sale, as well as CDs of Korean pop music, art books and books of art photographs. In Kaesong, the Folk Hotel has a couple of shops, and the Hyangsan Hotel at Mt Myohyang has a rather upmarket shop that must reflect its clientele. Back in the capital, the Diplomatic Shop in Munsu-dong has an arts and crafts and souvenir section, as does the Ragwon foreign currency department store near the Air Koryo office. You will also be able to buy ceramics, in particular modern copies of traditional green celadon ware. Prices for the latter can be high. The gallery shop at the Changgwangsan Hotel on Chollima Street in the same area as the Ragwon store has a good range of ceramics and paintings. Another place to look is in the shops attached to museums and galleries in Pyongyang and the provinces and even in the grounds of temples such as Pohyon at Mt Myohyang, many of which sell artistic products and sometimes reproductions of what is in their collections.

Several specialized outlets exist for the sale of arts and crafts and paintings. The Paekhu (White Tiger) Art Shop in Munhung-dong (East Pyongyang) near the Iranian embassy sells the usual range of celadon and other ceramics and also has scrolls. The same shop does inexpensive framing, but you have to supply your own glass. Be warned that all glass available locally is window glass, which can be very heavy. This shop will also copy pictures for you, so if you want an embroidered picture of your family, this is the place to go. It has an intriguing selection of paintings, some on strong religious themes, that have presumably not been collected.

The Minye art shop, part of the cultural complex that contains the Yun Isang concert hall and not far from the Koryo Hotel, has a good selection of celadon, scrolls and so forth, and sells souvenirs, including costumes. The biggest outlet is the Mansudae Creation Centre (see Chapter 5 above) on Saemaul Street in Pyongchon district, a huge complex that is home to artists as well as a large shop. The latter sells original artwork, including paintings, scrolls and a wide range of pottery. You can arrange to see the artists at work, which gives added interest, since many of them are technically very good. The lack of originality is disappointing, however, and attempts to discuss artistic techniques tend not to get very far. Prices can be high.

A small band of dealers also exists, prepared to act as intermediaries between artist and buyer for serious collectors with funds at their disposal. The latter will find they can buy original paintings in both ink and wash and oils, prints and original ceramics, all the work of contemporary artists. Themes may be revolutionary or traditional. Prices for paintings and ceramics can be high: hundreds, sometimes thousands, of dollars/euros. The main buyers in this field seem to be from neighbouring Asian countries and their taste tends to prevail in what is offered; for instance, oil landscapes, as opposed to landscapes in traditional ink and wash, appear to be preferred. It may be wise to check out the other outlets for prices before entering into negotiations with dealers and anyone else offering art works or books, if only to give yourself a framework for bargaining. Your travel guide or interpreter should be able to put you in touch with dealers, but be aware that this is an area of great rivalries.

A more modest group of entrepreneurs are the artists who, in the provinces, wait for you outside the temple, museum or site you are visiting with a selection of paintings, scrolls and small ceramic and craft goods. The paintings are generally copies, but are usually competently executed. Prices will be in hard currency and presumably go straight to those responsible for the display. Apart from the pleasure of a souvenir of a beautiful place, you can reflect that you are encouraging a nascent capitalism!

Philately

The philately bureau, or 'stamp shop' (see above under Eating out), located to the left as you face the front of the Koryo Hotel, sells catalogues of all the stamps, postal stationery and cancellations ever used by the DPRK, together with an amazing collection of stamps; not quite all that the country issued, but a surprisingly large number. The DPRK has acquired a bad reputation among stamp collectors because it issues so many stamps, often on themes that seem remote from the DPRK and its interests and because it reissues stamps when it thinks there are sales to be made. Real collectors will probably confine their attention to the catalogues and the definitive issues. Others may just see the stamps as colourful souvenirs. Postcards and some stationery material are for sale.

Books and posters

Hotel bookshops may be thin on foreign-language items, but the Foreign Languages Bookshop, just off Kim Il Sung Square and on the corner of the street housing the Folk Museum, will come to your help. The comprehensive (and expensive) *Illustrated Book of Ruins and Relics of Korea*, a twenty-volume series, can be bought here, though not all the volumes may always be in stock. Another attractive item is an album of photographs entitled *Celebrated Mountains of Korea* accompanied by appropriate stamps. As well as books, this is the place to go for hand-painted posters. All appear to be individually prepared copies of well-known models, giving you an original that is not an original. They are nonetheless very striking and good examples of socialist realist art that is still executed in a serious spirit and not as an ironic tribute. A catalogue displays the range of subjects, and orders may be placed. The themes reflect the DPRK's concerns and interests, so the military features prominently, but there are other subjects as well. 'Potatoes are a staple as well as a vegetable' is one we bought.

8

The Land and its Sights

THE LAND

THE 38TH PARALLEL is a purely political demarcation, chosen in 1945 as a means of dividing the peninsula to allow US and Soviet troops to receive the Japanese surrender in the southern and northern halves of the country respectively. The Demilitarized Zone (DMZ) forms the actual line of division between the DPRK and the ROK. This strip of land 4 km. (2.5 miles) wide runs 240 km. (151 miles) from below the 38th parallel on the west coast and ends north of the parallel on the east coast. Only at its western end, where the DMZ runs along the valley of the Imjin river and out 60 km. (40 miles) into the estuary of the Han river, does it approximate to a natural boundary. Elsewhere, it cuts right across both natural formations and pre-existing lines of communication. Thus, the famous Kumgang – 'Diamond' – mountains, although forming the northern end of the long Taebaek range that reaches down towards the southeast of the peninsula, are shut off from the south by the DMZ. Similarly, Kangwon province, which occupied the central eastern portion of the peninsula, is now divided into a northern and southern province, each called Kangwon. The railway that formerly linked Wonsan on the east coast and Seoul by following the line of the major fault running through the mountains is now truncated on both sides. Other traditional routes between north and south have likewise been cut.

While the DMZ forms the southern 'boundary' of North Korea, in the north the DPRK shares a long border of approximately 1400 km. (about 880 miles) with the People's Republic of China and a much shorter one of 16.5 km. (roughly 10 miles) with the Russian Federation. Most of this frontier is a natural one created by the Amnok (Yalu), North Korea's longest river at around 800 km. (497 miles), which flows west to the Yellow Sea, and the east-flowing Tuman river (520 km./323 miles), together with their tributaries. A short stretch of territory lies between the head reaches of the two rivers. Korea's tilted eastern seaboard means that, other than the

Tuman, most rivers emptying into the East Sea are very short. Those taking a westerly course, such as the Chongchon (around 200 km.–124 miles) and the Taedong (430 km.–267 miles), are longer. Few natural lakes have formed, and many of the large inland areas of water are reservoirs. Along the east coast, particularly around Wonsan, lagoons have formed behind sandbars, and there are some small offshore islands. The west coast of the DPRK is broken by wide river estuaries and is subject to high tidal ranges. The DPRK, as does the ROK, asserts a territorial waters limit of 12 miles (19.3 km.) and moreover claims jurisdiction within a wider 'military sea boundary'.

The whole of the Korean peninsula is generally exposed to the same basic patterns of climate, but the northern half experiences largely cooler temperatures, harsher winters, especially in the far north, less precipitation, particularly in the far northeast, and a shorter growing season than the south. Spring is estimated to arrive about one-and-a-half months later in the north and autumn about one-and-a-half months earlier. The mountainous inland areas of North Korea are cooler in summer, experience colder winters, and are generally somewhat drier than coastal sites. The northern portion of the DPRK has a high central mountainous core, with many peaks above 1500 m. (4900 feet). The peninsula's highest peak, Mt Paektu, (2744 m.–6560 feet), lies in this area on the Sino-Korean border. The north-central section of the border, especially the two landlocked provinces of Ryanggang and Jagang and the northwest portion of North Hamgyong province, is cut off by mountain ridges from the sea and is, instead, open to the north. Its 'continental' type of climate brings summer temperatures of 15°C to 22°C (59°F–71°F) and extremely cold winter temperatures that can sink as low as –30°C (22°F). Frosts can last for up to seven months, and snow cover is often heavy. The coldest place in winter in the DPRK and indeed the whole of Korea is said to be Chunggang, which lies on the Amnok in the central stretch of the frontier. This north-central region is heavily wooded with fir, spruce and larch. It also contains important reserves of iron ore. Its difficult terrain and harsh climate, however, have meant it has always been sparsely populated.

It enfolds two smaller areas, the Kaema upland and the area around Mt Paektu, that are in strong contrast with the geography of the rest of the country. Kaema is an isolated plateau in the highest part of Korea, extensively forested and receiving relatively low precipitation. To the northeast it adjoins the basalt plateau out of which rises Mt Paektu, an extinct volcano. The name signifies 'white head', from the snow that covers it in winter and, according to the German geographer Lautensach, in summer from the gleaming white pumice of which it is formed. The crater of Mt Paektu contains a small, deep lake, Lake Chon, or 'heavenly lake'. Lake Chon is frozen from the end of October to the following May, but in summer turns a deep blue. Hot springs are found along the north shore. Three rivers rise in the Mt Paektu plateau: the Amnok (Yalu), the Tuman and the Songhua, which flows north into China. With its north-facing aspect, the plants growing in the region have closer affinity with more northerly species. Furthermore, a number of previously unrecorded invertebrate and plant species are claimed for the area. The remote and alien qualities of the plateau have led the surrounding peoples to accord it traditional reverence as a sacred site. In the DPRK, Mt Paektu is now exalted as the claimed birthplace of Kim Jong Il and site of his father's guerrilla exploits.

The central mountainous core of northern Korea flattens out in the extreme northeast towards the Tuman river. As the coast runs south to Hamhung, so the mountains drop more abruptly down to the eastern seaboard, a narrow strip of land broadening out now and again. From Hamhung south to Wonsan, the ground flattens out again somewhat, but after Wonsan rises again sharply to form the Kumgang mountains. From the early 1930s, the Japanese colonial administration, drawing on the natural resources of the northeast region – iron ore, coal and water for hydroelectric schemes – intensified the economic and industrial development of both the interior and the seaboard of the region to meet its needs. The new republic restored this industrial region in the 1950s, but the economic decline of recent years has badly affected its productivity.

The western part of the DPRK slopes more gently from the central massif towards the coast. In the far northwest, the Amnok river takes a meandering course to the sea. The area southeast of the mouth of the Amnok was the site of an early land reclamation project undertaken by the Japanese, and the pattern of extracting some profitable use from tidal and coastal regions of the west coast through reclamation or the installation of salt pans has continued since. To the south of the Taedong estuary, the land juts out into the Yellow Sea before curving back inwards sharply towards the estuary of the Han river (which lies in South Korea). The flat, wide region contained within this curve has a relatively dry climate and a high proportion of cultivated land. By contrast, the high inland area stretching northeastwards across the peninsula towards Wonsan and the Kumgang mountains has some of the heaviest summer rainfall, well above the average of 1000 mm.

The extensive mountain ranges have not only limited the land available for agriculture and housing, but have kept communities isolated from each other. While modern roads and railways have modified this somewhat, even today there may be little contact between towns and villages separated by high mountains. This has been useful to the central government in imposing control over the country.

ARCHITECTURE

On liberation in August 1945, the country's housing stock was still mainly divided between Japanese colonial settlements and indigenous Korean housing. Such large buildings as existed, the railway station in Pyongyang, for example, as well as barracks, administrative offices, banks and business premises in the capital and the provinces, were the work of the colonial regime. The small foreign community, composed largely of missionaries and businessmen, generally clustered together in its own quarter, as it did in the northwestern part of central Pyongyang, where it built churches, schools and hospitals. Whereas the Korean districts in a town were distinguished by narrow thoroughfares and low, traditional houses, thatched or tiled, the Japanese sections were laid out in streets with two- to three-storey housing in Japanese style. Foreign visitors, such as the British traveller Isabella Bird Bishop, contrasted the wretchedness of a town's Korean quarter with the spacious regularity of its Japanese settlement. Bishop on her arrival around 1895 in Wonsan – then an open port with a large Japanese population – reported such differences even before Japanese annexation. In Pyongyang, the Japanese largely settled in the areas to the east and southwest of the railway station, in the southern portion of the city.

The new North Korean regime, supported by the Soviet occupying forces, set about improving the country's infrastructure and provision of public facilities. The first premises of the Central History Museum opened in 1945, and the DPRK's first university (now Kim Il Sung University) was built in 1948 in Pyongyang with Soviet assistance. Moranbong Theatre and the first offices of the Party newspaper, *Rodong Sinmun*, were also constructed in the capital as Kim Il Sung launched a new cultural and ideological programme for the nation. Housing was taken in hand, with Kim anxious to replace the traditional one-storey houses with collective living in apartment blocks. From 1950, he was given the opportunity to proceed on an almost clear field as aircraft under the UN Command progressively flattened Pyongyang and the rest of the country in relentless bombing raids that drove both the administration and the population to work and live underground. Not much was left standing at the armistice of 27 July 1953. Only three public buildings are said to have survived the war in Pyongyang: the old city hall, the Japanese-era building now occupied by the Party Founding Museum, and the Hwasin Department Store (also dating from the Japanese era; it was demolished in 1982). Kaesong, protected from bombing by its location within the zone designated for armistice talks, is one of the few places that have managed to conserve some old buildings. Temples and churches were heavily damaged.

The destruction of so much that had been classed as alien and old-fashioned allowed Kim and his architects and town-planners freedom to rebuild the country's towns and capital along new lines. Pyongyang received especially careful attention. To some extent the old pattern of streets was preserved, but roads were widened and realigned to open up and divide the city, and a new space, Kim Il Sung Square, was created in 1954 as the capital's central point. Much emphasis was laid on landscaping the city environment and on providing parks and green spaces. Enormous efforts went into rebuilding the capital, both in the use of voluntary labour by soldiers and civilians and in the devising of new techniques of prefabrication and standardization. Until they withdrew in 1958, the Chinese soldiers stationed in the DPRK assisted in the construction of public buildings, including the Russian embassy. Up to the early 1960s, people's accommodation was largely in temporary wooden housing or barracks. Then, from the 1970s into the late 1990s, new streets and self-contained neighbourhoods of high-rise blocks were built successively in Pyongyang to house or re-house the population, all incorporating the model of wide, landscaped avenues. Only in a few districts does an older style of single, one-storey housing persist. Though none of the DPRK's other cities are as large as Pyongyang, they too have been reconstructed on spacious lines with wide streets.

An evolution in design can be traced from the mid-1950s. The large buildings erected in Pyongyang during those years bear evidence of European influence in their pilastered facades, decorative capitals and friezes and the pitch of their roofs. This is not surprising, given that East European architects were involved in their construction and that Koreans were being trained as town-planners and architects in the Soviet Union and Eastern Europe. In a deliberate move away from foreign patterns, the Pyongyang Grand Theatre (1960) incorporated Korean-style roofs and tiles and other traditional features into its design. Thereafter, a plainer, rectilineal style developed for both large buildings and apartment blocks, relieved by occasional colour and decoration, with a return to native Korean inspiration for a number of big projects, the finest of which is the Grand People's Study House (1982). A few constructions break with the generally conservative approach with bold curves and rooflines. The high-rise towers in which many people live are undoubtedly reminiscent of both Soviet and Western design, but they are less brutal in their effect. In place of a monolithic approach, a certain dynamism can be sensed in the slender proportions of some blocks, their grouping and variations in height, the curving facades of some projects and the abundant use of landscaping.

The reliance on communal accommodation extends to the countryside, where small, three-storey blocks rise incongruously beside the fields. They are constructed out of large bricks made of sand and lime, and have pitched roofs, but do not appear to have any external facing and consequently may be only one brick deep. Elsewhere, new, single-storey houses are built in cement along traditional lines, with upturned eaves and tiled roofs. In the forested northern parts of the country, wooden chalet-like houses and log cabins are the style.

ESSENTIAL LANDMARKS AND SIGHTS

In one way, decisions on what are 'essential landmarks and sights' have already been taken for the traveller to the DPRK even before he or she arrives. Hosts or contacts will know what the truly significant places are that they should encourage, if not actually require, a visitor to see. Tourists in particular will find that an itinerary is presented to them on arrival. It may include visits to important sites and monuments, a model collective farm such as Chongsan-ri, a children's palace, possibly a school, some kind of cultural performance, and outings to the International Friendship Exhibition at Myohyangsan and the Joint Security Area at Panmunjom. Such an itinerary may prove satisfactory enough in that it will give visitors a chance to see much of Pyongyang and something of other parts of the country, as well as typical institutions. Tourists who can stay only for a week or ten days should not necessarily feel that they are being fobbed off and denied the chance to see the 'real' Korea, however they may define that, and to find out what people really think. Foreign residents may have the time to explore and to come into contact with a wider range of citizens, but they will not inevitably be the wiser on what their interlocutors' thoughts are and on what is happening in the country. A visit to the DPRK, however short, is an opportunity to see an extraordinary society, one that could be described as 'modelled' as few others are, which insists on imposing its own terms on the world, but which is nonetheless capable of warmth and friendliness to guests.

PYONGYANG

Foreign residents of Pyongyang are generally free to move about within the city's boundaries. The municipality extends up to 30–40 km. beyond the built-up area and takes in a fair amount of open country with its distinctive red loam. Signs on the main roads into and out of the capital mark the city limits. Police checkpoints further guard the approaches to the city, but usually wave foreigners' vehicles through.

Early remains

Pyongyang first assumed the title of capital in 427. The ruling Koguryo dynasty (*c.* AD 300–668) strengthened and extended existing walled fortifications and further rebuilt them in the sixth century. Taking advantage of the natural defences afforded by two rivers and a number of hills, the walled city lay between the Taedong and Potong rivers and stretched from the northern tip of Moranbong hill down to the southernmost curve of the Taedong. It was divided into four sections or forts: the north, inner, central and outer forts. Gates and stretches of fortification associated with the former north fort can be seen on Moranbong hill. These were the scene of heavy fighting between Chinese and Japanese forces in the battle of Pyongyang during the 1894–5 Sino-Japanese War, which was fought mainly on Korean soil.

Three structures in close proximity to each other on the west side of the Taedong immediately to the south of Okryu bridge are all associated with the old walled city, even if they are not all on their original sites. They are the Taedong gate, the Ryongwang pavilion overlooking the river, and the small pavilion housing the Pyongyang bell. The Taedong gate was the eastern gate of the ancient inner fort; and the site of the present Ryongwang pavilion is described as having formed the eastern command post of that fort. The present structures both date from the seventeenth century. The bell, dating from the eighteenth century, originally hung in the gate-tower of the Taedong gate and until the 1890s sounded the hour to the residents of Pyongyang. In the west of the old walled city, the Potong gate (destroyed in the Korean War and rebuilt on a slightly different site) was the west gate of the central section. In a central position between these two gates stand the Sungnyong (fifteenth century) and Sungin (fourteenth century) temples, both restored. The first houses memorial portraits and tablets to Tangun and Tongmyong (see Chapter 2 and below); the second, Sungin, is kept locked, since its contents, memorials of the Chinese commanderies, are considered too 'bad' to be viewed.

Taesong, meaning 'great fort', on the northeast outskirts of Pyongyang, was utilized as part of the defences of the city when it became the Koguryo capital. It follows the pattern of similar 'forts' elsewhere on the Korean peninsula, whereby walls linking together mountain peaks enclosed a considerable area of land, often high and wooded. Within the defences lay storehouses, armouries and barracks, plots of cultivated land and adequate supplies of water. Gateways guarded the entrances. The area thus fortified served as a place to retreat to in times of danger. The remaining stretches of wall on Mt Taesong have been restored and the south gate (Nam Mun) was reconstructed in 1978.

Those with an interest in archaeological remains may visit the site of Anhak palace, lying under the southern flank of Mt Taesong. The palace, built in the fifth century as a royal residence, covered an extensive area. The site is still bounded by four red earth walls that form a square pierced by six openings, where gates once stood. Inside the walls, lines of round or square granite blocks now sunk down into the soil mark the bases of columns and delineate the outlines of buildings and the walkways that connected them. Where the ground is open, it is cultivated, but is crossed by a footpath. The walls still rise to quite a height and can be walked along. They are most clearly visible in the winter and spring months. The site, just off the main road to Kangdong, is completely open, and only a white signboard set just inside the central south 'gateway' confirms that this is the place

Central Pyongyang

The high ground between the Taedong and Potong rivers has created two very different river landscapes. The Taedong opens up a broad vista from the tower of the Yanggakdo Hotel in the south to the huge curves of the May Day stadium (1989) on Rungna island to the north. At mid-point, the Tower of the Juche Idea (1982) and the Grand People's Study House (1982) face each other across the water. Gardens and riverside walks line each bank in this middle stretch of river, which is enlivened in summer by two high jets of water. Rowing boats can be hired on the west bank. Grouped around Kim Il Sung Square (1954) in the western section of the city are ministries and the Central History Museum (first opened in 1945) and Korean Art Gallery (1954). These last two are well worth visiting, the museum for its interpretation of Korean history, the gallery for its impressive display of ancient and contemporary art. Slightly to the north are the Folklore Museum (1956), another good place to visit, the No.1 Department Store, built in 1982 on the site of the former Japanese-era Hwasin Department Store, and the Mansudae Art Theatre (1976). Between the store and the theatre lies a beautiful fountain park where children paddle after school in the summer heat. Further grandiose buildings then carry the eye up over open ground towards the Mansudae Assembly Hall (rebuilt 1984), meeting place of the Supreme People's Assembly, and on to the Korean Revolution Museum and the gigantic statue of Kim Il Sung (both 1972). The ensemble formed by the statue against the backdrop of Mt Paektu, worked in mosaic on the facade of the museum, and the supporting groups of statuary, is known as the Grand Monument on Mansu hill. Still higher to the north is Moranbong hill. Pushing north from Moranbong you pass the Tower of Immortality, erected in 1997 at the entrance to the street leading to Kim Il Sung's mausoleum, to reach the Three-Revolution exhibition (rebuilt in 1993 to replace an earlier exhibition area) that displays the country's achievements in the juche doctrine and industry, agriculture, electronics and new products.

South from Kim Il Sung Square the ground rises again slightly to Haebang hill and the Central district, an area that was rebuilt early on after the Korean War. Large, substantial blocks line the streets, often with discreetly decorated façades. Noteworthy is Kim Chaek University of Technology on Yonggwang Street. The Central Post Office and the International Post Office, both dating from the late 1950s, are on Haebang Street. Further along on this street is the Party Founding Museum (opened in 1970), of clearly Japanese design. Originally the offices of a Japanese company, it served as headquarters of the Party Central Committee in the years between liberation and the Korean War. Kim Il Sung lived in a house in the grounds of this building. His second son, Kim Jong Il's brother, drowned as a child in a pond in the gardens. Haebang Street skirts the southeastern edge of the zone that houses the present Party headquarters and accommodates high Party officials. Entry, except on official business, is prohibited, and it is not possible to use the northern section of Changgwang Street to reach the Potong gate at the further end of it. Instead, everyone has to circumvent this zone, which occupies a similar central forbidden area as the imperial city did in Beijing. Guests staying on the north side of the Koryo Hotel can, however, look down on to this central zone. The southern portion of Changgwang Street runs past the hotel to the main railway station, rebuilt in 1958 after war devastation. It is an imposing building with an octagonal clock tower, designed in what might be called a Russo-oriental style and slightly reminiscent of a Chinese mosque. The clock now has a cracked note. The station is for external viewing only, since, unless you are arriving or leaving by train or greeting somebody, you will not be allowed inside. At the further end of Yonggwang Street, which runs northeast from the station, is the Pyongyang Grand Theatre (1960).

The east bank of the Taedong was traditionally less developed than the west bank, and parts of it are still semi-rural. The two diplomatic quarters are here, the vast maternity hospital (1980), the Catholic cathedral, many universities and hospitals and formerly, some industry. The central section of the riverfront is finely landscaped, particularly around the Juche Tower, with its flanking groups of bronze and granite figures and elaborate fountains that play in summer. The confident theme is carried north with a series of large buildings facing the river, constructed partly on the site of the former airport and designated for culture and leisure (you will spot the bowling pin of the Gold Lane bowling alley.) One block in from this row of buildings on the east bank is the Party Foundation Monument (1995). An attractive new hall on the riverfront, built largely in glass, is for exhibitions of Kimilsungia orchids and Kimjongilia begonias.

If the Taedong creates an expansive mood, the Potong river to its west offers a more intimate scene. The district used to be prone to flooding and was consequently poor and neglected, but now the river banks, fringed by the willows for which Pyongyang is famous, have lovely walks on both sides leading in an arc from the Potonggang Hotel round to the war museum. The section between the Sinso and Potong bridges has health and sports centres, the main Ragwon department store and the People's Palace of Culture (1974). The riverside park on the west bank brings you to the vast and impressive memorial to the Korean War, the Monument to the Victorious Fatherland Liberation War (1993) – the DPRK does not admit defeat. Ten dramatically sculpted groups of bronze figures portray North Korean victories in the war or praise the heroism of soldiers and civilians. A gigantic figure waving a flag of victory looms over the far end. The memorial leads on to the Victorious Fatherland Liberation War Museum (1974), which again is instructive for its very different interpretation of the Korean War. Along the river bank between the memorial and the museum is a series of older, more restrained statues that depict, in life-size figures, heroes and heroines of the Korean War. They form a pleasing contrast to the enormous ensemble of the memorial. Dominating the skyline in this part of town is the pyramid of the unfinished Ryugyong Hotel, an eerie, even unsettling presence. Further west, on another arm of the Potong, is the Monument to the Potong River Project (1971), a flood control scheme initiated in 1946. On the opposite bank to this monument is one of the two Protestant churches, Bongsu church. Billy Graham preached here on a visit in the early 1990s.

Monumental Pyongyang

What makes Pyongyang extraordinary is its large number of monuments and public buildings and the activities these commemorate: fraternal assistance from the Soviet Union and China, improvement schemes or production goals, political or Party attainments, and international events (the Korean War) and aspirations (unification). Several of the monuments were erected solely to eulogize Kim Il Sung; but around half of the big projects are museums, concert halls, theatres and sports stadia or are dedicated to study and culture, all with a clear didactic aim. The great originator of monuments was Kim Il Sung, who supervised or permitted a building programme that from restrained activity in the 1940s–1960s (two or three projects a decade) rose in a crescendo – at least sixteen projects – from the 1970s up to his death in 1994. His successor Kim Jong Il was associated with many of these monuments but has been a less active initiator of projects, and only five at the most can be attributed to him, three of them connected with his father: Kumsusan memorial palace and the Tower of Immortality, and the completion of Tangun's tomb.

Visitors will soon learn that many of the monuments are carefully built to provide numerical clues to their origins. Thus, the Juche Tower has seventy granite tiers, representing the seventy years of Kim Il Sung's life – it was constructed to mark his birthday in 1982. The Arch of Triumph, erected at the same time, has seventy azalea reliefs, for the same reason. Guides love to draw attention to such things.

Individual monuments may strike immediately by their sheer size; what are less obvious are the patterns that enmesh them. Playing on the city's natural features, the designers of these vast constructions have established poles of connection both visual and spiritual between many of them. The most obvious alignment is from the Grand People's Study House on Kim Il Sung square across the Taedong river to the Juche Tower on the opposite bank. These monuments were built in the same year, 1982, the Study House doubtless as a principal resource in the study of the juche idea. A parallel axis across the river was created in 1995 when the statue of Kim Il Sung on Mansu hill was linked with the Party Foundation Monument directly opposite on the further bank. Kim now gestures towards one of his chief creations. This symbolism is probably most easily perceived from the higher, west bank of the Taedong. From Mansu hill you can furthermore best appreciate the enfolding curves of the Taedong and the encompassing ring of mountains to the east. The immediate view is enhanced by the 'borrowed scenery' of the more distant one, expressing a concept that is deeply rooted in Korean notions of art and landscape. A further, less obvious line leads from the statue of Kim Il Sung through the high-flying horse of the Chollima statue (1961) down towards the Arch of Triumph (1982) under Moranbong hill. That arch, on the northern side of the city, is echoed by the Unification Arch (2001) over the road leading south from Pyongyang towards Kaesong. This deliberate alignment of significant buildings and monuments has its parallels elsewhere in the world; one has only to think of Washington DC and its long axis between the Capitol and the White House, with the Lincoln Memorial as another pole.

Parks

Besides the many open spaces and riverside walks, Moranbong, the wooded peak that formerly comprised the northern fort of old Pyongyang, now serves as a beautiful park. The line of fortification can still be traced, intersected by carefully restored gates and pavilions. The gardens, well planted and tended, are particularly attractive in spring. In fine weather they are popular with local people for Sunday walks and picnics, accompanied by singing, dancing, drumming and drinking. Moranbong Theatre, at the entrance to the park, has an unexpected neo-classical portico; it serves usually as a concert hall. From Ulmil pavilion, the view north and eastwards over the Taedong and the city is very striking. At this point, the Taedong divides to form a long island, Rungna island, laid out as a park, and the site of the May Day stadium. The narrow arm of the river curves sharply east and as it does so, cuts deeply into Moranbong hill, creating steep cliffs. Various groups of buildings are hidden in the woods here that function as state guest houses or possibly official residences. The area is protected by security guards, and casual visitors are not permitted. On the west side of Moranbong hill lies the Kaeson revolutionary site, where Kim Il Sung addressed his fellow Koreans on his return to his native country on 14 October 1945. The nearby Arch of Triumph, bearing the dates 1925 and 1945, commemorates Kim's alleged struggle against the Japanese during these twenty years. Set into this side of the hill is a funfair that contains, incongruously, one of the few Buddhist temples in the capital, Ryonghwa temple. Around Moranbong are located the monuments to Soviet and Chinese support to the North Korean regime. The Liberation Tower (1946, rebuilt 1985) on the southern edge of the park commemorates the role of Soviet troops in liberating Pyongyang in August 1945; the Friendship Tower (1959, enlarged 1984) marks the contribution of the Chinese People's Volunteers in the Korean War and the post-war reconstruction of the country.

On the opposite side of the city, in East Pyongyang, is a much smaller but equally attractive park, laid out on Munsubong hill to commemorate a visit by Kim Il Sung and his family on 6 April 1947 to plant a tree. The day is still marked as Reafforestation Day.

On the northeast outskirts of Pyongyang, the lower slopes of Mt Taesong are the setting for various amenities – the zoo, the botanical gardens and an intermittently operating funfair. A system of roadways constructed over the hillsides takes you to good picnic spots and magnificent views from the highest points. Access to your own transport is, alas, pretty well essential. If you can tolerate zoos, the Pyongyang zoo is not too bad an environment for the animals kept there and most of them appear to be quite well fed and cared for. An unexpected section is that devoted to dogs. On display are two breeds of Korean native dog: the Chindo, from the southwest of the peninsula, and the Pungsan, from the north. The accompanying information panels point out how much fiercer and hardier the northern breed is! The botanical gardens, beautifully designed and planted, provide an attractive spot to walk in. Pride of place goes to the Kimilsungia and Kimjongilia flower species cultivated there. A series of grass mounds along the northeast side of the gardens are identified merely as 'ancient tombs'. On the northwestern flank of Mt Taesong is Kwangbop temple, said to have been founded in the fourth century AD by the Koguryo kingdom as one of the nine temples of Pyongyang. It was twice destroyed, once by fire in 1700, after which it was rebuilt in 1727, the second time by enemy action during the Korean War. Only in 1990 was its reconstruction achieved as places of worship were again permitted. The present temple follows the customary layout of two entrance gates, the inner one housing the four heavenly kings or guardians, which lead into a courtyard. The main hall stands at the further side of this yard and is flanked by two side halls. The temple is finely decorated in traditional Buddhist style. The oldest relics are in stone: they are the remains of two ancient banner stands and tablets recording past benefactors and reconstructions.

Buddhist and Confucian buildings and old pavilions are some of the attractions on Mt Ryongak situated on the western side of the capital. This area is famed for its walks and views over Pyongyang, but is little known to foreigners. The Mangyongdae children's camp, built in 1971, is at the foot of Mt Ryongak.

Revolutionary sites

Some of the most attractive sites within the municipality are associated with Kim Il Sung or Kim Jong Il or their family. Some may be in quite secluded spots where one or other leader lived or was active at a stage of his or her life, and thus merit the epithet 'revolutionary'. Their location is usually signalled on a main road by a sign bearing a red flag and an arrow indicating on which side of the road the turning is. But beware: not all such sites are open, and a red flag may lead you to a revolutionary site but not one welcoming visitors!

The most famous revolutionary site in the Pyongyang area is undoubtedly Mangyongdae, 'platform of ten thousand views' and the location of Kim Il Sung's birthplace. A cluster of low houses, richly thatched, represent the spot where he is said to have spent his early years before leaving for northeast China. The spot is constantly visited by groups of Koreans, who arrive to the sound of swelling music and are guided round. If, as a foreigner, your visit is announced beforehand, a guide will be there to greet you in your own language; but if you come on a casual visit, you will be left to look round on your own. The garden is filled with natural and man-made features – a well, a spring, a rock – associated with Kim Il Sung. On the other side of the road from the birthplace, a row of trees in varying stages of growth commemorate the world leaders who planted them. None were added after Kim Il Sung's death. Not far away, on a wooded hillside, two sets of double burial mounds record Kim's parents, Kim Hyong Jik and Kang Pan Sok, and his paternal grandparents, Kim Po Hyon and Ri Po Ik. Their busts are displayed in front of the mounds. For some reason, this spot is guarded by a series of surly young security officials, who look on suspiciously as you walk around. In another part of the grounds is the straw-thatched school house where Kim Hyong Jik, who was a teacher, ran the school. A walk through Mangyondae gardens is always refreshing, especially when it culminates in the climb up to the viewing platform above the Taedong.

Not far north from Mangyongdae in the western suburbs of Pyongyang is Chilgol, where a small thatched house set in a neat park marks the birthplace of Kim's mother, Kang Pan Sok. It contains a low desk said to have been used by Kim as a young boy. Kang Pan Sok's statue (1972) stands in the park. The house is open to visitors without prior arrangement. Adjoining this site is Chilgol church, the second Protestant church in Pyongyang. Kim's maternal family were Christians. His mother taught at Sunday school in the Chilgol area, and the church, built in the early 1990s, may be on the site of the one that she attended.

Maekjon and Ponghwa, to the northeast of the capital on the main road to Kangdong, again commemorate Kim Hyong Jik. The site of the Maekjon ferry on the Taedong river, now replaced by a road bridge, is marked by a large painted board on the further bank depicting a young man – Kim Hyong Jik – leaving a ferry. Kim taught for a year and a half in 1916–17 at Myongsin school, situated two kilometres further on at Ponghwa-ri. Kim Il Sung, then aged five, lived with his parents at the village. The present extensive site can again be taken as a display of filial piety. Spots to visit are the schoolhouse and exercise ground, a fine old tree and a natural spring, which was probably a much earlier site of veneration.

O'un revolutionary site is one of the few commemorating Kim Jong Il, who spent six weeks (20 August-4 October 1962) there on basic military training during his student days. It lies north of Pyongyang on the eastern side of the main road leading to Sunan airport. Easily visited in the training area is the Taedae mess hall where he ate, his place and his utensils still marked and on display. Beyond the training zone is a small reservoir set in a ring of fine wooded hills threaded by walks. The area has become popular with both Koreans and foreigners.

The revolutionary dead are honoured in the Revolutionary Martyrs Cemetery (1975, enlarged 1985) on Mt Taesong, where rows of bronze busts mounted on marble tombstones record those who fell in the anti-Japanese struggles. On the road to Mt Taesong is the greatest funerary monument of all, the Kumsusan Memorial Palace, where Kim Il Sung, president in perpetuity of the DPRK, lies embalmed. Kumsusan served from 1976 as Kim's official residence. He died there on 8 July 1994 and it is there his body lay in state. The decision was taken to alter and enlarge the residence to create a vast mausoleum. Enormous amounts of material were expended in the reconstruction, and the mausoleum still consumes resources in the form of its own electricity supply and dedicated tramline. It can be visited, usually twice a week. Foreigners are permitted to visit alongside Koreans, but they must accept a lengthy 'purification' in which their clothes and persons are cleansed of outside contamination and they are led slowly through many turns and prepared emotionally through music and effects of lighting for the encounter with the eternal president. The ritual is to bow on all four sides of the glass case that contains Kim's remains; but this is not obligatory for foreigners, and each visitor must make his or her own decision on whether to do so. Many foreigners merely stand to attention. A great many Koreans visit, almost all in groups organized by their work, military or study unit. For most of them, one must assume, the experience offers a focus for devotion; and the role of Kumsusan in providing an emotional core to the state and its relationship with the people should not be underestimated.

A ring of tombs

Pyongyang's antiquity as a strong place and centre of administration is borne out by the variety and number of tombs dating from different eras that lie in and around the present city. Under a philosophy that demands that every significant object and event contribute to the accepted interpretation of the past, many of these sites are presented as evidence of particular achievements. Those that cannot meet this requirement are less publicized.

The Lelang tombs come into this second category. They are the most numerous remains of an ancient site known in Chinese as Lelang, in Korean as Nangnang or Rangrang (the sounds 'l', 'n' and 'r' in Korean are often interchangeable), that flourished during the middle centuries of the Chinese Han dynasty (206 BC–AD 220) as a 'commandery' or settlement established by the Chinese during a period of expansion into the Korean peninsula. As such, they are a reminder of a sensitive issue in the DPRK, which disputes the importance of the Chinese connection with these early settlements (see Chapter 2). Nonetheless, Lelang has survived in the form of Rangrang, the district immediately south of the Taedong at the start of the road to Kaesong. Lelang became a prosperous trading and administrative centre. Its inhabitants were interred in earth-mound tombs, the earliest of which are dated to the late first century BC. As many as 1,500 mounds have been identified, scattered over the countryside to the southeast of Pyongyang. Many of the tombs have been excavated, first by Japanese and later by Korean archaeologists, and yielded many rich and beautiful artefacts. A group of eight such mounds lie immediately to the east of the new Unification Arch, on the edge of the city, tucked in behind the very modern Army Film Studios. The tomb entrances are kept closed by metal doors, and a visit has to be specially arranged; but you can walk unhindered through and round the mounds. The spot is worth visiting for the strange, almost surreal juxtaposition of ancient and new, urban and rural.

In AD 313, the rising kingdom of Koguryo overran the Lelang commandery and brought an end for the time being to Chinese intervention in the peninsula. The practice continued, however, of burying people of high rank in stone-built chambers mounded over with earth. After the Koguryo capital was moved to Pyongyang in 427, the quantity of such tombs increased around the city. They were generally constructed in beautiful settings and surrounded by trees to enhance the harmony and dignity of the site. Some of the Koguryo tombs around Pyongyang have been excavated, revealing superb examples of wall paintings in various states of preservation and highly developed construction techniques, which form essential elements in the development of Korean art. Copies of the paintings are displayed in the Korean Art Gallery. UNESCO has already supported conservation measures in several of these tombs. In July 2004, the UNESCO World Heritage Committee agreed to inscribe a number of the tombs as World Heritage Sites (at the same time inscribing another concentration of tombs located in the earlier Koguryo territory on the middle stretch of the Amnok (Yalu) river, in Ji'an, now in China). Some of those around Pyongyang are open, but in the interests of conservation, visits are restricted and an entrance fee, said to be 100 euros, is charged, with additional payments for photography and video recording rights. Tombs dating from the fifth to the seventh century AD are located at Kangso, Tokhung-ri (dated precisely to 408), Susan-ri and Yaksu-ri to the southwest of Pyongyang, between the capital and Nampo. One of the finest, Anak No.3 tomb, is sited further south in Anak county of South Hwanghae province.

Another group, dated to the latter half of the sixth century, are situated southeast of Pyongyang on the road to Wonsan at what is now called Tongmyong's tomb. (The site may be familiar to some as Chinpa-ri, but is now known as Mujin-ri in Ryokpo district.) There is an entrance charge. Though the site is described as Tongmyong's tomb, it encompasses in all fifteen mounds, of which the principal one has traditionally been associated with him. The DPRK claims Tongmyong as the founder of the Koguryo dynasty in the third century BC. It is probably best to take him as a legendary figure, whose modern value lies in reinforcing the concept of the northern part of the peninsula as the wellspring of Korean civilization (see Chapter 2). He is honoured accordingly at his tomb with a hall painted inside with scenes of his life and of the military and cultural achievements of his reign. A stele in Kim Il Sung's hand, presented as a good example of his Chinese calligraphy, records the reconstruction of the tomb in 1993. Another four finely worked stelae relate the history of Tongmyong and commemorate the dynasty. Statues of four civilian officials and their horses on the right and four military officials and their horses on the left, all new but finely carved, flank the steps leading to the tomb. Two tigers, two columns, a lantern and a table for offerings are placed in front of the central mound. Behind and around stretches a wood of beautiful pine trees through which wind paths leading to the fourteen lesser mounds. You may find that one of these is open for visiting, though it contains nothing. It does, however, allow you to see the typical style of Koguryo tomb construction, of stepped stone beams and a lantern roof. If you walk beyond the mounds you can find evidence of much later tombstones that appear to date to the nineteenth century. Look out for the small, wiry red squirrels that live in the woods.

To the right of Tongmyong's tomb as you face it is Jongrung temple, rebuilt in 1993 to replace an older temple on the site that was destroyed during the Korean War. It is constructed and painted in what seems to be authentic traditional style, and the three halls are carefully maintained, but it is devoid of visitors, let alone worshippers, and has a forlorn air.

The most grandiose of the tombs around Pyongyang is Tangun's tomb, which occupies a large and magnificent site to the northeast of Pyongyang at Munhung-ri on ground just off the road to Kangdong. A small admission charge is made.

The tomb visitors see is of recent construction. It was completed in October 1994, a few months after Kim Il Sung's death, but from the outset was his project. It is built massively in white granite, in the form of a level-topped pyramid, and is reached by two long flights of steps, broken at mid-point by ten stelae of varying heights that form a kind of gatepost. Statues of twelve male figures, each about five metres high, flank the approaches to the tomb. Eight of these are said to represent Tangun's ministers; the four nearest to the tomb are presented as his sons. The customary stone offertory table, small lantern and sacrificial vessel are found in front of the tomb. Its four corners are guarded by large stone sculptures of tigers and dagger-shaped pillars, and the front two by additional columns. Inside the tomb are displayed the remains of Tangun and his queen.

The present monument should not be taken as an exact reconstruction of the tomb that undoubtedly existed on this site and which did yield human bones and other material remains in the course of earlier excavations. That older tomb had apparently long been associated with Tangun, who, as discussed above (Chapter 2), is a figure regarded traditionally throughout the peninsula as a mythical construct, the founder of the Korean nation. The significance of the present monument is that the bones found in the earlier tomb and displayed in the new one are claimed as the actual bones of a historical Tangun, dating back over 5000 years. The elevation of Tangun as the 'national father', whose remains are located in the north, aims to consolidate the DPRK's claim to be the true guardian of Korean identity and nationhood. The tomb's location near Pyongyang is intended moreover to emphasis the antiquity and importance of the capital city. Its message is heightened by the symbolism of the statuary around it: the traditional attendant figures of officials serving the king in death; the four sons, an innovation doubtless added to emphasize the actuality of a powerful ruler; the dagger-shaped pillars in the form of a weapon identified as distinctively Korean. Stone tigers habitually guarded the tombs of kings and queens, but had mild expressions; the tigers at Tangun's tomb are shown as fierce creatures, full of fight.

Other important sights

USS *Pueblo* and the *General Sherman*: For a taste of comparatively recent history, two side-by-side sites on the southern bend of the Taedong, right by the Chungsong bridge, commemorate two occasions when the Koreans got the upper hand over Westerners. The grey boat generally moored at the riverside here is the USS *Pueblo*, a US information-gathering ship captured off the east coast of the DPRK in January 1968 by North Korean patrol boats, assisted by fighter aircraft. The DPRK claimed the vessel was within its territorial waters. The North Koreans opened fire when the vessel tried to escape, killing one of the crew and wounding three others. The remainder of the crew, eighty-two in all, were detained until the end of December 1968, when they were released following negotiations and a US apology. The *Pueblo* was taken into the east coast port of Wonsan, where it stayed until 1999, when it was brought to Pyongyang, reportedly by sea around the south coast of the peninsula, sailing in international waters. On climbing aboard the ship, you may be greeted by an elderly naval man, one of those who took part in the original boarding. On occasion, the *Pueblo* disappears from its mooring place, for unexplained reasons.

The other victory recorded at this spot with a plaque and cannon taken from the boat is the burning of the *General Sherman* in 1866. The story of the destruction of this vessel and the killing of its crew and passengers can be read in Chapter 2. The point at which the boat was stranded is a little lower down the river, but the chance to juxtapose these two records of the humbling of Western might was clearly too good to miss.

Korean Film Studios: These are the main state film studios and are well worth visiting. The high value placed on the educational and artistic aspects of cinema in the DPRK, together with Kim Jong Il's long-standing interest in the medium, mean that considerable resources go into the film industry (see Chapter 5). The studios are located on the northwest edge of Pyongyang beyond the Potong river and are surrounded by fields. They were inaugurated by Kim Il Sung in 1947, were destroyed by bombing in the Korean War and were subsequently rebuilt. A large group statue of Kim Il Sung surrounded by film workers stands in the central square. Visitors are taken round the lots, most of them 'streets' variously representing Japan in the 1930s; northeast China – Manchuria – during the same period; a decadent-looking Seoul in the 1950s-1960s full of bars and clubs and exuding American influence; and a street of traditional Korean houses and buildings with magistrate's office. There is a village of thatched huts, very typical in its irregularity, and a small area planted with European trees and shrubs to provide a convincing backdrop to European houses. A mini-forest of pines has been cultivated and provided with log cabins to represent the area around Mt Paektu. Through these streets and sets, the many films made here are thus infused from the outset with the desired tone and atmosphere. Occasionally, filming may be done on location, at Mt Paektu or even sometimes abroad. As we were shown around, a goat and two kids, part of a herd that was browsing in the grounds, made themselves comfortable on 'Japan street'. They were doubtless an initiative on the part of the maintenance staff rather than extras.

There is also a film studio associated with the army, near the Rangrang Lelang tombs, but it does not seem possible to visit this. Some visitors have managed to get to the Animation Film Studios, not far from the Juche Tower.

NAMPO

Nampo, 55 km. (34 miles) to the southwest of the capital on the estuary of the Taedong, serves as the port for Pyongyang. Most deliveries for the west side of the DPRK come in here through the West Sea barrage, including much international food aid. A weekly service runs between Nampo and the South Korean port of Inchon, further down the coast. Since the construction of the barrage across the estuary 15 km. beyond Nampo, completed in 1986 after five years' labour, the Taedong is no longer exposed to the great tidal variations that mark the west coast and the port is able to accommodate fairly large vessels. The locks are navigable by ships of up to 50,000 tons. Nampo municipality has a population of 731,000 inhabitants and, like Pyongyang, extends over both rural and urban areas. The city itself has, or had, a certain amount of industry in addition to port work, and the municipality takes in smaller towns that were once beacons in the DPRK's rapid industrialisation. Now it looks to the more recent export processing zone set up near the city. Two roads, one an expressway completed in 2000 with much use of 'voluntary' student labour, link Nampo with Pyongyang. Apparently, the hope is eventually to amalgamate the two cities into a new capital area that would draw in trade and investment and support new residential sectors. It would have an inbuilt attraction in the form of the Pyongyang golf course laid out in 1987 around Lake Taesong. Several of the Koguryo tombs discussed above also fall within the same area; and the model cooperative farm of Chongsan-ri, fronted by a spirited group sculpture in bronze of Kim Il Sung flanked by farmworkers, lies just off the expressway.

A trip to Nampo is very agreeable as a means of spending a day by the sea, especially in the summer. Foreign residents with their own transport may drive there unaccompanied. For the fast journey take the expressway, which is generally deserted. The old road is more picturesque as it hugs the river in its early stages, but as it approaches Nampo it deteriorates into a dirt track. Either route leads into the main street of Nampo and down to the port area. This is a prohibited zone, so follow the road round to the right and out along beside the estuary past a long stretch of salt pans to the barrage. A fine monument in white marble commemorates the soldiers and workers who constructed it, sometimes at the cost of their lives. Turn left on to the barrage and cross over to the further side on to the small island there, which has an observation platform and an exhibition on the building of the barrage. Follow the road round the side of the island to arrive at a small sandy beach. There is a changing and shower block with a small shop and terrace built above. Swim suits can be hired from the shop. The swimming is quite good. It is best to bring your own food, as Nampo offers little in the way of restaurant or shopping facilities, apart from the Seamen's Club near the port area. The greatest pleasure at Nampo is to relax in the warm air and admire the spectacular views out to sea and across the estuary to the mountains beyond.

KAESONG

Kaesong, about 160 km. (99.5 miles) south of Pyongyang by the expressway, is in strong contrast to the capital. Smaller in size and population, it has kept many old buildings of considerable historical interest and has areas of low, traditional housing. Before the Korean War, the town was in South Korea. During the war it always remained within a neutral zone by virtue of the armistice talks that were carried out first in Kaesong, then at Panmunjom nearby, and thus escaped the heavy bombing that reduced most North Korean cities to ruins. There are also less immediate differences between Pyongyang and Kaesong, in a more relaxed atmosphere, despite being only 8 km. (just under 5 miles) away from the Demilitarised Zone and the site of the military headquarters that cover the DMZ. Patterns of speech are also different in that, whereas in Pyongyang and indeed most of the DPRK the most formal mode of address is common, in Kaesong the less strict, middle level of formality prevails in conversation, as it would in Seoul. The town indeed is closer to the capital of the ROK (which lies about 50 km. (31 miles) to the south) than it is to Pyongyang. The other, historical difference is that for nearly five hundred years Kaesong was the capital of the Koryo dynasty (918–1392), which took its name from the earlier Koguryo dynasty and ruled over a unified country. These factors, together with the town's location in the North, place the Koryo dynasty in high esteem in the DPRK.

Kaesong has a magnificent setting at the foot of Mt Songak. Koreans tell you that the outline of the mountain resembles a pregnant woman lying on her back – a very potent image. Spread in a wide arc along the lower levels of the mountain are the remains of Chomsongdae, an ancient astronomical observatory, the foundations of the former Koryo royal palace of Manwoldae, Anhwa temple and the ancient Confucian 'university' of Songgyunggwan. From Manwoldae, traces of the former outer fortifications can be identified snaking over Mt Songak. The centre of the town is divided by a low hill called Janam hill, topped by a large bronze statue of Kim Il Sung. Just below the hill is Namdaemun, the great south gate of the old inner fort, now standing bereft of walls in the middle of a crossroads. The gate was destroyed in the Korean War and has been reconstructed. It is furnished with a large bell. On the west side of Janam hill, the eighteenth-century Kwandok pavilion overlooks old houses and the Folk hotel. On its east side lies another former Confucian school, the Sungyang lecture hall with its heavily tiled roofs and courtyards rising one above the other up the slope. Northeast of Janam hill, on the road leading to Sunggyunggwan, is Sonjuk bridge, constructed in 1216. It was the spot on which Jong Mong Ju, an official loyal to the Koryo dynasty, was assassinated in 1392 by order of Yi Song-gye, the Koryo general who turned against the dynasty, overthrew it and in the same year established his own line, the Yi or Choson dynasty. Around this site and on the opposite side of the road are several 'monuments to loyalty' dating to the seventeenth, eighteenth and nineteenth centuries, marking Jong Mong Ju's steadfastness and commending his example.

Sunggyunggwan itself lives on as the Koryo museum. Founded in 992 as the Kukjagam, the principal educational institute of the Koryo dynasty, it was given its present name in 1308. The present buildings date from the first decade of the seventeenth century. It served both as a centre of Confucian learning and as a site for honouring eminent Confucians. Two spacious courtyards succeed each other, planted with ancient ginko and zelkova trees. The museum is housed in four of the buildings and displays an interesting and varied collection of artefacts connected with the history and achievements of the Koryo reign: metal type, woodblock printing, material on astronomy, ceramics, Buddhist statuary and relics, bronze mirrors and bells and so on. Of equal interest are the stelae, pagodas, stupas and stone lanterns, some over a thousand years old, brought from various temples to a small park on the west side of the main complex. It is little wonder that Sunggyunggwan is often used in filming.

The area surrounding Kaesong holds a number of natural and historic sites. In the hills north of the city are the Pagyon falls, a thread of water cascading gracefully over 37 metres (121 ft) from one pool into another. This lovely site has been popular for centuries as a place for picnicking. Carved into the rock face surrounding the fall are verses composed by visiting revellers. A steep climb further up the mountainside past Pomsa pavilion brings you to Kwanum and Taehung temples. The whole district formed a fortified zone known as Taehungsan, encircled by walls and entered through gates and intended to strengthen the defences of Kaesong. The city itself lies in an area known to be rich in archaeological sites. Discussions have begun between local authorities and cultural organisations in Kaesong and a British-led group of foreign experts including archaeologists on investigating and assessing the quality of what is in and on the ground. The long-term aim would be to develop and manage the tourist potential of Kaesong. Land to the east and south of the city is being developed as an industrial park in conjunction with South Korean business. To the west of the city lie two tombs, both dedicated to Koryo kings: Wang Kon (reigned 918–43), founder of the dynasty, and the thirty-first king, Kongmin (reigned 1351–74). Not long before his death, Kim Il Sung took Wang Kon's tomb, quite close to the city, in hand. Judging that the tomb of the founding king should surpass that of the later ruler, Kim ordered that the former stone grave attendants and furnishings, dismissed as too small, should be replaced by larger and grander versions. The result has a monumentality lacking in the original, but is still not wholly successful. An example of how royal tombs were traditionally constructed and ornamented is provided at the double tomb of Kongmin and his Mongolian queen, which lies somewhat further away from Kaesong at the head of a small valley. It was restored and landscaped in 1984, but appears to have been generally left in its original design. Guarding the twin tombs are alternating tigers and sheep, the first for the Korean king, the second for his Mongolian wife. It is one of the most beautiful sites in the peninsula.

Visitors must apply for permission to visit Kaesong and take an escort, and passes are checked at road blocks once inside the boundaries of Kaesong municipality. Inside the city itself, however, it seems you are free to walk about the streets and visit the monuments. The journey takes about two hours along a well-paved expressway. Sohung rest house provides a break. It was here that we bought our bottle of Daesong red wine. Along the route, opposite the turning for Sariwon, a road leads into the Mt Jongbang mountain resort and Songbul temple.

PANMUNJOM

In a land of surprises and contrasts, Panmunjom is one of the strangest, a scene of institutionalized impermanence, where the two Koreas, or rather their representatives, can come face to face. If a visit is possible, do not miss it.

The site was chosen in October 1951 as the meeting place for the armistice talks that had got under way earlier that year between the contending forces in the Korean War. The document eventually signed on 27 July 1953 designated Panmunjom as the location of the Military Armistice Commission (MAC) set up by both sides to monitor the armistice within the Demilitarized Zone. Maybe in acknowledgement of the provisional nature of the agreement ending the war, but more importantly of the potential for violent confrontation inherent in the arrangements of the MAC, the Joint Security Area (JSA), the name by which, strictly speaking, this neutral zone is known, is not large and contains no more than a minimum of personnel and installations. The most important of the latter is the MAC hut, the middle one of three low buildings painted in UN blue that lie astride the military demarcation line. This hut is the venue for such joint discussions on issues arising in the implementation of the armistice as still take place between the Korean People's Army (KPA) and the United Nations Command. A cord running down the middle of the negotiating table marks the demarcation line. Inside the hut, visitors may pass freely between north and south, but the building is only open alternately to parties from either side; there is no chance of mingling.

The JSA is now a considerably calmer place than it used to be. In the past, it was the scene of confrontations that sometimes ended in death or injury, and the approaches on the southern side were past several US army camps. Since 1991, South Korean troops have patrolled the area and the DMZ, and at the end of 2004, all US forces left the area. Clearly the South Korean soldiers are chosen with an eye to their height and burliness, since they dominate their North Korean counterparts physically. Visitors should match the outwardly low-key atmosphere within the JSA. This is not a place in which to start an argument about the apportioning of blame for the Korean War. Do not deviate from the route you are shown or try to wave to people on the other side – and they are very close. Be prepared for ROK and UNC observers to photograph you and when you are in the MAC hut, to stare closely though the windows at you. On days when visitors come from the South, KPA observers will be doing the same.

The expressway to Kaesong is protected towards its southern end by the occasional tall construction by the roadside that is designed to drop a block of masonry across the roadway. As you drive further south towards Panmunjom, the route becomes progressively more fortified, with tank blocks in the fields. At the entrance to the DMZ, which stretches for 2 km. (1.2 miles) on either side of the demarcation line, visitors are given a short briefing with the help of a small-scale model of the area and then proceed on their way with a military escort. (This is probably the closest you will get to a member of the KPA.) Some farming goes on in the Demilitarized Zone. Because of the relatively undisturbed conditions of the terrain, the DMZ is a haven for wildlife, as well as the site of a large number of landmines. The perimeter of the Joint Security Area is guarded by an electrified fence, along the outer edge of which runs a gravel strip raked to show up any footprints. Within the northern section of the DMZ, visitors can view the armistice discussions hall and the specially built hut in which the armistice was signed, and can take lunch at a resthouse. The charge is included in the fee for the trip.

WONSAN

Wonsan lies on the east coast, almost directly across the peninsula from Pyongyang. The eastern coastline, backed for considerable stretches by mountain ridges, is altogether more dramatic than the west coast as it falls abruptly down to the sea. The area around Wonsan forms the largest break in the northern section of this coastline. The port lies inside a vast natural harbour created by a hollowing out of the coast at this point and is protected from the outer sea by islands and spits of land. The advantages of the site have been exploited for centuries, and Wonsan has thrived as a shipping and trading centre. The town has developed around the port, but to both east and west are fine beaches with good swimming. Those to the northwest of the city centre, at Songdowon, are probably the more accessible, since they can be reached on foot by an attractive road that runs through gardens beside the beach. This resort, set among pines, has long been popular as a holiday centre. It boasts botanical and zoological gardens, a number of good restaurants and an international children's camp which was still catering to foreign children in the summer of 2001, when we travelled from Beijing to Pyongyang in company with groups of Thai and African youngsters. Mountains, pines, sand, sea and islets combine in a scene of amazing beauty. As yet, tourism is modest and controlled; it may not always be so.

The expressway between Pyongyang and Wonsan itself runs through fine countryside. Tongmyong's tomb (see above) is passed fairly soon after leaving the capital, then the road takes its course through a series of plateaux ringed by mountains and on into a mountainous region. The area is full of rivers and streams. The journey can be broken at the Sinpyong rest house, by the side of a lovely stretch of water. Between there and Wonsan, the road runs through a number of tunnels. Before reaching the coast, a detour can be made down the first leg of the new road to Hamhung, intended as a shorter route through the mountains. This road, constructed by the army, shows evidence of quite good engineering and execution, but is still a dirt track. The reason for venturing down it is to see another magnificent waterfall, which seems as yet to be unnamed. Kim Jong Il himself is said to have discovered it when the road was being cut. The site was opened up and made accessible in 2000–2001. The date 2001 is carved and painted in red on the rock face beside the fall, a sure sign that Kim at least visited the site in that year. Unfortunately, the desire to 'improve' on nature has not been resisted, and a succession of brightly coloured animal plaster statues lining the walk to the falls mar the splendour of the waterfall and its setting.

KUMGANG MOUNTAINS

Wonsan has traditionally been a stopping point en route to the Kumgang mountains that lie to the south of it. The region contains some of the loveliest and most renowned scenery in the Korean peninsula. The name Kumgang, or Diamond, refers to the needle-sharp granite peaks and serrated ridges of the mountains and their glittering appearance in the sun. In their folds are many Buddhist temples and hermitages, for the area offered a retreat from secular pressures. The extraordinary scenery, of steep ravines, rivers and streams, waterfalls, jagged pinnacles and curious rock formations, was a favourite subject with landscape painters. It is divided into three sections: Sea Kumgang, on the coast, where pillars of stone wade out to sea; Outer Kumgang, full of waterfalls and steep valleys; and Inner Kumgang, with more gentle scenery.

However, with seven counties along the eastern sector of the Demilitarized Zone closed to visitors, the mountains appear difficult of access to tourists approaching from the north. It is not easy to gain permission to visit from Pyongyang. The surest way of seeing Kumgang would seem to be to arrange a visit from outside of the country through one of the foreign tourist agencies that offer trips to the area via the DPRK, or to approach from the ROK. In 1989, the late founder of the Hyundai conglomerate, Chung Ju-yung (who was born in Tongchon county just north of the DMZ), negotiated an agreement with the government of the DPRK to develop the

Kumgang mountain region as a tourist destination. The privilege has cost Hyundai enormous sums of money. The Kumgang region itself – 530 sq km. (204.5 sq miles) – comprises about one-eighth of the total area that Hyundai, with exclusive rights for thirty years, hopes to open up for tourism along the east coast of the DPRK below Wonsan.

The first cruise organized by Hyundai took place in 1998. Since then, similar cruises offered visits to Sea Kumgang and Outer Kumgang, not to the inner recesses. In January 2004, however, Hyundai suspended tours by cruise ship, citing financial losses brought about by a diminishing number of tourists. Instead, the route now in use appears to be a land crossing up the east coast through the DMZ. (See the website run by the (South) Korea National Tourism Organisation http://english.tour2korea.com for some information on the tours.) A new hotel opened in July 2004 for tourists, largely staffed by North Korean personnel under South Korean management. Nonetheless, only a small area has so far been developed for tourism. The DPRK authorities, having granted access, albeit limited, to their territory to South Koreans and others, control their movements closely. It looks as if state concerns on one hand and business considerations on the other may keep Kumgang off the common tourist path for some time.

MT MYOHYANG

By contrast, this lovely site, lying about 120 km. (74.5 miles) to the northeast of Pyongyang, can be freely visited. It comes under the jurisdiction of the capital, which means that no previous authorisation is required to go there. The wooded mountain slopes that rise above the Myohyang river have been renowned for centuries for their calm and beauty and formerly sheltered many Buddhist temples and hermitages. A few of these remain and together with the abundant waterfalls form the stages on hiking routes up to and along the mountain tops. If all you want to do is picnic, there are many fine spots along the main river or up one of the side streams. Most people come on a day trip from Pyongyang, but if you want to stay, the resort has several hotels, of which the Hyangsan is the most luxurious. Exports of bottled mineral water from Mt Myohyang have started up to South Korea,

If you are travelling with Korean hosts, their prime reason for coming to Mt Myohyang will be to show you the International Friendship Exhibition. This is housed in two vast stone halls that opened in 1978, built largely with voluntary labour in traditional style with green hipped roofs, but constructed without windows.

Inside, a series of rooms with controlled lighting and temperature, kept at 18°C (64°F,) display the presents given to Kim Il Sung and Kim Jong Il by international leaders and visiting delegations. The exhibition is overwhelming in its scope but also in the ostentation and banality of many of the items. Especially unsettling is the section of gifts offered to Kim Il Sung *since* his death. The lavish use of materials – marble, bronze and so forth – and of resources – lighting and temperature and humidity control – is also disturbing when set against the impoverished state of much of the country's infrastructure. North Korean officials argue, however, that it is good that gifts given to the leaders can be seen by ordinary people.

It can be a relief to cross over the river to Pohyon temple on the opposite bank. Dating in its origins to 1042, but rebuilt several times since then, the temple spreads over various gates and halls set in beautifully planted gardens. The two pagodas are especially fine. A separate temple on the Pohyon site commemorates the priest Sosan and other 'patriotic' monks who joined in popular armed resistance to the Japanese invasion of Korea at the end of the sixteenth century. A small museum displays 80,000 woodblocks carved in Chinese characters with the Buddhist scriptures from which printed versions were made. The blocks are dated to the Koryo dynasty (918–1392). The souvenir shop has some nice objects. Despite the feeling that Pohyon is intended more as a museum than as a religious centre, it is a calm and refreshing place to visit.

The trip to Mt Myohyang is along a well-metalled highway, inaugurated in 1995. (This expressway runs for some distance north from the capital before dividing; the good road goes on to Huichon, just beyond the Mt Myohyang resort, the poor road proceeds all the way to Sinuiju and the Chinese border.) After Anju, the route follows the Chongchon river, into which the Myohyang river flows. At Kujang, an attractive small town on the Chongchon, you can admire the luxuriant coils of rice-straw thatch covering a small house described as an inn where Kim Il Sung stayed in 1925 on his trek north to China. From Kujang a road winds up into the mountains to the Ryongmun caves. The existence of caves in the region has long been known, but the vast cave system now open to visitors was, it appears, only discovered accidentally in 1959, when miners working in a nearby coalmine broke through. Kim Jong Il is said to have visited twice in the 1990s; certainly, the carefully installed pathways, stairs and lighting are all evidence of high-level interest. The spectacular impression is, alas, marred by the guide's presentation; rather than providing relevant geological and historical information, she is obliged to point out the fanciful likenesses of formations and entertain visitors with stories.

MT PAEKTU

Mt Paektu has become the most cherished site in the DPRK. It is not, however, an easy place to get to. It lies 385 km. (239 miles) northeast of Pyongyang on the Sino-DPRK border, in the angle formed by the sources of the Amnok and Tuman rivers. The journey can be made by air, then bus, or by train, though the rail trip can now take 30–40 hours. Where once, until the mid-1990s, resident foreigners were offered tours to Mt Paektu, the search for hard currency now imposed on the country has meant that in 2002 such trips were being priced at several thousand dollars. Time and cost discouraged us from attempting the journey, but foreigners do visit; and for young Koreans a trip to Mt Paektu has been an essential rite in their maturing as revolutionary adults.

The mountain, and Lake Chon that lies in its crater, are regarded as a place of mysterious and awesome beauty (see above for a fuller description.) Over the past quarter of a century, the potent associations of the region have fused with the desire to give substance to the claims to success of Kim Il Sung's guerrilla force during the anti-Japanese struggle. In this most sacred of places, Kim achieved his most telling blows against the oppressor – thus goes the story. A series of bivouacs and secret camps have been (re)constituted along the two Korean sides of the border running east and south of Mt Paektu and the sites of various engagements at Pochonbo and Musan are marked. The culmination of this reconstruction of the region is the placing of Kim Jong Il's birth in a log cabin on the flanks of Mt Paektu in 1942. In 1979, an extensive ensemble of sculpted groups and statues, including a statue of Kim Il Sung 15 m (49 ft) high, was inaugurated in the area at Lake Samji. This may have marked the beginning of the creation of Mt Paektu as *the* revolutionary site. No matter that other accounts of Kim Il Sung's activities in the late 1930s and the early 1940s and of the place of Kim Jong Il's arrival in the world are at odds with the official Korean line. It may be simpler to accept the Korean claim that 'the area of Mt Paektu serves as an open-air museum which educates our people in the revolutionary traditions of the Korean Workers' Party of Korea'.

▶ Part III

A Brush with History

9

Opening the British Embassy Pyongyang, 2001–02

J. E. HOARE

ON THE MORNING of 12 December 2000, at a brief signing ceremony in the office of the Permanent Undersecretary, Sir John Kerr, in the Foreign and Commonwealth Office (FCO) in London, Britain and the Democratic People's Republic of Korea (DPRK – North Korea) signed a document in which they agreed to exchange diplomatic missions. The signatories were Sir John Kerr for the United Kingdom, and Mr Kim Chun Guk, head of the European Department of the DPRK's Ministry of Foreign Affairs (MFA) for the DPRK. Within minutes, the news of this development had appeared on the FCO's website, and been announced throughout the world. Given the previous lack of contact between the two countries, some expressed surprise at the speed of developing relations. Among international news services, only Radio China International noted that Britain was the first Western permanent member of the United Nations' Security Council to establish diplomatic relations with the DPRK.

This is a very personal account of what came next. It is a shorter version of an essay that appeared in the *Papers of the British Association for Korean Studies* (Vol. 9, 2004). That had more detail on Britain's relations – or non-relations – with the DPRK from 1948 to the early 1990s, together with notes, but this version tells the same story.

BACKGROUND

Before 2000, Britain and the DPRK had tended to ignore each other. They fought each other in the Korean War, but thereafter there were few contacts. Following the 1945 division of the Korean peninsula, and the emergence of two separate Korean states in 1948, Britain, in common with most Western countries, had recognized the Republic of Korea (ROK – South Korea) as the 'only legitimate government' on the peninsula. The Korean War, though it made no legal difference, reinforced the position taken in 1948. The adoption of a resolution on 27 October 1950 establishing a United Nations Commission on the Unification and Rehabilitation of Korea (UNCURK) settled the question. UNCURK's mandate was the 'establishment of a unified, independent and democratic Government in the sovereign state of Korea'. Britain's legal view was that the existence of UNCURK meant there could be no British recognition of the DPRK.

The position changed in November 1973, when the United Nations wound up UNCURK by a consensus resolution. This freed the way for the establishment of diplomatic relations with the DPRK by countries that had hitherto believed that UNCURK prevented such a move. Britain took note, and at one point seemed ready to extend diplomatic recognition to the DPRK. But there was little interest in Britain in North Korea, and the moment passed. Some British businessmen, including Sir John Keswick of Jardine Matheson, thought that there were trading possibilities. Under Sir John's auspices, a Britain-DPRK Trade Council operated for a few years but the expected trade did not materialize, and the council faded away. John Gittings of *The Guardian* and two members of the University of Leeds, Dr Gavan McCormack and Aidan Foster-Carter, were the only scholars to take the DPRK's claims about itself seriously.

The late 1980s saw an increase in unofficial contacts between Britain and the DPRK but no change in the formal British position of non-recognition. That only came when both Koreas entered the UN in September 1991. Britain voted for the admission of both Koreas. The decision meant the recognition of the DPRK as a state, since only states can enter the UN. Ministers made it clear, however, that recognition did not mean diplomatic relations.

Yet Britain was cautiously moving forward. In November 1988, British officials were permitted to talk to DPRK officials in neutral settings. DPRK officials remained wary of any contact, so this did not amount to much. More significant was the agreement that two British officials could accompany the British delegation to the Inter-Parliamentary Union (IPU) meeting in Pyongyang in April 1991. These two became the first British officials to visit the DPRK soil since the Korean War, and as well as attending IPU-related functions, they were able to meet with the DPRK-UK Friendship Association and MFA staff.

From May 1991, there was also a permanent DPRK presence in Britain, with the establishment of a DPRK mission to the London-based International Maritime Organization (IMO). Britain was still not ready for diplomatic relations, but recognition made it easier for contacts to develop, and increasingly there were issues to discuss, including nuclear matters and concern about human rights. Thus, when two DPRK MFA officials visiting Europe in 1992 enquired whether they might come to Britain, the answer was positive, and in June 1992, an unprecedented exchange of views between British and DPRK officials took place in London.

Such talks would take place approximately every eighteen months for the following eight years. London was the most frequent venue, but there were also meetings in Geneva and, eventually, Pyongyang. They could be difficult occasions, as each side presented its concerns to the other without much meeting of minds. The atmosphere was often frosty, with minimum courtesy on the British side. Yet the talks were valuable in letting each side learn something of the other's preoccupations, and, slowly, establishing a little human rapport. The usual DPRK leader was Mr Kim Chun Guk of the MFA's European Department. Matters might have gone on like this for years, but for major changes on the Korean peninsula in the late 1990s.

Britain welcomed the election of the veteran South Korean opposition leader, Kim Dae-jung, as president of the Republic of Korea in 1997. He was in many ways an old friend of Britain and had spent six months at Cambridge University after failing to win the 1992 presidential election. His first overseas visit after becoming president was to the Asia-Europe Meeting (ASEM) in April 1998, held in London. Understandably, therefore, British ministers supported his new policy towards the DPRK – the 'sunshine policy'. But, given British concerns on nuclear and proliferation issues, it was equally understandable that the support given to closer links with the DPRK was cautious. Despite the new ROK government's positive encouragement to its friends and allies to develop links with the DPRK, Britain remained hesitant about any move towards establishing diplomatic relations. As late as January 2000, a Foreign and Commonwealth Office Minister, Mr John Battle MP, in a Written Answer to a question in the House of Commons, clearly stated that:

> At present, the United Kingdom is not planning to establish diplomatic relations with North Korea. We actively seek dialogue with North Korea and continue to press North Korea for progress on issues of international concern, such as missile proliferation and human rights abuses. Our future stance will largely depend on North Korean willingness to discuss these long-standing concerns.

But the international environment was changing. As well as the growing contacts between the two Koreas, Italy established diplomatic relations with the DPRK in January 2000, while Australia re-established them in early May 2000. The DPRK seemed finally to understand international concerns about missile proliferation, which paved the way for the resumption of normalization talks with Japan and generally improved the international atmosphere. Even United States-DPRK relations appeared to be on the move.

A CHANGE OF POLICY

These developments led Britain to keep under review its policy towards the DPRK but there was no immediate push for change. What proved to be the catalyst was the unprecedented summit meeting between the leaders of the two Koreas in June 2000. Subsequent revelations have shown that the summit was not set up quite as effortlessly as it was originally presented, and that much money passed across to the DPRK to get the desired result. However it came about, the meeting in Pyongyang in June 2000 was a remarkable achievement. The personal chemistry between the leaders seemed good, and real progress appeared possible on a number of issues. Whatever scepticism there was about motives, politicians around the world welcomed this new development.

Britain was no exception to the general euphoria. The same Mr Battle who had said in January that there would be no diplomatic relations, now praised the imagination and wisdom of the two leaders:

> I am greatly encouraged by news of the successful Summit meeting between President Kim Dae-jung and Chairman Kim Jong-il. The Summit is a testimony to the vision and dedication of both leaders, and a significant achievement for Korean and international efforts to ease tensions on the peninsula.

He went on to say that Kim Dae-jung had always had Britain's full support in his policy of engagement with the DPRK, and that Britain remained committed to that policy. Other British statements followed a similar line, though Prime Minister Tony Blair apparently struck a cautious note at a meeting of the Group of Eight world leaders a month later.

The general trend remained positive. Already in May 2000, the then head of the FCO's North East Asia and Pacific Department, Mr Peter Carter, visited the DPRK as part of the regular round of political contacts. DPRK officials did all possible to make his visit a success, and Carter was able to reach agreement on direct aid to North Korea in the form of an English-language teaching programme recruited by the British Council but funded by the FCO. From September 2000, therefore, two British teachers (later increased to three) became the first known Westerners to teach in DPRK universities, at Kim Il Sung University and Pyongyang University of Foreign Studies.

During that summer, the DPRK foreign minister wrote to those European countries that had not so far established diplomatic relations, suggesting that now might be the time to do so. None responded. However, the British prime minister and foreign secretary on their way to Seoul for the third ASEM meeting in October 2000 appear to have had a conversion worthy of St Paul, for almost immediately on arrival, Robin Cook, the foreign secretary, announced that Britain had decided to establish diplomatic relations with the DPRK. The decision came as a surprise to those of us working on Korean matters in the FCO, and to the British advance delegation already in Seoul. But the deed was done, and a positive response was now sent to the DPRK foreign minister.

In announcing the decision, Mr Cook linked it to the progress made between the two Koreas, and particularly the summit. He also made it clear that diplomatic recognition did not imply any approval of the DPRK's policies on matters such as human rights: diplomatic relations were a way of doing business, not a mark of approval or a reward. In an interview with the BBC's Radio 4, Mr Cook said that Britain had a number of issues of concern about the DPRK: 'If we have diplomatic relations we have a better channel for promoting our dialogue on that and exploring our concerns.' According to *The Guardian*, the prime minister said that 'momentous developments [were] underway on the Korean peninsula. The [June 2000] summit has created the real opportunity for lasting peace and reconciliation.'

IMPLEMENTING THE DECISION: JANUARY-JUNE 2001

There was no immediate follow-up. But when the DPRK MFA indicated that it would like to send a delegation to London in December 2000, as part of the regular political discussions, the FCO accepted. It was agreed that the question of diplomatic relations would be added to the regular topics for discussion. Three Koreans arrived: Kim Chun Guk, now MFA Director for Europe, Thae Yong Ho, Section Chief in the European Department, and Pak Kang Son, UK desk officer. The British side was led by Rosalind Marsden, Director for Asia-Pacific, and included Peter Carter, Sir Stephen Brown, former ambassador in Seoul, and myself, then head of the North Asia and Pacific Research Group. Other officials attended as needed.

The first part of the meeting was taken up with the type of regular exchange that Britain and the DPRK had been having for the previous seven years, including discussions on the current situation on the Korean peninsula and in Europe, and human rights issues. The Koreans were surprised when we did not criticise their human rights' record, but instead explained how the British Government handled criticism of its human rights record.

The meeting then turned to the question of diplomatic relations. Progress was remarkably swift. The DPRK officials confirmed that a future British embassy in Pyongyang could have a dedicated satellite-based communications system, and that British diplomats would be allowed to travel outside the capital provided they gave the requisite notice. After some initial hesitation, they also agreed that, as an interim measure, a British chargé d'affaires could be based in Seoul while steps were taken to set up an embassy in Pyongyang. For their part, the DPRK officials sought British assistance in establishing an embassy in London, and said that they too would initially appoint a non-resident chargé d'affaires, based in either Stockholm or Geneva. On that understanding, the agreed document was signed on 12 December 2000. Despite some concern that there would be media criticism of the move, none materialized.

The agreement on diplomatic relations had come rather faster than anybody had expected, and no arrangements were in place to implement the undertaking. However, as the only known person in the FCO who had expressed a willingness to go to the DPRK, I was now asked if I would become chargé d'affaires for an indefinite period, to establish the embassy. There was only one answer. It would be a temporary arrangement, but the general view seemed to be that I could expect to do the job for a year. However, nothing was to be said in public until both Koreas had agreed.

January 2001 saw a flurry of meetings. Initially, it looked as though lack of money would be a problem, but the FCO agreed that there should be four UK-based staff in due course. In addition, in order to take forward the December agreement, a delegation would go to Beijing, Pyongyang and Seoul later in January to present me to the Koreans and to begin the process of establishing an embassy. The same delegation would also make tentative plans for a visit by Sir John Kerr, planned for March 2001.

The practical arrangements proved surprisingly easy, and on 21 January, the delegation, led by Rosalind Marsden, and including Peter Carter, Stephen Brown and myself, left for Beijing. In Beijing, which like Pyongyang, was in the grip of the coldest winter for fifty years, much effort went into purchasing warm clothing, and Antony Stokes joined us from the embassy in Seoul. Then it was on to Pyongyang. The reception was warm, even if the weather remained bitterly cold and the charms of the Koryo Hotel, with no heating outside the bedrooms, somewhat limited. The DPRK had no problems with my appointment and the officials made no difficulty about our wish formally to inform the ROK before making a public announcement. We were also able to establish good contacts with the foreign community; the Swedish embassy proved particularly helpful, as they were to do on many further occasions.

As well as discussing current political issues, where a strong anti-United States feeling was already evident, the delegation made good progress on Sir John Kerr's proposed visit, and began work on selecting possible sites for the British embassy. The DPRK were clearly keen that any link with Seoul should be short-lived, and promised all assistance in finding premises in Pyongyang. We were shown what we all agreed was a good option, the former Swedish embassy offices, most recently used by the UN Children's Fund (UNICEF), but currently empty. We were also shown some typical diplomatic apartments, very much in the style of what some of us knew from Beijing (and others from Moscow), though smaller and less well-constructed. The Koreans made it clear, however, that all such accommodation was at a premium and that they would not be able to guarantee that we could be adequately housed. Other highlights of the visit included meetings with the British teachers, a visit to the opera, the willingness of the British chargé d'affaires-designate to sing at a Lunar New Year party organised by the MFA for the European residents of Pyongyang (and this on the day of our arrival!), and the whole delegation dancing on the bar at the Random Access Club (RAC) at the World Food Programme (WFP) offices on the night before their departure for Beijing and Seoul. In Seoul, the ROK proved equally content with my appointment, and the FCO announced it on 29 January 2001. The ROK press also showed some interest.

On return to London, I began the preparations that would be required for a posting, including seeking medical clearance, and other practical matters. Gradually, May emerged as the best time to plan to take up residence in Seoul. The FCO was still struggling with the funding issue, and there was some uncertainty about my exact status. My grade manager informed me on one occasion that mine was not a normal posting; rather, I was 'an administrative measure devised by the command. . . .' He later said that he meant to describe the slot I occupied rather than me personally, but it was an unusual way of putting things, and would have looked odd on my CV.

I returned to Pyongyang in late February 2001, in advance of Sir John Kerr's visit. The weather had but marginally improved; the temperature remained around freezing at best for the whole time I was there. Indeed, the first night I arrived, I almost gave up in despair. Marooned in the Yanggakdo Hotel on an island in the Taedong river – the Koryo was in use for meetings of separated families from North and South – I gazed out on snowy darkness, with not a light visible. Fortunately, Dr Hazel Smith and one of the staff of German Agro-Action, the German NGO, arrived to rescue me! Until they came, Pyongyang seemed very remote from the rest of the world.

In the course of the following two weeks, Antony Stokes from Seoul, my wife – Susan Pares – and Andy Cornell and Mike Tibbs, colleagues from the FCO Estates Strategy group, joined me. Gordon Slavin, from the British Council in Beijing, also arrived, to liaise with the British teachers. In addition, Elizabeth Wright, then of the BBC World Service, with whom I had shared a room in the FCO nearly thirty years before, Beth McKillop from the British Library, Dr Robert Anderson, Director of the British Museum, and Jane Portal from the British Museum's Department of Oriental Antiquities, all travelled to Pyongyang at that time. The British presence was suddenly rather pronounced! A dinner party for visiting and resident Britons saw some eighteen people around the table – and not all the visitors could be present.

Work now moved forward on the embassy front. I was shown a number of additional apartments, none very suitable. But once Messrs Tibbs and Cornell arrived, they wasted no time, but began to look seriously at what was on offer. They felt that the original building that we had been shown, the former Swedish offices, would make a good residence for the Head of Post, but was not really suitable for both residential and office accommodation, as the Koreans seemed to envisage. They were also not very impressed by the apartments that were available. They were able to put these concerns across in professional-to-professional discussions with their DPRK counterparts, and as a result, were shown a set of buildings that had clearly been designed as an embassy, but never used as such. These buildings, together with the old Swedish mission, seemed likely to give us enough office and staff residential space for some time to come. In the meantime, it was understood that we would have office space in the German embassy – the former East German embassy – that had originally been designated for a now aborted United States liaison office. Since the building, which dated from the mid-1960s, contained the Germans, the Swedish offices and the Italian aid agency, this looked like a good piece of European Union cooperation. With help from Susan and others, I was also able to do some work on cost of living and allowance matters.

Sir John Kerr arrived on 10 March. A programme of extensive political discussions with DPRK officials followed, and with some difficulty even included a call on a senior military officer. It became clear that the DPRK had perhaps over-optimistic expectations of the amount of British aid that was likely to be forthcoming, both for English-language training and for other sorts of assistance – this would become a recurring concern. There was a visit to a WFP project, and some cultural activities. During the visit, we held what was the first major British reception in Pyongyang. The novelty meant that we attracted a very large gathering of Koreans and foreigners, and the food barely held out – a useful warning for future occasions.

In addition, Sir John looked at the proposed embassy buildings. He decided that the new offer was a good one, but that we would want more than just the main office block that was being put forward. He did not oppose the acquisition of the former Swedish offices, but clearly felt that this was less important than the three buildings on the new site. And in a move that had a direct effect on my position, he decided that we should open up in Pyongyang as soon as possible, using the German premises as offices and putting staff into hotels until the other buildings could be prepared for use. This, it was estimated, should not be too long, since as well as making available offices, the Germans were also prepared to lease staff accommodation, though this too would require work to be done. Sir John made it clear to the Koreans that the further expansion of the British embassy would mean the introduction of satellite communications, to which they made no objection – I had begun to suspect, however, from my discussions with them, that what the DPRK officials understood by satellite communications was not the same as we were proposing. Sir John left Pyongyang on 13 March, together with Susan and me, Antony Stokes and the British Library and British Museum Group. We found ourselves carrying large pots or pictures that Jane Portal had acquired for the British Museum's collection. Some nifty diplomatic footwork at Beijing airport ensured that Jane was not compelled to have them all x-rayed or to pay duty before we were allowed out!

After a few days in Beijing, where we found that there was already some concern in the embassy that the opening of Pyongyang would mean extra work for them, Susan and I went on to Seoul, where we found much media interest in our Pyongyang experiences. Alas! The main stories were due to appear on 22 March 2001, but the founder of the Hyundai group, Chung Ju-yung, died the night before, and I was largely driven off the front page. There was sufficient coverage nevertheless to show that there was no ROK hostility to the developing British links with the DPRK, which I was able to link closely to the improvement in ROK-DPRK relations since 1997.

Back in London, all was activity. The decision that we would open as soon as possible in Pyongyang was a relief in some ways, since life there would be on a far simpler scale than if I was going to Seoul. There were still many things to do. Money now seemed less of a problem; we purchased laptops and printers for the embassy and ordered cars from Japan. Family matters needed sorting out, dental examinations undergone, and so on. One of the best developments was the arrival on the scene of Eilidh Kennedy, who had volunteered to be my temporary management officer, and who proved lively and full of new ideas. Another was the appointment of a project officer, Robert Fitchett, whose job was to 'manage' the Pyongyang project. His role was to represent our interests to the FCO, and the FCO's interests to us. A certain amount of briefing was required.

There was also the Joint East Asia Associations' Conference in Edinburgh to attend, where I presented a paper based on my experiences up to that time with the DPRK – it caused as certain amount of wry amusement. Finally, I left London on 5 May, bound initially for Boston and my elderly aunt, the last surviving relative from my parents' generation. After a few days in Washington, where there was much eagerness to find out anything about the DPRK, I arrived in Seoul on 10 May, to another round of media activity. There was less competition this time, and European relations with the DPRK were high on the local agenda, following the visit of an EU delegation led by the Swedish prime minister to Pyongyang on 2 May. Some of the grandiose claims that were attributed to me about the purpose of my mission were unlikely to be fulfilled. An unexpected but welcome diversion was giving a speech to the annual ceremony to commemorate the British journalist, Ernest Bethell, whose early twentieth-century campaigns against Japanese domination in Korea are well remembered.

May–June 2001 would prove to be a busy period. I arrived back in Pyongyang on my own, to find that Mr Pak Kang Son was no longer the UK desk officer, having been replaced by Mr So Chol since my last visit. Mr So was already known to me, since we had met at the FCO's conference centre, Wilton Park, in February 2001, when he had been a member of a DPRK team. Mr Thae, as before, remained as a fixture on our horizon. A few days after I arrived, Eilidh and Robert Fitchett came. The latter was on a week's visit, to familiarize himself with Pyongyang. This would be useful, we thought, as work on the embassy progressed. A week after that, Messrs Tibbs and Cornell returned, to take forward planning on the proposed embassy premises and to see what work needed to be done in the temporary offices. They would be frequent visitors right up to the time of our final departure. Soon after my return, the Koreans had withdrawn the offer of the old Swedish offices, so we were now limited to the new site that they had proposed, plus whatever staff apartments we might be able to rent. (The old Swedish offices would become the

World Health Organization offices later in 2001, so I would attend meetings in what had been planned as my dining room!)

From the beginning, we faced the problem that DPRK officials tended to see us as a visiting delegation, rather than, as we saw ourselves, the advance guard of the embassy. They were quite happy to arrange sightseeing or similar activities but less keen on our acting as an established diplomatic entity or undertaking commercial visits. We had great difficulty in persuading them to issue us with diplomatic identity cards, even though we knew that our DPRK counterparts in London had been able to claim their ID cards from the moment that they had arrived there. (The fact was that the ID cards were virtually never required, and we could probably have managed without them; but there was a principle involved.) On most issues, we would get there in the end, but it was hard work. In general, we found it easier to get work-related calls when the Koreans wanted something; a huge list of aid requests had begun to build up by now. Working out of the Koryo Hotel was also less than satisfactory, as was our dependence on hired cars.

The biggest problem, however, turned out to be the question of communications. Now that we were on the point of beginning work on converting buildings for our use, it was essential that there should be no doubt that we would be able to install and operate our satellite-based communications system. The MFA became cagey, saying that the matter was out of their hands, but pointing out that other embassies and the UN agencies were able to have e-mail via servers in China or through the international airline link, SITA. Explanations about the difference between what was acceptable to our host government and what we needed fell on very stony ground. Eventually, I was referred to the Ministry of Communications. Here there was no doubt; DPRK law forbade the use of satellite communications except by DPRK state authorities, and we could not operate such communications. The answer 'no' came not once, but four times.

At that stage, we had committed ourselves to nothing, so it was easy enough to stop the work on the proposed premises, especially since most of the essential measuring and other tasks were done. However, to make the point, I called Messrs Tibbs and Cornell off the site, and we all went to a collective farm instead. For the rest of their stay, they concentrated on work on the offices, and on the two temporary apartments that the Germans were willing to make available. They also began to look more seriously at the possibility of developing a derelict block on the German compound, which they thought could be used for both an ambassadorial residence and for staff apartments. The North Koreans expressed some concern that we would not proceed with the premises we had been offered, but remained adamant that there could be no change on the communications issue.

The German embassy held their premises outright, as did the DPRK in Berlin – they ran a nightclub in the basement at one time – and there was nothing stopping the Germans from leasing part of the buildings to others. And so it was that the brass plaques of the British Embassy were fixed to the walls of the German embassy

Determined to show that we were a real embassy, we held the first-ever Queen's Birthday Party (QBP) in Pyongyang on 2 June 2001 – it was not entirely a coincidence that this was my absent wife's birthday. As with our March reception, we tried to get away from the stilted formula that marked so many national day receptions in Pyongyang. To some extent it worked, though it was clear that not everybody was happy at standing rather than sitting during the evening. The lack of long speeches however, was clearly a welcome development. The event also engendered some publicity for what was then the newest of British embassies. In addition to the QBP, we held an exhibition of science and technology publications from Britain, and attended a 'Friendly Get-together' organized by the Committee for Friendship with Foreign Countries and the Korean-British Friendship Association. We had arrived.

Meanwhile, practical needs required much attention. Both Eilidh and I intended to leave in mid-June, returning the following month. By now London had decided that the embassy would be formally opened by Christopher Hum (now ambassador in Beijing), who was the then Chief Clerk, or head of the administration. For this, we had the two brass plaques but little else. Korean staff had to be sought from the General Service Bureau for the Affairs of Diplomatic Missions (known generally as the GSB), and we had to negotiate with the same people for telephones. Furniture was on order, but until it arrived, we were to make do with what remained of the old East German furniture stock. Some ten years on from the closure of the East German embassy, there was not much furniture left, and what there was, tended to fall apart when picked up. But we managed to salvage enough to make habitable two offices and a reception room for the interpreter. Work on the telephones needed assistance from Beijing.

One of the many issues that Eilidh sorted out was that of allowances; London agreed that as we were now functioning as an established post, we should start to receive proper allowances. However, in solving one problem, we created another, at least for me. According to London, I had neither medical nor dental clearance, and without those, not only would I get no allowances, but, as one of the FCO's medical staff pointed out in a rather heated telephone conversation, I should not even be at post. When I pointed out that I was, the reply was: 'Well, we didn't say you could.' A flurry of activity in London produced both the dental clearance, and the medical report. My teeth were fine, but unfortunately, the medical report, put away without action, indicated a problem. Frantic phone calls to London to assure them that I had never felt better – true, as it happened – cut no ice.

Consequently, when I arrived back in London on 19 June, my carefully arranged programme disappeared in the need for medical examinations and tests. Meanwhile, Eilidh stayed on, sorting out telephones and other matters, though she too left on 23 June.

As well as the medical tests, there were more briefings and meetings, plus some 'media exposure training'. For the latter, I was lucky enough to have a morning's session with Harvey Thomas, widely credited with having improved Lady Thatcher's contacts with the media. I hope he did the same for me. Until the go-ahead on the medical side was given, however, a question mark hung over my return to Pyongyang, and of course, over allowances. (Long afterwards, I learnt from a 'reliable source' that unless I had actually dropped down dead, I would go to Pyongyang since there was at that stage nobody to replace me. . . .) Finally, I was cleared, with strict injunctions to report anything amiss, and a couple of new sets of tablets to take, and Susan and I left for Beijing on 24 July. We had one night there, and flew on to Pyongyang via Shenyang on 27 July. Eilidh, who had arrived earlier in the week met us at the airport, where our cars and drivers were also waiting. Flying the flag proudly on Car no.1, we set off for the embassy!

AN EMBASSY AT LAST: JULY 2001 ONWARDS

There was to be no rest. On 28 July, Christopher Hum arrived for the formal opening ceremony to be held on 30 July. Like all visitors, he also wanted a more extensive programme, so we made calls and went on field trips over the weekend. Then, on an overcast and muggy morning, with large numbers of diplomatic colleagues, the British community, and a small delegation of Koreans led by Vice-Minister Choe Su Hon, we gathered in front of the German chancery (office) building for speeches and flag-raising. The MFA had indicated that the Vice-Minister would be quite happy to dress informally, without jackets and ties, but the Chief Clerk felt that we should be properly attired for this occasion. It was a contingent dripping with sweat, therefore, that made speeches. We had decided not to do a conducted tour of the very ramshackle offices, but we drank champagne and ate canapés outside instead. Christopher left the next day, and our new life began with a very enjoyable dinner with

Glyn Ford, a Labour Party Member of the European Parliament, and a regular visitor to the DPRK.

The building where we now had our offices had suffered from years of neglect. On most days, there was no water from around 10.00 until perhaps 16.00, since the East Germans had not installed a storage tank – we had to remember not to use the lavatories! The lights were weird and wonderful. Most of our first week was spent waiting for the next set of lights to start burning and then explode, although the frequent power cuts reduced the pressure on the lighting. Even without power cuts, the voltage, at perhaps 180 volts rather than the theoretical 220, and the cycles, perhaps 43 or 44 hertz (later there would be spells of 40–41 hertz) instead of the official 60, sent machinery haywire at regular intervals. We could retreat to our hotel, with hot water available from 07.00 to 09.00 and from 18.00 to 22.00, but the power cuts pursued us there as well. In the summer, we could often not run the air-conditioners, while in winter the heating barely functioned – the pipes and radiators were rusted and the pumps inefficient. As winter progressed, we turned to space heaters but these too had their drawbacks. Chinese-made, they were often badly assembled and gave off shocks. They also put a strain on the electricity, to the consternation of the German officer in charge of housekeeping, and there were periodic banning orders on their use.

Our diplomatic community was small, some twenty-three missions, the same number as when the Swedes opened in 1975, although the composition had changed. The Russians and the Chinese were big and kept themselves to themselves. Of the others, the Indonesians and the Poles were the largest, at about six staff. Most embassies were in Pyongyang to show solidarity and friendship, whether of the socialist or the non-aligned kind. Some, such as Cambodia and Egypt, were once close to the DPRK because of personal rapport between their leaders and the late President Kim Il Sung. Those links did not survive Kim's death in 1994; his son and successor, Kim Jong Il, was not interested. Some may have had military purposes; Egypt again, and possibly Iran, Pakistan and Libya. India and Pakistan both admitted that for each of them their role was to watch the other.

Even our European colleagues were not quite what they seemed. The Swedes, who established relations in 1973, and closed in 1994, re-opened in 1995, mainly to act for the United States. With only two staff, they had not been able to do much beyond that, except that they were always unfailingly helpful to all visiting Western diplomats. The Germans were an interest section until March 2001. Large by local standards, with five people, they had not been allowed to have formal links with Koreans or other embassies. This changed during our time in Pyongyang, and the Germans became very active, especially after the arrival of an ambassador in January 2002.

Then there were the UN organizations. The UN Development Programme (UNDP) and WFP each had around fifty expatriates working for them, and there were a number of resident NGOs, closely associated with the UN bodies. While many UN staff had diplomatic status, the Koreans appeared to treat the UN organizations somewhat differently from other diplomatic missions. The very tight controls of the past had gone. Aid workers were not confined to the Koryo Hotel, as they had once been, but were still watched carefully, a process aided by the presence of many Korean 'national officers' in all UN organizations. The UN officials had to work with their Korean hosts, which made it difficult to push too hard. Despite receiving massive aid, the Koreans still viewed the UN, and even more the NGOs, with suspicion. The UN bodies wanted to modify the Koreans' attitude, and they made up the largest single group of foreigners in the country. But they had to tread carefully if they wished to continue their programmes.

The Koreans were wary of us; indeed, they were wary of all diplomats, and in the past had done their best to control and corral them. At one time, the embassies were more or less in the centre of Pyongyang, near the Party and state organs, but now only the Chinese and the Russians remained there. The rest had long since moved either to Munsu-dong, some six kilometres from the centre, where we now were, or Munhung-dong, a little further away, where we had been looking to go. The Koreans would have liked us to stay in our enclaves, preferably without contact with each other; if they gave something to one embassy, they always suggested that we should not mention it to others. Munsu-dong had a club and a shop for diplomats, so in theory there was no need to go anywhere else, apart from the older diplomatic club beside the Taedong river.

Communication was by Note, directed at the appropriate geographical department in the MFA or to the Protocol or Consular Departments. We issued 132 Notes between May and December 2001, perhaps not a world record but it must have been nearly so. They were rarely answered in writing when we first arrived, though this was beginning to change before left; instead, something did – or more likely – did not happen. Long lead-ins were demanded for travel and other activities at first but this too was beginning to change by the time I left. Some heads of post found their courtesy calls arranged with alacrity, with scarcely time to draw breath. Others moved in slower time, especially if anything out of the ordinary was requested. Protests were met by assertions that this was how it was done in the DPRK, and appeals to international norms fell on the deafest of deaf ears. Attempts to bypass the MFA by direct approaches to other organs or ministries were not welcome, though they sometimes worked.

Control was the name of the game, and control extended to all areas. Visiting delegations had their days filled with programmes that allowed for little or no deviation. Strenuous attempts were made to prevent visiting groups from meeting with their own diplomats. There were normally no briefings and no press conferences. If you requested information, you would be told to look at the press. Even Korean speakers could learn little, since they could not have easy contact with ordinary Koreans. Links with the outside world were also limited. In the past, some embassies had clearly used radio; the masts are much in evidence. Grudgingly, the Koreans allowed the use of e-mail but lines were poor and contacts sometimes difficult. The Internet was unavailable, since low voltages and servers outside Korea made it a difficult and expensive task to log on. The Koreans banned the use of all satellite communications, including satellite phones. Mobile phones and other forms of wireless communications were also not allowed. Telephone directories were unavailable so local staff had to ring the MFA for numbers. We could not have contact telephone numbers for our staff. Theoretically, the MFA provided an emergency contact service for out-of-hours crises, but nobody could ever raise a response on the number provided.

A further form of control was the imposition of DPRK norms as much as possible. Diplomatic missions were expected to present flowers to Kim Il Sung's statue on formal occasions, and no major state anniversary was complete without a 09.00 visit to the Great Leader's mausoleum. Failure to do so meant close questioning by the local GSB staff, whose main role was to keep a check on our activities. Heads of mission were expected to send birthday cards to Kim Jong Il – and our Korean hosts prepared suitable cards in advance. As far as we could tell, none of the embassies felt it was any part of their role to challenge this strange world that the Koreans had created. Some bemoaned the lack of opportunities to travel, but did not do much about it, apart from blaming the Dean of the Diplomatic Corps for not pressurizing the Koreans. The exception was visiting the mausoleum, where there had been minor rebellions. The previous Nigerian Ambassador announced that seeing a corpse on 1 January would mean a bad year ahead. The Egyptian Ambassador on one occasion announced at a dinner that unfortunately, he thought that he was going to be ill next day. He was.

Into all this, the British had now come. Others greeted us with high hopes of bringing new ideas and a fresh approach. The diplomatic community may have been small, but it was friendly, with political differences put aside, a welcome change from the experience of Erik

Cornell, the first Swedish diplomat, in the 1970s. One colleague from the Middle East was a devoted follower of the Royal Family, and constantly pestered me for information on their doings. Representatives of former British colonies must have embarrassed any Koreans listening as they sang the praises of the British imperialists, who had brought good government and efficient services to their countries. All applauded our stand over communications, even if nobody else was trying the same thing, and few held out much hope of success. Our ELT programme was seen as positive. Hopes were high that we would establish a library and a school, as an alternative to that provided by the Koreans. No amount of explaining that we were destined to be a small mission would persuade colleagues that we would not make a difference.

In practice, while foreign visitors and especially journalists were often subject to very tight control, diplomats were free enough in and around Pyongyang. In May and June 2001, Eilidh and I had spent hours wandering about the town in the evenings and at weekends, without once being stopped or questioned. Later, once we had the embassy cars, we were able to extend our journeys into the surrounding countryside and even further afield, without problems. Nobody raised any objections when I took the BBC's Brian Barron around the town in my car, even though he stopped to film from time to time. He also did a very sympathetic interview, putting a positive spin on Britain's relations with the DPRK. I was able to do the same with other journalists as well. Even when we needed permission to travel, we found it relatively easy to acquire. On one occasion, with less than twelve hours' notice, and without an interpreter, I accompanied the BBC's Seoul correspondent to the east coast to look at flood damage. Other journeys were often arranged equally swiftly. In general, as far as we were concerned, the rules seemed more relaxed than they had been for others in the past.

Another way in which we induced the Koreans to modify their position was by inviting academics and journalists as guests of the embassy. Not only did this work in terms of getting visas, but we also found that DPRK officials would actually help with the programmes for such visitors. They were also most helpful in laying on programmes and entertainment for family visitors.

We could help scholars in particular in other ways too. The Koreans proved co-operative over tracking down films – and without charge – for one academic, and the Grand People's Study House eventually produced some beautifully copied and bound editions of the journal *Chosun Munhwa* (Korean Culture), for another. Later, we were able to provide direct support and assistance to the second British Library/British Museum visit to the DPRK in May–June 2002. These various efforts contributed to the preparation of papers presented at study days in London in December 2001 and December 2002.

These were perhaps small victories, but they did at least show that DPRK behaviour could be modified. Eilidh had battles over her driving test, which was regularly cancelled – she eventually won, getting a licence without any test. (As head of post, I did not need to take a test, which she found particularly galling!) There were some problems with clearing containers until the Koreans learnt that a) we were not going to bribe them to do their job; and b) Ms Kennedy did not give up.

For much of autumn 2001, we camped out in our East German-furnished offices. Susan, meanwhile, had found work with UNICEF, which introduced us to another group of contacts. An embassy outing for all of us to Nampo and the seaside was a great success; we would repeat it the following year, and we also had bowling expeditions. In September, after one disagreement too many with the Koryo Hotel, where rooms were rarely cleaned and staff would come in when they felt like it, we moved to the Potanggang Hotel. The Potanggang is somewhat older than the Koryo, but it had locking doors and understood the need to clean the rooms occasionally. It also had a better, if more expensive restaurant, where for £30 it was possible to buy a decent bottle of Chablis.... Susan and I lived in great splendour, with a vast sitting room, a small sitting room, a dining room, and river views. Only as the winter drew on did the drawback of no heating become obvious, and one by one our grand rooms were abandoned.

A steady stream of visitors, both official and private, provided plenty to do. Occasionally, they attracted some publicity from the Koreans, though it was hard to tell what the Korean Central News Agency (KCNA) would cover and what it would not. From the Beijing embassy, we had regular visits from the engineers sorting out our telephones and faxes, and the embassy nurse, Jayne Senior, came to advise on medical matters. Other visitors included Nick Archer, Peter Carter's successor as the head of the North East Asia and Pacific Department of the FCO, and an exploratory trade delegation from the British Consultancy Board. This required much work and coincided with one of our worst-ever battles over containers. Some of the group expressed an interest in following up on the visit, but only the International Mining Corporation was able to do so and then much later.

I also began to get some of the over fifty calls I had asked for but on which, apart from a call on the Korean Workers' Party, the Koreans had taken no action from July to September. These varied in value, but in general, I felt that I was learning something about how the DPRK worked – at least at the theoretical level. Field trips with the UN groups or NGOs also added to our knowledge. I have seen more DPRK hospitals than I care to count! But I also took part in UNICEF's immunization campaign, saw farms and villages, and was able to make some personal assessments of conditions in rural areas. And from time to time, we escaped to Beijing, taking and collecting official mail.

Contacts with the FCO could be frustrating. The fax machines suffered badly from the frequent power cuts. During British Summer Time, there was generally a window of opportunity when we could talk to the newly arriving staff in London just before we prepared to go home. But communications remained an annoyance. As to what happened to the letters, faxes and notes that I sent back to London, I do not know. Often they seemed to fall into a black hole, with no action taken, not even onward copying. So information that I later learnt would have been of interest to Australian and other foreign ministries sat, I suspect, unread in London cupboards, because not in e-mail form.

Nevertheless, friends and colleagues did not forget us.

Many wrote to say that they had seen me being interviewed by Brian Barron, and were puzzled as to why it was taking place in a taxi – so much for our magnificent and comfortable Toyota Landcruisers! I must have received at least six copies of a piece by Peter Hitchens in the *Mail on Sunday,* making a heavy-handed comparison between the alleged personality cult of Prime Minister Blair and that of Kim Jong Il.

Our builders, headed by Vernon Schofield, arrived in November. Most of their time would be spent on preparing our temporary apartments, but they also began work on the offices. They were a cheerful group, mixed British, Australian and Ugandan, all multi-skilled, and a welcome addition to the small local community. Once they started work on the offices, there was a distinct improvement. A large water tank meant that there was water for the lavatories and for a washing machine. Electric lights stopped exploding, which was just as well since a couple of our office rooms could not be used after dark by now, as all the lights had failed. It also meant that we were living in the middle of a building site, with dust and noise everywhere.

November saw the arrival of a new Polish ambassador, who immediately enrolled himself in the ranks of the more active embassies. For our part, we were preparing for what we had decided, optimistically, to call a British Week, to mark the first anniversary of diplomatic relations. We also decided to throw in St Andrew's Night for good measure, ordering haggis from Beijing for the occasion, while Susan began teaching Scottish dancing at the club. (The best dancer turned out to be the German logistics officer with WFP, who had learnt while in Rome at WFP headquarters.) Eilidh tracked down a band that would come and play for nothing. Orders went to London for books for an exhibition (promised since March, but which had up until then failed to arrive), a British Council-sponsored exhibition celebrating innovations, and films. Tough negotiations took place over the films. In the end, the Koreans agreed that we could show them in English, but they would decide the Korean audience. A suggestion that 'Wallace and Gromit' should be shown to children got nowhere, since the Ministry of Education refused all requests for a meeting. But venues were booked for all planned events in the fond hope that they would all materialise. There was clearly some Korean apprehension about the dinner-dance concept, but in general, we were promised full cooperation.

From all this, Susan and I escaped for three weeks in London in November-December 2001. Our time in London was hectic, but I was pleased to be told that the embassy was doing a good job in what everybody realized were very difficult circumstances.

British Week was originally planned to start on 3 December. However, since we were not due back until 4 December, we postponed it by a week, and since we had a large number of events, we decided to make it two weeks. It was just as well. On 6 December, forsaking the increasingly cold Potanggang Hotel, we moved into our temporary apartments. Ours was finished, but Eilidh's was not. She was determined to move before she left on 15 December, however, and to have a farewell party. That night, for the first time ever, the German generator failed, and we all woke up very cold. But in general, we were to find that the new apartments were comfortable and well equipped. Eilidh had her party through most of Sunday, 9 December, with the majority of the foreign community present at one time or another. For our part, our first entertainment in the new apartment was a dinner party for Caroline Gluck of the BBC and Peter Smurfit of the *Far Eastern Economic Review*, both of whom were in Pyongyang as our guests. My failure to realize that in the DPRK tomatoes are tinned in sugar produced the worst ratatouille ever!

The FCO's Public Diplomacy Department had warned us that events such as ours 'need careful and early planning'. I fear that neither Eilidh nor I were very good at careful and early planning, but since we had put in our orders for books as long ago as March, and for the exhibitions and the films in October, and had been assured that everything would be with us by 4 December, we were full of optimism. In fact, only the Innovations exhibition had arrived by the time of our return, and that without the 2000 leaflets that were to accompany it. No sign of the books, although these, too, were supposed to be on their way, as were the films. Frantic calls to London led to more promises, but we now had a very anxious Friendship Society, with venues booked and nothing to show. On the positive side, the Koreans had become quite enthusiastic about the dinner and the dancing, and had borrowed some tapes and music to learn more. In the meantime, we had lost the band, for they had put in their visa applications one day late and the Koreans would not be moved.

Came the day. Hugo Shorter, deputy head of the FCO's North East Asia and Pacific Department was visiting, so we billed him as in town for the celebrations. The Koreans sprang an anniversary dinner the night before ours, having shown no sign of doing anything up until then, They gave the British community and us six hours' notice. Not surprisingly, many of the community did not turn up – some never got the invitation.

Our dinner the following night was by consensus of foreigners and Koreans alike probably the best there had ever been in Pyongyang. It began conventionally enough, with speeches from Vice-Minister Kim Yong Il, standing in for Vice-Minister Choe, then in London, and myself. My speech was a light thank-you rather than the solemn fare on such occasions. There was much whisky. All who ate the haggis, foreigners and Koreans, including the vice-minister, pronounced it excellent. We then had some singing, with contributions from the head of the European Department, our old friend Mr Kim Chun Guk. Next was to be Scottish dancing, but we were preempted by the Koreans, who announced that there would be a Korean dance performance. Four professionals then performed Korean dances, followed by Scottish dancing with Korean characteristics; this included a four-person eightsome reel. The dancers had clearly studied our video very carefully, and the music had been transcribed using electronic instruments – they had found the original uninteresting, they said. The result was indescribable. The Friendship Committee, whose work this was, were very pleased, and suggested, hopefully, that we might like to pay for the performance. Our own amateur dancing, by contrast, was more shambolic but more accurate and fun, and there were even Koreans in the floor. It was 21.30 before the vice-minister left, and the party went on for some time afterwards; such late hours were unheard of normally. Another first was that we had all our Korean staff, from interpreters to the cleaner, as guests.

Came the dawn. The joint Innovations and book exhibition was due to open at 11.00 on Thursday, 13 December. When nothing came on the 11 December flight, it was clear that the books were not going to arrive in time. Eilidh improvized by gathering every booklet and pamphlet we had in the embassy and sending them off to the Friendship Committee. The result, if you did not look closely, was not too bad. The committee had taken a very large room at the Grand People's Study House and the staff had done their best to make what was available look respectable. It was clear, however, that there was disappointment at the meagreness of what was on display. There was also concern that there were still no films. Friday morning, 14 December, brought the delivery of the 170 books originally asked for in March, and firmly booked in August, and the 2000 Innovations leaflets, asked for in September. (The leaflets had been shuttled back and forth between the British Council and the FCO's bag room, which kept refusing to take them because they had no barcodes...) We sorted the books into the various categories, added display labels, and sent the lot off to the Friendship Committee. There were still no films but things were looking better.

Saturday, 15 December saw the departure of Eilidh, at the end of her temporary duty, and also of Hugo Shorter, the BBC's Caroline Gluck, and the builders. I now had to face British Week alone. On Monday, I was summoned to the Friendship Committee to explain the non-arrival of the films – not an easy task, since I had been assured by London that the films had left and should have reached me, and of course I had no idea why they had not. I also received notification that the Committee had not been over-impressed by the books, and that the Innovations and book exhibition would close the next day. On asking what was wrong with the books, I was told that there were only about seventy, which was not sufficient for a proper display. A quick visit to the exhibition hall at the Grand People's Study House showed that well over half the books had not made it from the Friendship Committee to the exhibition site. It was a pity because our unannounced visit revealed that many people were in fact looking at both books and exhibition. A couple of rather frosty discussions with the Friendship Committee saw all the books returned to us – those missing had been 'borrowed by scholars'.

British Week was by no means over. On 19 December, the films arrived. The Friendship Society was silent for a couple of days and then informed me that we were invited to the opening ceremony of the British film festival at 17.00 on 25 December. We declined, and instead attended a second opening on 26 December. The temperature in the hall was well below zero, and we sat in coats, hats and gloves to watch 'Notting Hill', in English, as promised but with a deadpan Korean version read out just loud enough to drown out the dialogue. Overall, we were told that 1700 people saw the various films between 25 and 30 December. Certainly, for weeks afterwards, when I called on universities and institutions, people said that they had enjoyed our films.

But it was still not the end of British Week. On 9 January 2002, I sat in my office and watched in disbelief as the drivers brought in twelve very large diplomatic bags. These contained 1600 special wallets, overprinted 'British Embassy Pyongyang', ordered in October, which had been ready for despatch in mid-November, and had been promised for the beginning of December. I never did find out why they were delayed. We were still giving them away when I left in October 2002.

Despite all the problems, the event was a success. No other embassy, not even the Chinese and the Russians, had done anything like it before, and it made a big impact. KCNA ran three stories on the anniversary of diplomatic relations and on British Week, which was also covered in *Rodong Sinmun*, the Korean Workers' Party newspaper.

It was perhaps just as well that British Week went on as long as it did, for with the departure of Eilidh and the builders, the embassy became a very quiet place. There was plenty to do, for I now had to do Eilidh's work as well as my own. With just two of us, and with absences for various reasons, we had always had to be flexible, and I had, somewhat late in the day, already learnt how to tie up a diplomatic bag and other skills. Now whatever there was to do was all mine, and being on my own meant that there would be no escape to Beijing until Eilidh's successor, Jim Warren, arrived.

Christmas and New Year proved surprisingly good fun. The winter was not as savage as the previous year, and the small number of foreigners who remained in Pyongyang did a good job of entertaining each other. Christmas day was spent with our German colleagues; we contributed more haggis and a Christmas pudding, both very popular. A fair amount of time was spent furnishing the offices, for new furniture had arrived. I cannot say that I was sorry to see the old go, but it had served its purpose. It was too cold and dangerous for travel outside Pyongyang, but I was able to do some calls within the city – after long delays, the Koreans were now arranging calls thick and fast, and I was even able to see a general, which had hitherto been 'too difficult'. I also began a project to look at religion in the DPRK. Now that we were in our apartment, we were able to do some more informal entertaining. Among those who came were Vice-Minister Choe, who seemed quite at home and happily adopted the self-service principle, for our dining area was too small for a waiter.

Meanwhile, London was silent, apart from a thank-you note from Hugo Shorter. Eventually, after three weeks' silence, I telephoned just to make sure all was all right. I was assured that it was; they had been too busy to contact us.

Jim Warren arrived on 28 January. Like Eilidh, he was Scottish, and he was to prove equally doughty in tackling the Koreans. He brought with him the first confidential mail to reach us since the beginning of December. It was a surprisingly thin collection, failing to include even the material on Vice-Minister Choe's visit to London in early December. His arrival allowed us to escape, and we spent a week in Beijing and Seoul over the Lunar New Year. Once again, the press in Seoul were very eager to see me, and the embassy there arranged a full programme of interviews and briefings. Since my visit came but a few days after the US President George W. Bush had made his 'axis of evil' speech, there was much interest in preliminary DPRK reactions. As I had seen both a representative of the People's Army and Vice-Minister Choe just before leaving, I was able to report that their comments to me had been relatively low-key, emphasizing that whatever Mr Bush said, the DPRK was anxious to resume a dialogue with the United States. This was taken as reassuring, and was widely reported.

Now I made a mistake. In answer to a question from the press about DPRK knowledge of the outside world, I mentioned that officials whom we met often had seen Western films and videos. I mentioned *Titanic*, *Mary Poppins*, and, most popular of all, *Sound of Music*. I did not know it but a very accurate account of what I had said appeared in the London *Financial Times*. There was nothing about politics in the story, as there had not been in my answer, but the sub-editor chose to head the report, 'Sound of Music counters "axis of evil" image', while the *FT*'s web-page had 'More "Sound of Music" than "Axis of Evil" in Pyongyang'. This would return to haunt me!

We returned to Pyongyang via Shenyang and a very cold visit to the Manchu 'Forbidden City', and plunged into a round of calls, dinners and all the rest of diplomatic activities. Vernon and the builders returned on 26 February, and we were again on a building site. Most of their effort was now concentrated on refurbishing our accommodation block, but there was also much more to be done to the offices. Once again, dust and noise filled our days. Visitors who came to sign the condolence book for HM The Queen Mother in April only reached the haven of calm that was my office after clambering through the construction work on the landing outside it. (We had received official notice of the Queen Mother's death, but no instructions on what to do. Still, that was an improvement on Princess Margaret's death. As far as I know, the Pyongyang embassy to this day has not received formal notification that Princess Margaret has died.)

As the weather improved, so official and private visitors began to flow into Pyongyang once more, and we could again go travelling further afield. Our courier trip to Beijing in March brought an unpleasant surprise in the form of a very critical letter from London – it was now that the 'Sound of Music' and the 'axis of evil' as evidence that I was anti-American came back to plague me, though this was not all that was covered in a very nasty letter. After several attempts, I finally drafted a reply to my satisfaction, but decided in the end not to send it. Since the drafter of the original had by then moved on, this was probably a wiser move than I could have anticipated. But it left a bad taste, especially when I learnt later that most of those concerned in London did not appear to share the same view.

April 2002 brought 'Arirang', a mass display and performance of music, dancing and gymnastics, and for once the Koreans seemed positively keen to have journalists visiting. They also agreed to a visit from the International Institute of Strategic Studies, a breakthrough in overcoming some years of resistance to contact with the Institute. We further extended our ELT programme by sending a group of doctors and other medical workers to the UK for language training, but the bankruptcy of the British NGO, Children's Aid Direct (CAD), caused problems. CAD owed large and unrecoverable sums to Chinese and DPRK companies. The bankruptcy had no direct effect on relations with the UK, but there were difficult moments for the European Community's Humanitarian Office and its British head. London's attitude was, quite rightly, that CAD was not an official body and had no British money in it, but it was not easy to get the Koreans to accept this.

In May, the embassy staff increased, with the arrival of John and Naomi Dunne. They had to be accommodated in a hotel at first, but they were cheered by the evident progress being made on the apartment block. By the time the next arrivals, the Duncans, reached Pyongyang at the end of July, they were able to move straight into their accommodation.

The 2002 QBP, which also marked The Queen's Jubilee, took place on 1 June. In keeping with the tradition that British parties were different, we hired the river steamer Pyongyang No. 1, and cruised and dined on the Taedong river, to music supplied by the Pyongyang Conservatoire. We had wanted young musicians from the Music and Dance University but this was turned down, at the last minute, because the Conservatoire was more suitable for an embassy function. Our wishes did not count, but at least there was no charge. The GSB also insisted that we should have a piano as well as strings. My threat to throw the piano into the river failed to have an effect, and we duly had a piano.

Our guest of honour was Ri Gwang Gun, the Minister for Foreign Trade, who had visited Britain in March. In my speech, I reminded the Koreans that there were still a few problems before there could be a British ambassador in Seoul, and also that we were there in the spirit of the June 2000 summit.

We had been worried that the Protocol Department would object to the venue, but we need not have been. The Koreans were delighted to come, since not many of them had ever been on the river. Mr Ri, the minister, said to me privately that it would be a good idea if all receptions were as informal as ours. As well as the minister, we had four vice-ministers and a huge turnout at the director level. Robert Anderson and Jane Portal from the British Museum, and Beth McKillop from the British Library, were our main outside guests. For the last time, we made it to the pages of KCNA.

A TRIUMPH AND AN ENDING: JUNE-OCTOBER 2002

At no point had we given up on the question of satellite communications, and I had taken every possible opportunity to remind our hosts that this was essential if the work of the British embassy was to advance. Officials noted my remarks but nothing happened. Then, at a party at the Swedish embassy at the end of June 2002, the MFA informed me that it had been agreed that we could install satellite communications.

It was perhaps not appreciated in London how big a victory this was, but it seemed to surprise the MFA; one member of the European Department said that they had no idea how it had happened. If the FCO did not understand how great a victory this was, the other missions and the UN organizations did. Now they pressed for, and got, the same concession. The WFP head in Pyongyang's first e-mail message on their own system, which I received just after our return to the UK in December 2002, made it clear how important a development this was:

> Jim: As promised, this is the FIRST e-mail message being sent from the new WFP VSAT facility in Pyongyang. Unfortunately, I couldn't find your own e-mail address, so must depend on the good offices of John to forward it to you (our techie lads were far too excited to wait even a few more minutes!).
>
> Hoped to say something profound – one small message for man, one giant – but couldn't come up with anything appropriate. I guess a BIG THANKS will have to do. You will be remembered for this.
>
> Best regards to you and Susan,
>
> No longer Internet challenged in Pingpong, Rick.

The remainder of our time in Pyongyang sped by, but there was little space for reflection. The flow of visitors did not abate. In early August, along with my Polish and German colleagues, I attended the concrete-pouring ceremony for the KEDO nuclear reactors on the east coast. The tone of the foreign speeches was not optimistic. We had the pleasure of hosting a party for the North Korean 1966 World

Cup team and the VeryMuchSo company that produced 'The Game of Their Lives'. The documentary won a special prize at that autumn's Pyongyang film festival, which also saw six other British films on show. Indeed, the Asian premier of Ealing Studios' 'The Importance of Being Earnest' took place at the festival, and we were able to arrange a special showing of the film as one of our farewell events. A mixed Korean and foreign audience seemed to enjoy both the film and the drinks provided.

Just two weeks before we left, we were able to move into the newly finished residence. While unusual for ambassadorial residences in that it was semi-detached, it had been designed and built to the highest specifications. We were sorry that we had such a short time in it, but were glad that we had seen it to completion. We were even gladder since the Germans had started to redo the other buildings, beginning with the one in which were our temporary apartments. Drills under the bed at 07.00 were not much fun. The concession on satellite communications meant that further work was needed in the offices, so my last week as chargé, like so many others, passed to the sound of hammers and drills.

Our main farewell party was to have been a combined circus and dinner evening, but the Protocol Department intervened, and suddenly the circus was unco-operative. We might have changed some attitudes, but there was clearly a long way to go. On 11 October, Susan and I danced on the bar at the Random Access Club, to rapturous applause. A more sedate farewell dinner took place on 14 October at the Minjok restaurant, where we had a slight victory over the Protocol Department by refusing to organize a top table. On 15 October, we left Pyongyang for the airport at 07.40 for the last time with the flag flying. Two hours later, at 09.40, as the Air Koryo flight passed over the Amnok (Yalu) River into China, my time as British chargé d'affaires Pyongyang was over.

EPILOGUE

My successor, David Slinn, whose appointment as ambassador had been many months before, was due to arrive in Pyongyang on the Saturday after we left, 19 October 2002. However, as we left Beijing on 17 October, the news leaked in Washington that the DPRK had apparently admitted to breaching the Agreed Framework during the 3–5 October visit by US Assistant Secretary of State James Kelly. David Slinn's departure was postponed indefinitely. Eventually, when it was clear that there would be no speedy resolution of the problem, he was allowed to go to Pyongyang in December 2002. By then, we were back in London and Pyongyang seemed far away.

References/Bibliography

BOOKS AND ARTICLES

Anderson, Robert, 'Behind closed doors', at www.dur.ac.uk/BAKS/PYtpt2.html, accessed 1 November 2004.

Armstrong, Charles K., *The North Korean Revolution 1945–1950*. Ithaca and London: Cornell University Press 2003.

Asendorf, Olaf, and Wolfgang Voigt (eds), *Botschaften: 50 Jahre Auslandsbauten der Bundesrepublik Deutschland*. Bonn: Bundesamt für Bauwesen und Raumordnung, 2000,p.180

Atkins, Peter, 'A seance with the living: the intelligibility of the North Korean landscape', in Smith, Rhodes, Pritchard and Magill (eds), *North Korea in the New World Order*, 1996, pp. 196–211

Barnes, Gina L. (ed.), *Hoabinhian, Jomon, Yayoi, Early Korean States*. Oxford: Oxbow Books, 1990.

——, *The Rise of Civilization in East Asia: The Archaeology of China, Korea and Japan*. London: Thames and Hudson, 1999.

Bartz, Patricia M., *South Korea*. Oxford: Clarendon Press 1972.

Bermudez, Joseph S., Jr., *The Armed Forces of North Korea*. London and New York: I. B. Taurus, 2001.

Bird, Isabella, *Korea and Her Neighbours*. London: John Murray, 1897. Reprinted London: KPI, 1985.

Bonner, Nick, and Dan Gordon, *The Game of Their Lives. The Greatest Shock in World Cup History*. Sheffield: VeryMuchSo, [2002] + video 'The Game of Their Lives'.

Breen, Michael, *Kim Jong-il: North Korea's Dear Leader: Who He Is, What He Wants, What To Do About Him*. Chichester, UK: Wiley, 2004.

Brinkoff, Thomas, 'North Korea', at http://www.citypopulation.de/cities.html, accessed 1 November 2004.

Buzo, Adrian, 'North Korea – Yesterday and Today', *Transactions of the Korea Branch of the Royal Asiatic Society*, 56 (1981), pp. 1–27.

——, *The Guerilla Dynasty: Politics and Leadership in North Korea*. London and New York: I.B. Taurus, 1999.

——, *The Making of Modern Korea*. London and New York: Routledge, 2002.

Campana, Andrea, *Corea: Una nazione divisa: relazioni internazionali nel Nord-est asiatico 1945-1996*. Rome: Koine, 1997.

Central Bureau of Statistics, *Report on the DPRK Nutrition Assessment 2002*, Pyongyang: Central Bureau of Statistics, 2002.

Central Office of Information, *The Korean Question and the United Nations*, London: Central Office of Information Reference Division, 1953.
Cha, Victor D., and David C. Kang, *Nuclear North Korea: A Debate on Engagement Strategies*. New York: Columbia University Press, 2003.
Ch'oe, Yongho, Peter H. Lee, and Theodore de Bary (eds), *Sources of the Korean Tradition*. New York: Columbia University Press, 2 vols., 1997.
Choi, E. Kwan, E. Han Kim, and Yesook Merrill (eds), *North Korea in the World Economy*. London and New York: RoutledgeCurzon, 2003.
Christen, Roberto, 'Agriculture in DPRK', forthcoming.
Cieslik, Thomas, 'Mit der Maus nach Pyongyang: Nordkorea im Netz', in Patrick Köllner (ed), *Korea 2002: Politik, Wirtschaft, Gesellschaft*, pp. 232–241.
Clark, Donald N. (ed), *Korea Briefing, 1993: Festival of Korea*. Boulder, Colorado; San Francisco, California, and Oxford: Westview Press, 1993.
——, 'Protestant Christianity and the state: religious organisations as an example of civil society in South Korea', in *Papers of the British Association for Korean Studies*, vol.9 (2004), pp. 19–32.
Conroy, Hilary, *The Japanese Seizure of Korea: 1868–1910: A Study of Realism and Idealism in International Relations*. Philadelphia: University of Philadelphia Press, 1960.
Cornell, Erik, translated by Rodney Bradbury, *North Korea under Communism: Report of an Envoy to Paradise*. London and New York: RoutledgeCurzon, 2002.
Cox, Caroline, and David Alton, 2003, *Report on UK Parliamentary Delegation to the DPRK*. September 2003.
Cumings, Bruce, *The Origins of the Korean War I: Liberation and the Emergence of Separate Regimes 1945–1947*. Princeton, New Jersey: Princeton University Press, 1981.
—— (ed), *Child of Conflict: The Korean-American Relationship, 1943–1953*. Seattle, Washington: University of Washington Press, 1983.
——, *The Origins of the Korean War II: The Roaring of the Cataract 1947-1950*. Princeton, New Jersey: Princeton University Press, 1990.
——, *Korea's Place in the Sun: A Modern History*. New York: W. W. Norton, 1997.
——, *Parallax Visions: Making Sense of American-East Asian Relations at the End of the Century*. Durham, North Carolina: Duke University Press, 1999.
——, *North Korea: Another Country*. New York and London: The New Press, 2004.
Dashwood, Christopher, and Kay Möller (eds), *North Korean Scenarios (1999-2003) and Responses of the European Union*. Baden-Baden, Germany: Nomos Verlagsgesellschaft, 1999.
Democratic People's Republic of Korea. Pyongyang: Foreign Languages Publishing House (FLPH), 1958.
Deuchler, Martina, *The Confucian Transformation of Korea: A Study of Society and Ideology*. Cambridge, Mass: Harvard University Press, 1992.
Duus, Peter, *The Abacus and the Sword: The Japanese Penetration of Korea, 1895–1910*. Berkeley, California; Los Angeles and London: University of California Press, 1995.
Eberstadt, Nicholas, and Judith Banister, *The Population of North Korea*. Berkeley, California: Institute of East Asian Studies, 1992.

Eberstadt, Nicholas, and Richard J. Ellings, *Korea's Future and the Great Powers*. Seattle, Washington, and London: National Bureau of Asian Research, 2001.

Eckert, Carter J., et al., *Korea Old and New: A History*. Seoul: Ilchokak for Harvard University Press, 1990.

Epstein, Stephen, 'Encountering North Korea Fiction: The Origins of the Future', *Words without Borders: The Online Magazine for International Literature*, at www.wordswithoutborders.org.article.php?lab=Encountering, accessed 31 October 2004.

Euro-Asia Business Consultancy Ltd., *The Three Koreas: An Introduction to the Economy, Business, and Opportunities in South and North Korea and in Yanbian*. Liphook, Hampshire, UK: Euro-Asia Business Consultancy Ltd., 1998.

European Union Chamber of Commerce in Korea, *Practical Business Guide on the Democratic People's Republic of Korea*. Seoul: European Union Chamber of Commerce in Korea, 1998.

Facts About Korea, Pyongyang: FLPH, 1962.

FAO/WFP, *FAO/WFP Crop and Food Supply Assessment Missions to the Democratic People's Republic of Korea*. Rome: FAO/WFP, October 2001; July 2002; October 2002.

FAO/WFP, *FAO/WFP Crop and Food Supply Assessment Mission to the Democratic People's Republic of Korea*. Rome: FAO/WFP, October 2003.

Feffer, John, *North Korea South Korea: US Policy at a Time of Crisis*. New York: Severn Stories Press, 2003.

Fendler, Karoly, 'Economic assistance from socialist countries to North Korea in the postwar years: 1953–1963', in Han S. Park (ed), *North Korea: Ideology, Politics, Economy* (1996), pp. 161–173.

Flake, L. Gordon, and Scott Snyder (eds), *Paved with Good Intentions: The NGO Experience in North Korea*. Westport Connecticut, and London: Praeger, 2003.

Foley, James, *Korea's Divided Families: Fifty Years of Separation*. London: RoutledgeCurzon, 2002.

Foot, Rosemary, *A Substitute for Victory: The Politics of Peacemaking at the Korean Armistice Talks*. Ithaca and London: Cornell University Press, 1990.

Foreign Languages Publishing House, *The Outline of Korean History (until August 1945)*. Pyongyang: FLPH, 1977.

——, *100 Questions and Answers: Do You Know About Korea?* Pyongyang: FLPH, 1989.

——, *The Criminal Law of the Democratic People's Republic of Korea*. Pyongyang: FLPH, 1992.

——, *The Civil Law of the Democratic People's Republic of Korea*. Pyongyang: FLPH, 1994.

——, *The Family Law of the Democratic People's Republic of Korea*. Pyongyang: FLPH, 1994.

Foster-Carter, Aidan, *Korea's Coming Unification*. London: Economist Intelligence Unit, 1992.

——, *North Korea after Kim Il Sung: Controlled Collapse?* London: Economist Intelligence Unit, 1994.

——, 'North Korea in Retrospect', in Kim Dae Hwan, and Tat Yan Kong, *The Korean Peninsula in Transition*. Basingstoke, UK: Macmillan Press Ltd, 1997, pp. 116–148.

Frank, Ruediger, 'North Korea: gigantic change and a gigantic chance', Nautilus Institute Policy Forum Online 03-31, 9 May 2003, at: http://nautilus.org/fora/security/0331_Frank.html, accessed 1 November 2004.

Franken, David, 'Travel Diary: Amidst Snow and Lies 1994: A North Korean Odyssey or Strangers in a Strange Land', http://members.ozemail.com.au/_davidf/homepage/nk_1994.htm, accessed 10 May 2003.

French, Paul, *North Korea: The Paranoid Peninsula: A Modern History*. London: Zed Books, 2005.

Gills, B.K., *Korea versus Korea: A Case of Contested Legitimacy*. London and New York: Routledge, 1996.

The Geographer, Department of State, *China-Korea Boundary*. International Boundary Study No. 17, Washington DC: Office of the Geographer, Department of State, 29 June 1962.

Goncharov, Sergei, John W. Lewis, and Xue Litai, *Uncertain Partners: Stalin, Mao and the Korean War*. Stanford, California: Stanford University Press, 1993.

Goodkind, Daniel, and Loraine West, 'The North Korean famine and its demographical impact', *Population and Development Review*, vol. 27, no. 2 (2001).

Gorenfeld, John, 2003. 'The producer from hell', *Guardian Review*, 4 April 2003, pp. 2–4.

Harris, Stuart, and James Cotton, *The End of the Cold War in North East Asia*. Melbourne: Longman Cheshire, 1991.

Harrison, Selig S., *Korean Endgame: A Strategy for Reunification and U.S. Disengagement*. Princeton, New Jersey: The Century Foundation, second printing with a new forward, 2003.

Harrold, Michael, *Comrades and Strangers: Behind the Closed Doors of North Korea*. Chichester, UK: Wiley, 2004.

Harvie, Charles, and Hyun-Hoon Lee, *Korea's Economic Miracle: Fading or Reviving?* Basingstoke, UK, and New York: Palgrave Macmillan, 2003.

He, Jiangcheng, 'Educational reforms', in Han S. Park (ed), *North Korea: Ideology, Politics, Economy*. Englewood Cliffs, New Jersey: Prentice Hall, 1996, pp. 35–48.

Henderson, Gregory, *The Politics of the Vortex*. Cambridge, Mass., and London: Harvard University Press, 1978.

Hoare, James, 'North Korean Foreign Policy', in Kim Dae Hwan and Tat Yan Kong (1997), *The Korean Peninsula In Transition*, pp. 172–196.

Hoare, James, and Gordon Daniels (eds), *The Korean Armistice of 1953 and its Consequences*. Suntory and Toyota International Centres for Economics and Related Disciplines International Studies IS/04/467, (February 2004)

Hoare, J. E., 'The centenary of Korean British diplomatic relations: aspects of British interest and involvement in Korea 1600-1983', *Transactions of the Korea Branch of the Royal Asiatic Society*, 58 (1983), pp. 1–34.

——, *Britain and Korea 1797-1997*, Seoul: British Embassy, 1997.

——, 'North Korea: Suspicious and Cautious', *The World Today*, vol. 59, no. 4 (2003), pp. 15–16.

——, 'People's Paradise, scholars' purgatory,' *Times Higher Educational Supplement*, 9 May 2003, p. 18.

——, 'A Brush with History: Opening the British Embassy Pyongyang, 2001–2002', *Papers of the British Association for Korean Studies*, vol. 9 (2004), pp. 57–87.

——, 'The Korean Armistice North and South: The Low-Key Victory' in Hoare and Daniels (eds), *The Korean Armistice of 1953 and its Consequences* (2004), pp. 1–10.

——, *Culture Smart! Korea: A Quick Guide to Customs and Etiquette*, London: Kuperard, 2005.

Hoare, J. E., with the assistance of Susan Pares. *Korea.* (World Bibliographical Series Vol. 204.) Santa Barbara, California: Clio Press, 1997.

Hoare, James E., and Susan Pares, *Korea: An Introduction.* London: KPI International, 1988.

——, *The simple guide to customs and etiquette in Korea.* Folkestone, Kent, UK: Global Books 1996; new revised edition published as *Simple Guide to Korea: Customs and Etiquette*, 2000.

——, *Conflict in Korea: An Encyclopedia.* Santa Barbara, California; Denver, Colorado, and Oxford: ABC-CLIO 1999.

Howard, Keith (ed), with Susan Pares, and Tessa English, *Korea: People, Country and Culture.* London: School of Oriental and African Studies, 1996.

Howard, Keith, 'Juche and culture: what's new?' in Smith, Rhodes, Pritchard and Magill (eds), *North Korea and the New World Order* (1996), pp. 169–195.

——, 'Korea 1. General; (iii) North', in Stanley Sadie (ed), *The New Grove Dictionary of Music and Musicians*, Basingstoke, UK: Macmillan, 2001, vol. 13, pp. 815–817.

——, 'Dancing for the eternal president', in Portal and McKillop (eds), *North Korean Culture and Society: Papers from the British Museum and BAKS study days 2001 and 2002* (2004), pp. 45–49.

Hwang, Eui-Gak, *The Korean Economies: A Comparison of North and South.* Oxford: Clarendon Press, 1993.

Hyun, Peter, *Darkness at Dawn: A North Korean Diary.* Seoul: Hanjin, 1981.

Institute for North Korean Studies, compilers, *The Son also Rises.* Seoul: Institute for North Korean Studies, 1980.

Jo, Am, and An Chol Gang (eds), *Korea in the 20th Cenury: 100 Significant Events.* Pyongyang: FLHP, 2002.

Kang, Chol-hwan, and Pierre Rigoulot, translated by Yair Reiner, *The Aquariums of Pyongyang: Ten Years in the North Korean Gulag.* Oxford: The Perseus Press, 2001.

Kim, Chan-dong, 'Korean culture and arts foundation art center', Curator's Concept for 'The Past & Present of Fine Art in North Korea', Kwangju Biennale, 2000, at www.gwangju-biennale.org/lastbiennale/2000/english/speciex-concept-no.htm#no.2, accessed 1 November 2004

Kim, Dae Hwan, and Tat Yan Kong, *The Korean Peninsula in Transition.* Basingstoke, UK: Macmillan Press Ltd, 1997.

Kim, Hakjoon, *Unification Policies of South and North Korea, 1945–1991: A Comparative Study.* Seoul: Seoul National University Press, 3rd. revised and enlarged edition, 1992.

Kim, Han Gil, *Modern History of Korea*. Pyongyang: FLPH, 1979.
Kim, Han-kyo (ed), *Studies on Korea: A Scholar's Guide*. Honolulu: University Press of Hawaii, 1980.
Kim, Ilpyong J., *Historical Dictionary of North Korea*. Lanham, Maryland, and Oxford: Scarecrow Press, 2003.
Kim, Il Sung, *Works*. Pyongyang: 39 vols., FLHP, 1984.
——, *Reminiscences: With the Century*. Pyongyang: 8 vols., FLHP, 1994.
Kim, Jong Il, *On the Art of the Cinema*. Pyongyang: FLPH, 1989.
——, *Let us carry out the Great Leader Comrade Kim Il Sung's Instructions for National Reunification*. Pyongyang: FLPH, 1997.
Kim, Samuel S., and Tai Hwan Lee, *North Korea and Northeast Asia*. Lanham, Maryland: Rowman & Littlefield, 2002.
Kim, Sung Ung (editor in chief), *Panorama of Korea*. Pyongyang: FLHP, 7th edition, 1999.
King, Ross, 'Language, politics, and ideology in the postwar Koreas', in David R. McCann (ed), *Korea Briefing: Toward Reunification*. Armonk, New York, and London: M. E. Sharpe, 1997, pp. 109–144.
Kirkbride, Wayne, *North Korea's Undeclared War: 1953–*. Seoul: Hollym, 1994.
——, *Panmunjom: Facts About the Korean DMZ*. Seoul: Hollym, 1988.
Köllner, Patrick (ed), *Korea 1998: Politik, Wirtschaft, Gesellschaft*. Hamburg: Institut für Asienkunde, 1998.
—— (ed), *Korea 2002: Politik, Wirtschaft, Gesellschaft*. Hamburg: Institut für Asienkunde, 2002.
—— (ed), *Korea 2003: Politik, Wirtschaft, Gesellschaft*. Hamburg: Institut für Asienkunde, 2003.
Korea Pictorial, *Songun, Banner of Victory*. Pyongyang: Korea Pictorial, 2003.
Korea Stamp Corporation, *Korean Stamp Catalogue (1946–1998)*. Pyongyang: Korea Stamp Corporation, 1998.
—— *Korean Postal Stationery and Maxicard Catalogue (1948–1998)*. Pyongyang: Korea Stamp Corporation, 1999.
Korea Tour: DPR Korea. Pyongyang: National Tourist Administration, 1997.
Korea's Tourist Map, Pyongyang: Korea International Travel Company, 1995.
The Korean Art Gallery/Le Musée des Beaux-Arts de Corée, Pyongyang: FLPH, 1985.
The Korean Central History Museum, Pyongyang: The Korean Central History Museum, 1989.
Korean Film Art, Pyongyang: Korean Film Export and Import Corporation, 1985.
The Korean Folklore Museum, Pyongyang: Cultural Relics Publishing House, 1992.
Kumatani, Akiyasu, 'Language policies in North Korea', *International Journal of the Sociology of Language*, 82 (1990), pp. 87–108.
Kwak, Tae-hwan, et al (eds), *The Two Koreas in World Politics*. Seoul: Institute for Far Eastern Studies, Kyungnam University, 1983.
Kwon, Soyoung, 'Changes in North Korea, reflected in *Rodong Sinmun* editorials, 1980-2002', in Portal and McKillop (eds), *North Korean Culture and Society: Papers from the British Museum and BAKS study days 2001 and 2002*, pp. 23–32.
Kyowon Sinmun (ed.), *President Kim Il Sung and Education*. Pyongyang: Kyowon Sinmun, 1990.

Lankov, Andrei, *From Stalin to Kim Il Sung: The Formation of North Korea 1945–1960*. London: C. Hurst, 2002.

Lautensach, Hermann, trans. and ed. Katherine Dege and Eckart Dege, *Korea: A Geography Based on the Author's Travels and Literature*. Originally published Leipzig, 1945. Translation published Berlin and New York: Springer-Verlag, 1988.

Lee, Dong-Bok, 'The Soviet events and inter-Korean relations', *Korea and World Affairs*, XV, no.4 (Winter 1991), pp. 626–639.

Lee, Hyangjin, *Contemporary Korean Cinema: Identity, Culture and Politics*. Manchester and New York: Manchester University Press, 2000.

——, 'Images of otherness and "sleeping with the enemy" in North Korean cinema', in Portal and McKillop (eds), *North Korean Culture and Society: Papers from the British Museum and BAKS study days 2001 and 2002*, pp. 33–38.

Lee, Hyun-bok, 'Differences in language use between North and South Korea', *International Journal of the Sociology of Language*, 82 (1990), 71–86.

Lee, Ki-baek, *A New History of Korea*. Trans. and expanded by Edward W. Wagner and Edward J. Schultz. Cambridge, Mass: Harvard University Press, 1984.

Lee, Ku-yol, 'Fine arts in North Korea: changes and characteristics'. *Korea Journal*, vol. 31, no. 4 (Winter 1991), pp. 79–86.

Lee, Soon Ok, *Eyes of the Tailless Animals: Prison Memoirs of a North Korean Woman*. Bartlesville, Oklahoma: Living Sacrifice Book Company, 1999.

Lee, Woo-shin, Tae-Hoe Koo, and Jin-Young Park, *A Field Guide to the Birds of Korea*. Seoul: LG Evergreen Foundation, 2000.

Lew, Young Ick (ed), *Korean Art Tradition*. Seoul: The Korea Foundation, 1993.

Lim, Gill-Chin, and Chang Namsoo (eds), *Food Problems in North Korea: Current Situation and Possible Solutions*. Seoul: Consortium on Development Studies and Ewha Woman's University Human Ecology Research Institute, Yanbian Center, 2003.

Lim, Un, *The Founding of a Dynasty in North Korea: An Authentic Biography of Kim Il-song*. Tokyo: Jiyu-sha, 1982.

Lone, Stewart, and Gavan McCormack, *Korea since 1850*. Melbourne: Longman Cheshire; New York: St Martin's Press, 1993.

Lowe, Peter, *The Origins of the Korean War*. London: Longman, 1986; 3rd edition 2000.

McCormack, Gavan, 'Britain, Europe and Korea', in McCormack and Selden (eds), *Korea North and South: The Deepening Crisis*, pp. 188–198.

McCormack, Gavan, and Mark Selden (eds), *Korea North and South: The Deepening Crisis*, New York and London: Monthly Review, 1978.

McCune, Shannon, *Korea's Heritage: A Regional and Social Geography*. Rutland, Vermont, and Tokyo: Charles E. Tuttle Company, 1956.

——, *Views of the Geography of Korea 1935–1960*. Seoul: Korean Research Center, n.d.

MacDonald, Donald S, *The Koreans: Contemporary Politics and Society*. Boulder, Colorado: Westview, 1988. 3rd edition, edited and revised by Donald N. Clark, 1996.

McKillop, Beth, 'Creating History: Tomb Building in the DPRK in the 1990s', in Portal and McKillop(eds), *North Korean Culture and Society: Papers from the British Museum and BAKS study days, 2001 and 2002*, pp. 3–12.

Mack, Andrew (ed.), *Asian Flashpoint: Security and the Korean Peninsula*, St. Leonards, NSW: Allen & Unwin, 1993.

Mercado, Stephen C., *North Korea and the Internet: Hermit Surfers of P'yongyang*. (2004). At www.cia.gov/csi/studies/vol48no1/article04.html, accessed 1 November 2004.

Merrill, John, *Korea: The Peninsular Origins of the War*. Newark, New Jersey: University of Delaware Press, 1989.

Morris, Warwick, 'UK Policy towards North Korea', in Smith, Rhodes, Pritchard and Magill (eds), *North Korea in the New World Order* (1996), pp. 86–92.

Myers, Brian, *Han Sorya and North Korean Literature: The Failure of Socialist Realism in the DPRK*. Ithaca and London: Cornell University Press, 1994.

Naewoe Press, *North Korea: The Land That Never Changes – Before and After Kim Il-sung*. Seoul: Naewoe Press, 1995.

Nahm, Andrew C, *A Panorama of 5000 Years: Korean History*. Seoul: Hollym, 1983.

——, *Korea: Tradition and Transformation – A History of the Korean People*. Seoul and Elizabeth, New Jersey: Hollym International, 1987.

Nahm, Andrew C., and James E. Hoare, *Historical Dictionary of the Republic of Korea*. Lanham, Maryland, and Oxford: Scarecrow Press, 2nd edition, 2004.

Nam, Jon Chol, *A Duel of Reason between Korea and US: Nuke, Missile and Artificial Satellite*. Pyongyang: FLPH, 2000.

Natsios, Andrew S., *The Politics of Famine in North Korea*. Washington DC: United States Institute of Peace, Special Report, 1999 at http://www.usip.org/pubs/specialreports/sr990802.html, accessed 1 November 2004.

——, *The Great North Korean Famine: Famine, Politics, and Foreign Policy*. Washington DC: United States Institute of Peace Press, 2001.

Nelson, Sarah Milledge, *The Archaeology of Korea*. Cambridge, UK: Cambridge University Press, 1993.

Noland, Marcus, *Avoiding the Apocalypse: The Future of the Two Koreas*. Washington DC: Institute for International Economics, 2000.

——, *Korea after Kim Jong-il*. Washington DC: Institute for International Economics, 2004.

—— (ed.), *Economic Integration of the Korean Peninsula*. Washington DC: Institute for International Economics, 1998.

Oberdorfer, Don, *The Two Koreas: A Contemporary History*. London: Little, Brown and Co., 1998.

Oh, Kongdon, and Ralph C. Hassig, *North Korea through the Looking Glass*. Washington, DC: Brookings Institute, 2000.

O'Neill, Tom, 'DMZ: Korea's dangerous divide', *National Geographic*, vol. 204, no. 1 (July 2003), pp. 2–21, 24–27.

——, 'Due North: A Brief Visit above the DMZ', *National Geographic*, vol. 204, no. 1 (July 2003), pp. 22–23.

Pai, Hyung Il. *Constructing 'Korean' Origins: A Critical Review of Archaeology, Historiography and Racial Myth in Korean State-Formation Theories*. Cambridge, Mass: Harvard University Asia Center, 2000.

Palais, James B., *Politics and Policy in Traditional Korea*. Cambridge, Mass., and London: Harvard University Press, 1975.

Panorama of Korea. Pyongyang: FLPH, 7th edition, 1999.

Park, Han. S. (ed), *North Korea: Ideology, Politics, Economy*. Englewood Cliffs, New Jersey: Prentice Hall, 1996.

Park, Kyung Ae, 1996: 'Ideology and women in North Korea', in Han S. Park (ed), *North Korea: Ideology, Politics, Economy* (1996), pp. 71–85.

Park, Young-Han, Ki-Suk Lee, Hee-Yul Lee, Ill Son, and Jeong-Rock Lee (eds), *Atlas of Korea*. Seoul: Sung Ji Mun Hwa Co., 2000.

Pihl, Marshall R., 'Contemporary literature in a divided land', in Donald Clark (ed), *Korea Briefing, 1993: Festival of Korea* (1993), pp. 79–97.

Pohl, Manfred, 'Nordkorea 1997/98: Wirtschaft und Politik', in Patrick Köllner (ed), *Korea 1998: Politik, Wirtschaft, Gesellschaft* (1998), pp. 267–280.

——, 'Politik und Wirtschaft Nordkoreas 2001/2002', in Patrick Köllner (ed), *Korea 2002: Politik, Wirtschaft, Gesellschaft* (2002), pp. 221–231.

——, 'Politik und Wirtschaft Nordkoreas 2002/2003', in Patrick Köllner (ed), *Korea 2003 Politik, Wirtschaft, Gesellschaft* (2003) pp. 205–216.

Portal, Jane, *Korea: Art and Archaeology*. London: British Museum Press, 2000.

Portal, Jane, and Beth McKillop (eds), *North Korean Culture and Society: Papers from the British Museum and BAKS study days, 2001 and 2002*. London: British Museum Research Publications, No. 151, 2004.

Pratt, Keith, and Richard Rutt, with additional material by James Hoare, *Korea: A Historical and Cultural Dictionary*. Richmond, Surrey, UK: Curzon, 1999.

Pucek, Vladimir, 'Impact of juche on literature and the arts', in Han S. Park (ed), *North Korea: Ideology, Politics, Economy* (1996), pp. 51–70.

Pyongyang. Pyongyang: Korea Pictorial, 1990.

Pyongyang Review. Pyongyang: FLPH, 1995.

Ri, In Mo, *Memoirs: My Life and Faith*. Pyongyang: FLPH, 1997.

Robertson, David, *A Dictionary of Modern Politics*. London: Europa Publications, 1993.

Robertson, James C., 'North Korean cinema, 1947–1987', *Papers of the British Association for Korean Studies*, vol. 7 (2000), pp. 253–265.

Ryu, Hun, *Study of North Korea*. Seoul: Research Institute of Internal and External Research, 1966.

Sanford, Dan C., *South Korea and the Socialist Countries: The Politics of Trade*. London: Macmillan, 1990.

Scalapino, Robert A., and Chong-sik Lee, *Communism in Korea*, Part I: *The Movement*; Part II: *The Society*. Berkeley, California, Los Angeles and London: University of California Press, 1972. Reprinted Seoul: Ilchokak Publishers, 1992.

Scalapino, Robert A., and Kim Jun-yop (eds), *North Korea Today: Strategic and Domestic Issues*. Berkeley, California: University of California Press, 1983.

Scalapino, Robert A. (ed.), *North Korea Today*. New York and London: Frederick A. Praeger, 1963.

Scenic Spots and Historic Relics in Korea, Pyongyang: Cultural Relics Publishing House, 1995.

Seliger, Bernhard, 'Die nordkoreanischen Sonderwirtschaftszonen – eine

Wiederholung des chinesischen Erfolgsmodell?', in Patrick Köllner (ed), *Korea 2003: Politik, Wirtschaft, Gesellschaft* (2003), pp. 262–285.

Sigal, Leon U., *Disarming Strangers: Nuclear Diplomacy with North Korea*. Princeton, New Jersey: Princeton University Press, 1998.

A Sightseeing Guide to Korea: Collection of Materials, Photographs and Maps, Pyongyang: FLPH, 1991.

Smith, Hazel, Chris Rhodes, Diana Pritchard, and Kevin Magill (eds), *North Korea in the New World Order*. Basingstoke, UK, and London: Macmillan Press; New York: St. Martin's Press, 1996.

Smith, Hazel, *Overcoming Humanitarian Dilemmas in the DPRK (North Korea)*. Washington DC: United States Institute of Peace, Special Report 90, 2002.

Snyder, Scott, *Negotiating on the Edge: North Korean Negotiating Behavior*. Washington DC: United States Institute of Peace, 1999.

Springer, Chris, photos by Eckart Dege, *Pyongyang: The Hidden History of the North Korean Capital*. Budapest: Entente Bt., 2003.

Steuck, William, *Rethinking the Korean War: A New Diplomatic and Strategic History*. Princeton, New Jersey, and Oxford: Princeton University Press, 2002.

Suh, Dae-Sook, *Documents of Korean Communism 1918–1948*. Princeton, New Jersey: Princeton University Press, 1970.

——, *Korean Communism 1945–1980: A Reference Guide to the Political System*. Honolulu: University of Hawaii Press, 1981.

——, *Kim Il Sung: The North Korean Leader*. New York and Chichester, UK: Columbia University Press, 1988.

——, *Leadership and Political Culture in Korea*. Seoul: Institute for Modern Korean Studies, Yonsei University, 2000.

Tennant, Agnita, 'Impressions of North Korean literature today: the unification theme', in Portal and McKillop (eds), *North Korean Culture and Society: Papers from the British Museum and BAKS study days 2001 and 2002*, pp. 39–44.

Tucker, Spencer C. (ed), *Encyclopedia of the Korean War A Political, Social and Military History*, 3 vols. Santa Barbara, California; Denver, Colorado, and Oxford, UK: ABC-CLIO, 2000.

U, Chang Sop, *The Chamo System of Dance Notation*. Pyongyang: FLHP, 1988.

UNICEF, *The Democratic People's Republic of Korea: Nutrition Survey: A Study Undertaken by UNICEF, WFP and EU in Partnership with the Government of DPRK*. Pyongyang: UNICEF, 1999.

UNICEF, DPRK, *An Analysis of the Situation of Children and Women in the Democratic People's Republic of Korea*. Pyongyang: UNICEF, 1999.

Wein, Roland, 'Recent developments in North Korea's economic policy', in *Politics and Economics in Korea in 1994*, Proceedings of the 4th Korea Seminar, February 1994, University of Newcastle upon Tyne. Department of Politics, University of Newcastle upon Tyne, 1994, pp. 1–9.

Wells, Kenneth M., 'The place of religion in North Korean ideology', in *Papers of the British Association for Korean Studies*, vol. 9 (2004), pp. 33–48.

Williams, James H., David Von Hippel, and Nautilus Team, 'Fuel and famine: rural energy crisis in the DPRK', *Asian Perspective*, vol. 26, no. 1 (2002), pp. 111–140.

Willoughby, Robert, *North Korea: The Bradt Travel Guide*. Chalfont St Peter,

UK: Bradt Travel Guides Guilford, Connecticut: The Globe Pequot Press, 2003.

Winert, Betina. 'FDI in North Korea – future Prospects'. M.Sc. thesis, University of Sheffield, November 2004.

Wit, Joel S., Daniel B. Poneman, and Robert L. Galluchi, *Going Critical: The First North Korean Nuclear Crisis*. Washington, DC: Brookings Institute Press, 2004.

Yang, Sung Chul, *Korea and Two Regimes: Kim Il Sung and Park Chung Hee*. Cambridge, Mass: Schenkman, 1981.

——, *The North and South Political Systems: A Comparative Analysis*. Boulder, Colorado: Westview Press; Seoul: Seoul Press, 1994; revised edition Seoul: Hollym, 1999.

Yeon, Jaehoon, 'How different is Pyongyang speech from Seoul speech?', in *Papers of the British Association for Korean Studies*, vol. 7 (2000), pp. 241-251.

Yoo, Jae-kil, 'North Korea art today', Curator's Concept for 'The Past & Present of Fine Art in North Korea', Kwangju Biennale, 2000. At, www.gwangju-biennale.org/lastbiennale/2000/english/speciex-concept-no.htm#no.2, accessed 1 November 2004.

NEWSPAPERS AND PERIODICAL PUBLICATIONS

*Bulletin of the Cold War International History Project (*Woodrow Wilson International Centre for Scholars) (Also web page via wwics.si.edu/index.cfm?topic)

DPRK Business News Bulletin, Beijing: Korea Business Consultants, 2000–

The Economist, London.

Far Eastern Economic Review, Hong Kong.

FBIS-EAS reports.

The Guardian, London.

JoongAng Daily, Seoul.

Korea Annual. Seoul: Yonhap.

Korea and World Affairs, Seoul.

Korea Focus on current topics, Seoul: Korea Foundation.

Korea Herald, Seoul.

Korea Journal, Seoul.

Korea Times, Seoul.

Korean Central News Agency (KCNA), Pyongyang.

Korean Journal of National Unification, Seoul.

The Military Balance: London: International Institute for Strategic Studies (IISS).

News and Views, London: Foreign and Commonwealth Office.

Pyongyang Times, Pyongyang.

Rodong Sinmun, Pyongyang.

Strategic Survey, London: IISS.

Summary of World Broadcasts, Caversham: BBC.

Yonhap News Agency, Seoul.

CD-ROMS, DVSS, VIDEOS

Christian Solidarity Worldwide, *North Korea: Suffering in the Secret State.* Video. New Malden, Surrey, UK: Christian Solidarity Worldwide, 2003.

Hoffman, Frank, Matthew J. Christensen, and Kirk W. Lansen, compilers. *The Harvard Korean Studies Bibliography: 80,000 references on Korea.* CD-ROM. Cambridge, Mass.: Harvard University Korea Institute, 1999.

Korea National Computer Corp, *Pyongyang.* CD-ROM. Korea National Computer Corp., 2001.

Korea Stamp Corporation, *Korean Stamps 2001.* CD-ROM. Pyongyang: Korea Stamp Corporation, 2001.

——, *Korean Stamps 2002.* CD-ROM. Pyongyang: Korea Stamp Corporation, 2002.

——, *Korean Stamps 2003.* CD-ROM. Pyongyang: Korea Stamp Corporation, 2003.

Pyongyang Computer Centre, *Samchonri.* CD-ROM. Pyongyang: Pyongyang Computer Centre, 2001.

Pyongyang Computer Centre, *Samhoung.* (English-Korean – Korean-English Dictionary.) CD-ROM. Pyongyang: Pyongyang Computer Centre, 2001.

VeryMuchSo Productions, *The Game of Their Lives.* Video. Sheffield, UK: VeryMuchSo Productions, 2002.

——, *A State of Mind.* DVD. Sheffield, UK: VeryMuchSo Productions, 2004.

WEBPAGES

http://nk.chosun.com
http://dprk.accesshost.com
http://210.145.168.243/pk/main.htm
www.bbc.co.uk/radio3/world/andykershaw.shtml
www.cankor
www.clickkorea.org/
www.dh.gov.uk/PolicyAndGuidance/HealthAdviceForTravellers
www.dprknta.com.english
www.dprk-trade.com/
www.fao.org
www.fco.gov.uk
www.humanitarianinfo.org/dprk
www.kcc-europe.de
www.kccp.net
www.kimsoft.com
www.korea-publ.com
www.koryogroup.com
www.nautilus.org
www.nkhumanrights.or.kr
www. nkzone.typepad.com
www.pyongyangartstudio.com
www.pyongyangsquare.com [some items can only be accessed

on a subscription basis]
www.regent-holidays.co.uk
www.reliefweb.int
www.skas.org/
www.thegameoftheirlives.com
www.tour2korea.com
www.unicef.org/dprk
www.vnc.nl/korea/tours.htm
www.wfp.org
www.who.int/csr/don/en
www.who.org

Index